How to Roast a Lamb

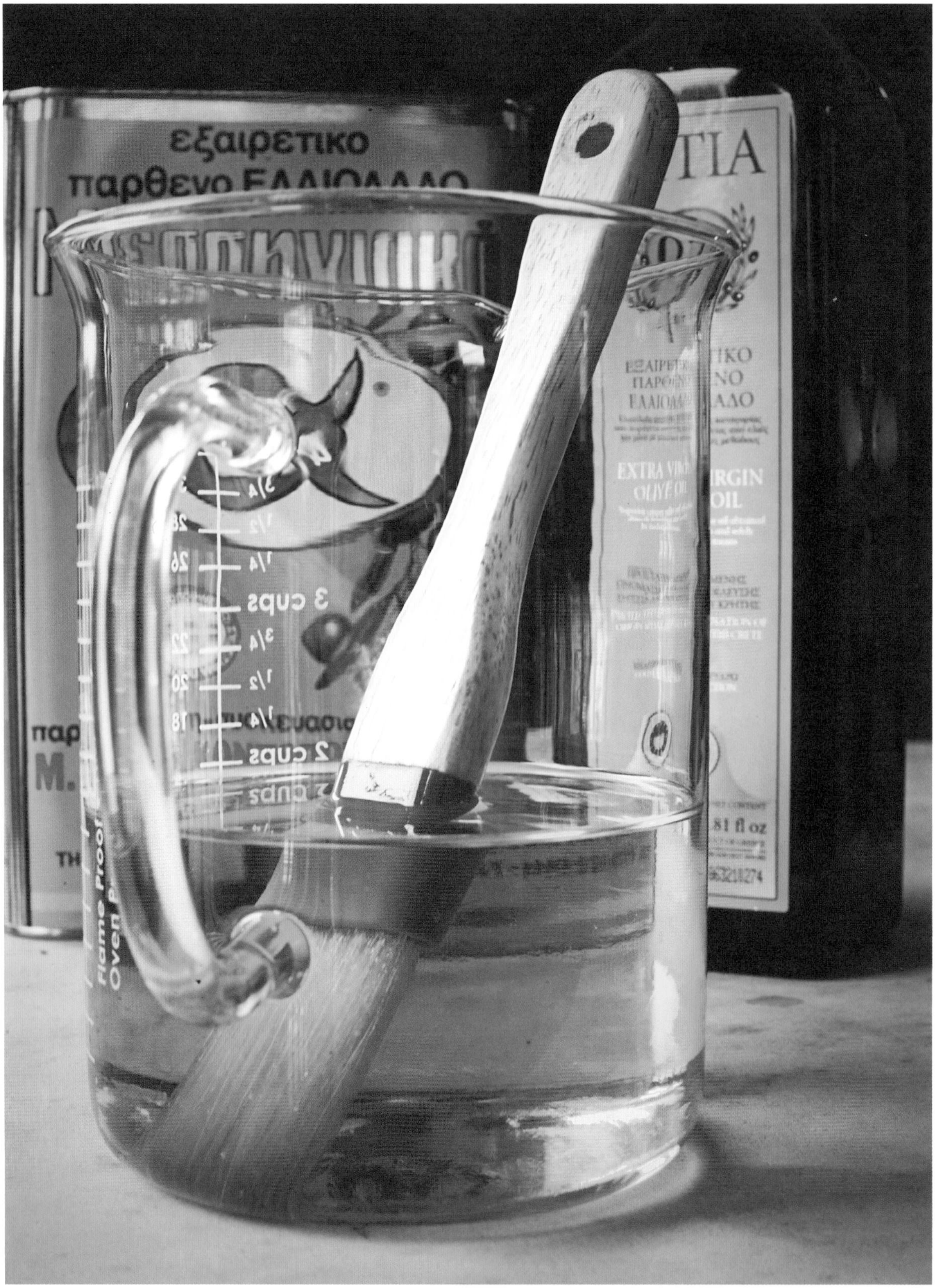
εξαιρετικο

How to Roast a Lamb

new greek classic cooking

Michael Psilakis

with

Brigit Binns ◉ Ellen Shapiro

Foreword by Barbara Kafka

Photography

Christopher Hirsheimer & Melissa Hamilton

Little, Brown and Company
New York Boston London

Little, Brown and Company
Hachette Book Group
237 Park Avenue, New York, NY 10017
Visit our website at www.HachetteBookGroup.com

First Edition: October 2009

Little, Brown and Company is a division of Hachette Book Group, Inc.
The Little, Brown name and logo are trademarks of Hachette Book Group, Inc.

Library of Congress Cataloging-in-Publication Data

Psilakis, Michael.
    How to roast a lamb : new Greek classic cooking / Psilakis, Michael ;
foreword by Barbara Kafka. — 1st ed.
        p.   cm.
    Includes index.
    ISBN 978-0-316-04121-8
    1. Cookery, Greek.   2. Cookery, Mediterranean.   3. Psilakis, Michael.   I. Title.

TX723.5.G74P75 2009

641.59182'2 — dc22   2008054932

10 9 8 7 6 5 4 3 2 1

Imago

Design by Christopher Hirsheimer and Melissa Hamilton

Printed in Singapore

FOR MY FATHER

In my mind, you are still here, with me, our daily conversations helping, guiding,

and illuminating right from wrong, as they do in the stories that follow.

You are my hero.

❖ ❖ ❖

FOR MY MOTHER

Know that a lifetime of meals spawned from your love has become the foundation

of who I am today as a chef and a person.

❖ ❖ ❖

FOR ANNA & GABRIEL

Forgive me for unknowingly asking you to sacrifice to help me realize my dreams.

Forgive me for the hours you spent waiting for me to return. Forgive me for allow-

ing food to become my addiction. Forgive me for trying to be the man you both

deserve and for not fully appreciating the suffering this has sometimes caused.

Forgive me for being me.

But know this: without you both I would be nothing.

Know that you are truly the center of my world.

I love you.

CONTENTS

Foreword

Barbara Kafka

It is a rare experience to find a brilliant new chef. Usually, they do not remain a secret. Instead, they become famous. I had this experience a few years ago when a friend told me that I must try a new restaurant, Kefi. I did, and the friend was correct. Michael Psilakis, whose book you have in front of you, was the chef, and he had all the attributes of a great chef. The acclaim has come along with two more restaurants and the growth of Kefi from a small establishment to a larger one in a new location.

The new restaurants are Anthos and Mia Dona. Go and enjoy.

What are the attributes that make a great chef? First, there is a sound grasp of the many techniques that make a cooked food what it is; but technique is not enough. As with any major creative talent, great intelligence and passion are necessary. Michael has these and a love for his family and for what food means to him and them.

It is creative. Based on the flavors he loves, he constantly creates variations and new dishes. The first recipe section of the book, crammed with delightful salads and vegetable dishes, illustrates the outcome of these talents. Many of these recipes are inspired by his dearly loved father's ardent gardening. These foods are joyous with loving memories.

They and the other recipes in this book are contemporary Greek cooking and deserve to join the pantheon of other great foods of the world. You won't find a recipe for the old familiar Greek salad any more than the many splendid wines of Greece today are like the retsinas of yore.

While the book is replete with wonderful recipes for poultry, meats, fish, innards, and game, the wealth of vegetables, salads, and meze also make it a wonderful resource for vegetarians and those who feed them.

The recipes obviously derive from Michael's Greek heritage, but they take off with new ideas and sail over new seas. There are a few elaborate recipes, but most are well within the scope of the home cook and even take budget into account.

Everyone who reads this book—a delight of love and memory—will come away made richer with an understanding of how and why to cook in a certain way. They will not only have found a treasure trove of excellent and original recipes but will also be tempted to invent their own based on Michael's hints.

I owe Michael a debt for wonderful meals, for being such a warm and generous person, and for being as good a chef as I had hoped he would be, and for sharing his family stories and his own recipes. Not the least of the thanks is for this wonderful book.

THIS COOKBOOK IS AT ONCE a collection of recipes and a collection of reminiscences. These stories reflect on memories, emotions, and insights that transpired throughout my childhood and into early adolescence. They illuminate the years that would stand as the building blocks for my growth from boy to man and ultimately to chef. The importance of my childhood and the events that are chronicled within this book as chapter introductions are vital to the path that led me to my destiny in the kitchen. Without this foundation, I would be unable to experience the bliss of standing behind a stove and creating dishes that express my emotions in much the same way as a poet, painter, or musician might.

Through these chapter introductions, I invite you, the reader, into my soul as a chef. In following my muse, I have created a book of soulfully integrated chapters—with collections of recipes that flow from the critical stories. This makes for a seemingly haphazard compilation with appetizer, entrée, fish, vegetable, and meat recipes within any given chapter. While this format is somewhat unconventional by the standards of a traditional cookbook, it was more important to me to convey the pride I feel when tying on an apron than to stick to the mold. My hope is that by illustrating the emotion that inspires my labors in cooking, it will bring you closer to the food and ultimately to the passion that defines a true chef—that is, the passion behind the gift that is food.

To combat any confusion, I have included a second listing of recipes set up in a traditional manner, by type of dish, on page 280. This will be helpful if you are interested in using the book in a more conventional and straightforward way— as a means of introducing yourself to the wonders of Greek cuisine. I believe this is the underlying beauty of this book. It may be read as a book of prose with philosophical undertones relating to the soul of Greek food or as a cookbook that allows you to explore its identity through recipes or, as I have intended, both!

❧ ABOUT THE RECIPES ❧

☀ THIS SUN ICON AT THE END of many recipes denotes extra, optional steps. Ingredients called for in optional steps are not included in the ingredients list.

Although the use of stock is an integral part of achieving wide-ranging depth of flavor, for this book I've chosen to use only water, just as my mother did when I was a child. This is not to say that I don't recommend the use of stocks. To the contrary, a stock will always help to enrich the final product. The logic here, however, is to promote my desire to keep these recipes accessible to the home cook. It's more important to me that you begin to cook Greek food than it is for you to spend hours making a stock. Instead, I always add plenty of fresh, aromatic herbs and spices, season aggressively with salt and pepper, and often add tomato paste or my essential Garlic Puree for body. However, if you have some stock lying around or you have a favorite brand that you purchase when you want to go the extra mile, you have not only my permission to use it, but also my blessing!

In this book, wherever possible, I offer optional shortcuts by doing things like using really good store-bought products (like roasted red peppers in a jar) in lieu of making everything from scratch. If using water instead of stock and store-bought peppers instead of homemade will get you into the kitchen to cook recipes from this book, I'm all for it.

I know everyone is busy, so there are very few fancy techniques. I want my food to be accessible to everyone, to get you started falling in love with Greek flavors. At the end of the day, if you make four building blocks from "The Aegean Pantry," you can make twenty dishes with them. The Garlic Confit is really important. Yes, you see it in many of the recipes, but if you take the time to make it you have a whole bunch of recipes that become really easy to execute.

At the Greek table, appetizers are rarely served on individual plates, and there is never just one. Instead we serve *meze*, morsels of stand-up finger food that promote a relaxed flow of friends and family around a table of tempting variety.

For main dishes (or any dishes meant to be eaten hot), I suggest you warm your plates before serving.

❖ ABOUT THE INGREDIENTS ❖

CAPERS

Capers are the pickled, immature buds of a plant related to nasturtiums, and are ubiquitous in Greek cuisine. Most capers are packed in brine, and for the recipes in this book require draining, but no rinsing. Occasionally you can find salt-packed capers, which are larger and meatier, with a more pronounced caper flavor. However, they are often very salty and should be well rinsed, well drained, and, depending on the dish, roughly chopped to a size similar to that of brined capers (most commonly the small French variety known as *nonpareil*, which means "without equal").

CHEESE

Substitutions can be made as follows, if you don't live near a market that stocks a good selection of cheeses:

Graviera: Gruyère   *Manouri:* Ricotta salata
Mizithra: Ricotta salata   *Kefalotiri:* Pecorino Romano

Ricotta: Supermarket ricotta just isn't going to cut it. This is one of those places where you have to try very hard to get the best ingredient, because otherwise whatever you make will be too wet. The first choice is very fresh (preferably sheep's milk) ricotta. Try an Italian grocery, an artisanal cheese shop, or the cold counter of a really good market. On the Internet, you can get excellent frozen ricotta from Italy.

Feta: Shifting boundaries in the eastern Mediterranean and Balkans make it difficult to trace the origins of this beloved cheese: at one point, half of Greece was Bulgaria and half of Bulgaria was Greece. It is believed that the Greeks have been making a fetalike cheese since the twelfth century, even if it was called something else. While Greece is home to several other wonderful cheeses (like *mizithra, graviera, kefalotiri,* and *kasseri*), in northern Greece at least, any and all "cheese" is assumed to be feta. Traditionally, feta is made from 100 percent sheep's milk, which yields the creamiest, richest product, but sheep don't always produce enough milk, so regulations permit up to 30 percent goat's milk. Feta can be sold at the age of two months, but many enthusiasts prefer a cheese between six and twelve months of age. Younger feta is often eaten alone; the mature cheeses are perfect as a component of salads and other dishes.

Feta deteriorates when not stored in brine, so try to buy it in brine and, if at a service counter, ask for a little more brine to be ladled over your cheese. Or you can make more brine at a ratio of 1 quart water to ¾ cup kosher salt, dissolved. If you buy feta in bulk and store it in brine, keep your fingers out of the container to avoid introducing bacteria; retrieve what you need each time with a clean pair of tongs.

I recommend using Greek feta wherever feta is called for in these recipes. However, if you can't find Greek feta, you may substitute French feta. French feta has become widely available in the U.S. (the business evolved as a way of using the excess milk from Roquefort production); it tends to be moister and milder in flavor than Greek feta. American-made feta lacks the characteristic tang and can be squeaky on the tooth.

OIL

At Anthos, we use extra-virgin olive oil for every application except deep-frying. At Kefi, where it is important to keep costs down, I use blended oil. (If I used extra-virgin for every application at Kefi, I'd have to add a dollar to the price of each dish.) If you like, use extra-virgin olive oil wherever blended oil is called for in these recipes.

For salads, vinaigrettes, and any other dishes that are either not cooked or barely cooked, I use a Greek extra-virgin olive oil.

For cooking any protein, I use a blend of vegetable oils—canola, safflower, or best of all, grapeseed—plus extra-virgin olive oil, usually in a ratio of 10 percent extra-virgin to 90 percent vegetable.

For confit vegetables, I suggest using blended oil in a ratio that makes sense for you—tastewise and financially—anywhere from 10 percent to 90 percent as above, to 50/50 percent, or even a higher ratio of extra-virgin to the vegetable oil.

For cooking vegetables—and any time you are making a pan sauce—I prefer to use a mild-flavored extra-virgin olive oil. There's no need to waste full-bodied or peppery oils here, but stay away from anything labeled "extra-light virgin olive oil." This product is marketed under the pretense of being more healthful. In truth, the process of its extraction involves heat, which breaks down the polyunsaturated fats that give olive oil its health benefits.

OLIVES

I use three kinds of olives: oil-cured black olives, brine-cured black olives, and cracked, brine-cured green olives. Some people are put off by the excessive brininess of these olives. You can tame the briny-salty flavor of olives, capers, caperberries, pepperoncini, and/or sun-dried tomatoes by blanching them for four or five minutes in boiling water. This plumps the fruit and lets its own flavor shine through.

OLIVE VARIETIES

Tsakistes, or cracked, brine-cured green olives: These olives are picked when still green (immature), then cracked (or slit) and brined, often with herbs and lemon and/or garlic. Any forward-flavored, brined green olive, such as Picholine, may be substituted if *tsakistes* are unavailable.

Thássos, or oil-cured black olives: These olives are picked when black (ripe) and cured in oil rather than brine. They are often sold loose without any liquid, and usually appear somewhat shrunken and wrinkled. Any oil-cured black olive, such as Niçoise or Moroccan, may be substituted if Thássos are unavailable.

Kalamata, or brine-cured black olives: Picked when ripe, as with Thássos, but cured and then packed in brine. Kalamata olives are widely available.

OREGANO

Greek oregano is wild, so it has a very different flavor from the usual oregano. If you can't find oregano specifically labeled as "Greek," look for "wild-harvest oregano."

PEPPERONCINI

I use pepperoncini to add heat to many of my dishes. I always chop them whole, seeds and all, but if you don't want quite as much heat, remove the seeds before chopping.

"PICKED HERBS"

I call for picked herbs in most of my dishes, because the bright flavor of fresh herbs is, for me, what makes Greek cooking so wonderful. To "pick," take a sprig of thyme, parsley, dill, or rosemary, and gently pull your fingers backward down the central stem, releasing the small, very tender stems and leaves. Discard any tougher or woody stems. If the resulting sprigs are large, pull them apart into smaller pieces, getting rid of any remaining tougher stems as you do. All parsley is flat-leaf. All measurements should be considered "loosely packed."

SUN-DRIED TOMATOES

Try to find large, plump, and pliable sun-dried tomatoes. Or use oil-packed sun-dried tomatoes, well drained. If all you have are dry-packed sun-dried tomatoes that are dark purple, very dry, and papery, reconstitute them in hot water for twenty minutes, then squeeze dry.

TOMATOES & TOMATO SAUCE

I don't worry much about peeling or seeding fresh tomatoes. That's the way they come and that's the way I use them.

Crushed tomatoes: Lift the tomatoes from a can of good Italian plum tomatoes and crush with your hand as you add them to the pot.

Tomato purée: This is just a simple, thin tomato sauce. You can also use a good-quality marinara sauce from a jar.

YOGURT

All yogurt in the book is Greek yogurt. Almost all markets now carry this thick yogurt, but if you can't get it, you will have to drain whole-milk yogurt overnight in the refrigerator, in a colander lined with doubled cheesecloth or a clean towel.

Introduction

I t is with great joy and an open heart that I invite you into my kitchen, into my home. Food has always been an integral part of my family life and of my culture. You could even say that food was the tie that bound us all together while, as new immigrants, my parents and their respective families adjusted to the ways of a new country, language, and culture. Food and cooking were an integral part of our lives, not just for nourishment, but also for the lessons taught and lessons learned between generations. Nothing happened in our homes and in our lives—no one was born, no one died, no accomplishment was celebrated, and no occasion was marked—that didn't involve food and drink.

It was never specifically my dream to write a cookbook. My passion is for the kitchen and I love sharing this passion for food and my Greek culture with other people. Being in the kitchen cooking, creating, and feeding people in body and soul has always sated me. But in 2007, as my father's health declined and I spent hours and long nights with him sitting in his hospital room and revisiting the wonderful life I was fortunate to share with him, the idea for this book was born. Telling these stories, the pictures of my childhood, and coupling them with the food of my youth would be a way to honor my father.

My parents were emigrants from Greece. They left the country, the people, the culture, the food, and the language they loved behind not because they wanted to, but because they had to in order to survive—in order not to starve. Like many places in Europe after World War II, my father's native Crete was hit hard and many of the people were impoverished. My father was among them. Like many other emigrants, he left all he knew and came to America with minimal education and, literally, the shirt on his back and the seeds in his pocket—nothing else. He came because he wanted to do more than just survive; he wanted a better life for his family.

While my father's Greek national pride was undeniable, the pride he had for being Cretan was paramount. Cretan men are known to be strong, stoic, and self-

Facing page, clockwise from top: Michael's mother's family, the Karropouloses, Kalamata, Greece, 1954; Costas Psilakis, right, bicycling in Athens; Costas Psilakis, right; Costas Psilakis, front, in Athens, 1952

sacrificing—men among men. Even among the Greeks (and that's saying something), Cretans are thought to be opinionated, stubborn, and unbending in their convictions. My father met every aspect of this description. As children, we knew that my father had his own set of rules and principles to live by, and in his house you just didn't break them.

My father gave up everything and worked himself to the bone to give me and each of my three siblings a better life. But I was his heir. As the firstborn son in a Greek family, I was expected to stand in my father's stead, to uphold his name, and to provide for our family should that need arise. From birth, I was groomed to be the next man of the family, the next patriarch, the way my father was for our nuclear family and also for our extended family. He taught me how to hunt, garden, fish, and how to kill and skin a goat—how to provide for a family in the ways he knew.

I spent my entire life trying to make him proud of me and doing things he would admire. But no matter how much I achieve, no matter how much I accomplish, I know that he sacrificed so much to give me a head start that I'd be proud to be one tenth the man he was.

My early childhood was the stuff of fairy tales. Every day of the week I was surrounded by people who loved and nurtured me. Whether it was one of our birthday dinners that brought us together or my mother and *theias* (aunts) cooking for days to prepare for a party in honor of my father's name day, we were always together. But growing up as the son of Greek immigrants in a middle-class suburban Long Island neighborhood wasn't always seamless. It was when I entered school that I had the first glimmer of a life different from my own. In my teen years I questioned everything and everyone, causing my parents—and especially my mother—no end of heartache.

When I started kindergarten, I didn't know a word of English. I had grown up in a Greek bubble. Everyone I knew and socialized with was Greek. My *theios* (uncles) and *theias* and my cousins—these were the people I saw on a daily basis; this was my family and my social network. When I went to school, my mother dressed me in a suit with dress shoes and black socks. I got the sense that all of the kids were laughing at me, but I couldn't understand what they were saying. When I first distinguished the words "black socks" and understood them, I finally knew why they were laughing at me. They were all wearing jeans and white tube socks. I was the immigrant kid dressed for school as if he were going to church. They were eating hot dogs and hamburgers for lunch. I was eating *souvlaki* and *spanakopita*.

Some things got easier—I learned the language and made a lot of American friends—but other things got more difficult and more complicated. I straddled two worlds: the Greek world I lived in at home after school and on weekends— a world my parents knew and trusted—and the American world I inhabited at school. And in each world, I was a different person.

I wavered between these two worlds because I loved my family; the foundation and principles with which I had been raised; the pride of culture, cuisine, and heritage—but I also resented it and my parents, specifically my mother, because she was essentially the one who raised us. My father was always at work and my mother made the rules in our house. The way I saw it, she was the one who stood in the way of me really integrating into the local culture. As a result, she, not my father, was the one who bore the brunt of my frustration.

But as my mother hoped and knew I would, at the end of those rebellious years I came out on the other side with a great appreciation for my family ties, roots, and Greek heritage. While I was growing up under different circumstances, my youth wasn't all that different from that of my suburban Long Island peers. Happy childhood, rebellious and troubled teen years, and an early adulthood with a loving and caring family: I still sat at my mother's table and devoured every- thing she cooked every night of the week at our daily family dinners.

Many people believe in fate, luck, serendipity. You can call it whatever you want. There are so many junctures in my life where, had I turned left instead of right, it would have altered my path—*would have changed my life dramatically*. Some people know what their passion is from a very young age, some people never figure it out, and, for some, destiny delivers it to their door.

After college, still living at home in my parents' house, I was working as an accoun- tant and I was unhappy. This was not the career for me, but, admittedly, I was lost and didn't know *what* career path I wanted to take. As many of us who weren't quite sure what to do with our lives did at that time, I decided to go to law school.

I had lived at home during college and now I wanted the opportunity to live on my own. My plan was to apply to law school in California and, after I had saved enough money, move out there and go to school. I needed a job with flexible hours so I could attend classes but still earn enough money to pay my way through school. Becoming a waiter or bartender seemed like obvious choices. But back then, you couldn't just walk in off the street and get a job in the front of the house (restaurant-speak for the dining room staff). The restaurants wanted a résumé of related experience.

After a month of applying to countless restaurants, one day I commiserated with my sister Maria, who told me that she had a sorority sister whose boyfriend was the manager at a T.G.I. Friday's. The restaurant was in the next county, a twenty-five-minute drive from where I lived. I never would have applied there were it not for Maria. Maria's friend asked her boyfriend, and I had a job.

From the minute I hit the floor, I loved working as a waiter. I couldn't believe what a perfect match it was for me. It was as if I had been groomed from childhood specifically for this role. From a very young age, it was always my job in my parents' house to make sure that everyone who crossed our threshold was made to feel welcome, to feel at home. I asked people what they wanted to drink and delivered it to them. I made sure their glasses were full and that they had enough to eat. I committed their favorite drinks to memory and for years to come would remember what they liked and be able to serve it to them before they could ask. They were happy and, in turn, that made me feel happy.

It was at T.G.I. Friday's that I met Anna, the woman who later would become my wife, and James and Jim, two painter friends who would play pivotal roles in connecting me to the path of my future. Anna and I started dating and we were able to work together for a while, but dating among staff was frowned upon at the restaurant and we were being scheduled on alternate shifts—one of us on days, one of us on nights. If we didn't work together, we never saw each other.

In their off-hours, James and Jim were painting the interior of a restaurant called Café Angelica, which was owned by two Greek brothers. Knowing the problem we were having with our schedule, James suggested that I come over to Café Angelica and meet the owners. It was a beautiful restaurant, and they were cooking what seemed to me to be progressive food. All of it was new to me: fresh pasta, homemade

Psilakis family, 1979

focaccia, foie gras, wine service. Growing up in that Greek vacuum, I had never been exposed to any of this. I had never heard of focaccia; I didn't know what foie gras was. But I came to the restaurant and James introduced me to the owners. I was Greek; they were Greek. It was like a reunion with long-lost friends. They asked me if I spoke Greek and when I answered *in Greek*, just like that, I had a new job. Not being Greek, however, it wasn't quite so easy for Anna. She went through a full interview process but ultimately got hired as well.

I threw myself into this new job with a passion. I waited tables day and night and started studying cookbooks as if they were textbooks. I wanted to learn more about cuisine and cooking. I was like a sponge, absorbing every bit of information I could. Despite my interest in this "new" style of cooking, I continued working part-time at Friday's. I didn't want to resign until I knew that Café Angelica was financially viable.

A few months in, Café Angelica was struggling. I wasn't making nearly as much money as I had at Friday's. I was just about to call it quits and return to Friday's full-time when Café Angelica received a positive review in the *New York Times*. Then all hell broke loose. The restaurant became fantastically busy and success-ful, and there was a new need for organization and management. I volunteered. In addition to waiting tables at lunch and dinner, I started doing the restaurant's inventory, making the schedule for the front of the house, entering the chef's spe-cials into the computer, cashing out the drawer at the end of the shift, and staying until the cleaning crew finished so I could lock up. I was always the first guy in the restaurant in the morning and the last guy out at night.

The restaurant was open seven days a week and, after about four months, the brothers asked me to take the Sunday shift as restaurant manager so they could have a day off together. I went out and bought some suits. On Sundays I was on the floor in a suit with added managerial responsibilities, and every other day I was an acting manager in waiter's clothes. I was working seven days a week, living at my mother's house, and saving every penny.

Café Angelica was doing well, and the brothers wanted to open a restaurant in Scarsdale, New York—Central Square Café. They asked me to be a partner in the venture. I was twenty-three years old, and I owned a 25 percent share in a 300-seat restaurant. I learned quickly that running a 300-seat restaurant was completely different from running a 100-seat restaurant, which I had been doing successfully to date.

I continued to work crazy hours but earned less money and felt no joy in running the restaurant. After a year of this, I approached the brothers and asked them to buy me out—it just wasn't working for me. Buying into that restaurant turned out to be a terrible decision.

After a legal battle, the brothers offered me Café Angelica in trade for my 25 percent share of Central Square Café. It seemed like a great opportunity. What I didn't know was that in the year since I left Café Angelica to run Central Square Café, Café Angelica had taken a nosedive—and now it was mine, all mine. I had the seven-year note to prove it.

I could not afford to operate this restaurant on my own. Anna's father, my future father-in-law, bought in as a partner. By this time, all thoughts I had had of going to law school in California were a faint memory. Somewhere along the way, I realized that I had found my calling. Not only did I *want* to be in the restaurant business, but also this was what I knew I was *meant* to do.

I proposed to Anna on the first night I took over Café Angelica. Anna did the books for the restaurant and was the hostess, and I was the manager. But still the restaurant was losing money.

I had a good chef, Cary, and I did every possible thing I could think of to get Café Angelica into the black. In the morning I'd go in and chop vegetables, then I'd change into a waiter's uniform to work lunch. I did the same for dinner, and as before I was always first in and last out.

Five months into my ownership of Café Angelica, Cary told me that he was totally burned out and needed some time away. He gave me unlimited notice to find a new chef, but still I was overwhelmed with the added burden of having to replace him.

I hired a chef, Maureen, and she hired a sous-chef named John. Maureen fell while on the job and went on disability. John, however, turned out to be a talented young chef and he slid into her position seamlessly. Because of our financial situation, I couldn't afford to get him a sous-chef, but John rose to the occasion. He became like family to me, and I embraced him with open arms and an open heart.

The restaurant became something of a functional three-ring circus. John worked six days. On those days, I was the manager, bartender, and waiter. On John's day off, Anna was the manager and I became the chef, cooking the six pasta dishes I now knew how to make.

One day, I arrived at the restaurant and found the three cooks standing outside. No John. I started calling around and no one seemed to know where he was. This was so unlike him that I started to get frantic. Finally, one of the cooks pulled me aside and told me that he thought John had left for good. He had overheard John talking about opening his own restaurant. John never told me and never returned. We were down to the cooks and me.

It was a very dark time for me and, while I didn't recognize it then, this disaster put me on the path to my destiny. I told Anna that I had had enough: I was never going to be at the mercy of a chef again—*I was going to be the chef of my restaurant.* Anna, of course, thought I had lost my mind. After all, what did I know about being a chef? But what had I known about being a waiter, manager, or owner—and I had done that. I told Anna that I would learn. She would run the front of the house and I would cook. We would do this thing together.

As the new chef of my restaurant, the first thing I did was go to the bookstore and stock up on cookbooks. I bought more than a dozen and studied them as if I were cramming for the exam of my life. It was then that I started to fall into my mother's cooking—her food, her flavors. We were still an Italian restaurant, but I was learning, so essentially everything I cooked was an experiment.

My schedule continued to be chaotic, with me prepping and making fresh pasta before changing my clothes to wait tables for lunch and dinner. Anna continued to be hostess and bookkeeper and, on Friday and Saturday nights, manager when I worked full-time as chef in the kitchen.

Station by station I learned to cook. I would work the fish station until I felt I had a good handle on it and then go on to another station until I felt that I had mastered that too. I wrote the menus and, along with two cooks by my side in the kitchen, we got the food to the tables.

By this time, I was thirty-two; about eight years had passed since that fateful day when I first set foot in Café Angelica. Things were looking up. We paid off the note on the building and, finally, the restaurant started to make money.

Chefs Harris Sakalis, left, and Michael Psilakis, right, Anthos kitchen, 2008

Over the next year, my skills in the kitchen improved and so did the restaurant's bottom line. I wanted to open a new restaurant, but my father-in-law, having seen me through the hard times, was happy that the restaurant was thriving and was not on board with a new opening. So we compromised. We closed the restaurant, Anna redesigned it, we renovated, and renamed it Ecco. This restaurant had *our* soul.

I had been in the kitchen for a year and a half and I was very happy with my blend of Italian-Greek-Mediterranean cuisine. This restaurant was more formal than Café Angelica, and I wrote a menu to reflect that. Anna really started getting into wine and she began to build our wine list. We got two stars from the *New York Times*.

Our wine purveyor, Pano, said he would introduce us to "a guy he knew," Maurizio, who, he told us, would help us develop our wine list further. Maurizio came out to the restaurant from New York City and, of course, I fed him lunch. After lunch, Maurizio looked at me somewhat quizzically before pronouncing, "This is remarkable." And I countered with: "If you think this is good, come back for dinner and I'll do a tasting menu. This was only lunch."

Maurizio came back with Donatella Arpaia, the woman he was dating at that time. I cooked them a twelve-course tasting menu, and they brought the wine. They told me that I should open a restaurant in New York City. Donatella told me that *we* should open a restaurant together. I pshawed. It didn't seem possible. Who was I?

Over the next couple of years, Maurizio and I became very close. Anna and I went from being a twosome, going out for elaborate dinners in Manhattan on Monday nights when Ecco was closed, to a foursome with Maurizio and Donatella.

Anna found her passion and started working in the shoe business, commuting into Manhattan. So instead, on Mondays, Maurizio and I would go out for elaborate fifteen-course lunches, smoke cigars, discuss in great detail what we had eaten, and then meet the women for our Monday night dinners—to do it all over again. At all of these meals, I was tasting and learning. I was studying what other chefs were doing, tasting their flavors and spicing. My world continued to open as my taste buds developed and I gained a new understanding about the depth of food and flavors.

Maurizio got a call from Gael Greene, the *New York* magazine food critic. She was looking for a restaurant recommendation for some dear friends who lived on Long Island. Maurizio suggested Ecco. These friends, the Zausners, called for a reservation and asked if they could bring their own wine. I thought, Oh no, it's *those* people. They're going to show up with a $5.95 gallon of wine in a box to circumvent our wine list. I gave them my spiel on how if we had the bottle of wine on the menu they could get it here but if they had a special bottle of wine and we didn't have it, they could bring their own. At the other end of the line I heard, "Do you have a '62 Petrus?" I told them they could bring their own wine.

And so began our relationship with our dear friends the Zausners. They would bring us all sorts of fresh vegetables from their garden and wines I had never hoped to savor—and always, there was a glass sent into the kitchen for me to taste. The Zausners hosted a ten-person dinner at Ecco and among the invited guests were Gael Greene, and Maurizio, who brought the wine. I cooked them a seventeen-course meal that seemed to impress Gael Greene enough that she decided to write an article about us in *New York*. And the phone started ringing off the hook. Everyone was calling—from customers to other chefs, waiters, and restaurateurs. It was at this time that I finally thought to myself, Hey, maybe I *can* do this in New York City.

I decided that I wanted to give it a try. I wanted to open a restaurant in New York City with a purpose—to teach people about what I had learned as a child, to transmit that culture and heritage through my Greek cuisine. My goal was to elevate Greek food to its place alongside French and Italian food. If I was going to hit the big city, it would be with this goal in mind, and if I didn't succeed at least I would not live with the regret of not trying.

I sold Ecco and found a small space in Manhattan. I was struggling. We weren't making any money and I was back to the old days when I had to do everything myself because I couldn't afford to hire enough staff. No one seemed to understand what I was trying to do with Greek cooking, and there I was, a struggling, no-name chef fighting to stay afloat. It seemed that I had chosen the wrong restaurant, in the wrong neighborhood, with the wrong cuisine.

My publicist asked me if I could do something special, something unique that could get some media attention. I came up with an eight-course offal tasting menu.

She put the word out and writers started to come in, but only for offal. I got coverage in *Newsweek*, *Time*, and *BusinessWeek*—all articles about *offal*. I guess you could say that I became the offal king of New York City—not exactly what I was hoping for. With all of the hype, Anthony Bourdain came into my restaurant to try my offal menu and I made him a twelve-course all-offal meal. He looked at me and declared, "You will be a star." My bank account, however, indicated otherwise.

I was on the verge of closing and losing everything. Then, at long last, Frank Bruni from the *New York Times* came in and reviewed the restaurant. He gave it two stars. Calls for reservations started flooding in, and the restaurant was full.

Once again, Donatella approached me with a project. This time, I was ready to open the door to luck and welcome it in. Donatella had a restaurant, Dona, that she wanted me to re-create. This was a big-name, 130-seat, glamorous restaurant. This could be my "Broadway debut." But I had my goal, another objective: I still wanted to show the world what Greek cuisine was and what it could be.

Donatella and I made a deal: I would do Dona with her, with a menu of Italian-Greek fusion, and then we would open a Greek restaurant showcasing my dreams. Dona was a smashing and critical success. In 2006, we were named Best New Restaurant by *Esquire* magazine and received *Bon Appétit*'s Best Dish of the Year honors. In 2007, *New York* included Dona in their Top Ten Best New Restaurants.

Then we opened Onera, which means "dreams." This was "my" restaurant and I was cooking rustic Greek food my way. We were getting great and enthusiastic media attention. And then we were approached by our landlord. He was going to be renovating the building all around us for the next seven years, and we could either stay and endure it or get bought out. We already had plans under way to open another Greek restaurant, Anthos, so we moved ahead with that and, in the meantime, I opened Kefi.

It was now not only my goal but also my mission to teach people about my vision for new Greek cuisine. At Kefi, I took the food of my childhood and executed it with my own twists. I told all of the journalists who came in, "Taste this food at Kefi and when you come to my new restaurant, Anthos, you'll see how I have evolved that same dish to something new—a whole new level."

Looking back, it is amazing to me how many twists and turns my life has taken to bring me to where I am now. Had Maria not had the friend from the sorority whose boyfriend was the manager at that T.G.I. Friday's, I would not have had my start in the restaurant business, or met my wife—the two most important things in my life (and not necessarily in that order!). Had James and Jim not introduced me to the two Greek brothers, Anna and I would never have gone to Café Angelica. Had John come to work that day, I might never have made the final move from the "front of the house" in hospitality to the "back of the house" as chef in my own kitchen.

When I've been honored with awards and accolades, I've thought back to my childhood, the foundation upon which the rest of my life and all that I have accomplished has been built. I can never be as great as my father was, or as much of a success, but it gives me joy to make my customers feel like guests in my home and to share with them a taste of my childhood and a look at what I've dreamed of as "new" Greek cuisine.

When my father passed away in September 2007, there was one thing left unsaid: my father was my hero. In the pages that follow, I wish to honor the man who had the greatest influence on my life, who taught me and groomed me to be a man myself and who shaped me into the man I am today.

Life, love, and learning; food, family, and friends. These are the things that I hope to share, from my table to yours. Like the ingredients of each of the recipes in this book, to me, they are all intertwined—one cannot exist without the others. It is through sharing these recipes with you that I hope you can take some of this love and learning and share it with your own family and friends.

The reminiscences in this book that begin each chapter are the backbone of my youth, and the recipes that follow are what nourished us, day after day and night after night at my mother's table, at family parties, in celebrating happiness and commemorating sorrow. It is my sincerest hope that you will take the time to cook some of these recipes for family and friends, for the people you love. I promise that you will derive great joy from the food you have created, from the happiness of cooking for people who are dear to you, from feeding people and bringing them together. And you will be amazed at the outpouring of love you get in return from those you have invited to share your table.

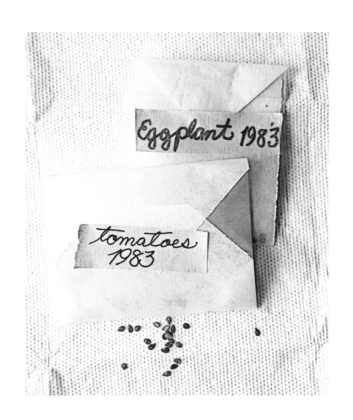

my father's garden

I knew gardening season was near when my father brought out the seed bag. He kept all of our seeds in a single bag, each variety encased in its own paper-towel envelope. The original seeds—the ones my father used for his first garden in America seasons before I was born—came over with him from Greece. And these, the ones we used every year until my father was no longer strong enough to tend the garden, were direct descendants.

The ritual of the seed bag started long before actual work in the garden. As if handling rare and precious jewels, my father would select a packet and gingerly unfold the paper towel until the seeds were revealed. First, we'd look for the tomato and pepper seeds. These were birthed inside so that, when it was time to plant outside, we'd already have seedlings to go into the garden. All the other vegetables and fruits, my father would explain, were vines that would start outside from seed. After days, sometimes weeks, of anticipation, at long last he would make the pronouncement: "Tomorrow we're going to work in the garden."

I was ten before I truly had the strength to help my father with the tilling, but that didn't diminish my eagerness to contribute in any way I could. As soon as my father walked out the sliding-glass doors onto the patio, I'd race ahead of him to the garden shed and drag the pick mattock (a hoe on one side of the head and a pick on the other) across the yard, struggling over the clumps of crabgrass and weeds. It felt as if I were dragging cinder blocks, and I'd have to rest several times along the way, but I was determined to pitch in. Exhausted and triumphant, I'd lay the smooth wooden handle at his feet while he assessed the work ahead, then I'd run back to the shed to work on delivering the pitchfork. Compared to the mattock, the pitchfork was easy—like pulling a well-waxed toboggan on snow.

My father would bring the pick mattock effortlessly up over his head and swing it down into the soil in a smooth, arcing motion. He would till the whole garden—a rectangle equivalent to about half the size of a tennis court—by hand this way. When I was strong enough, I would follow behind him with the pitchfork as he worked with the pick mattock, further breaking up the soil.

As was his manner, my father laid out the garden in a very specific and practical way. The rows ran from right to left from fence post to fence post. First were the cucumbers. We used many of them, so there were always at least three rows. Then came three rows of tomatoes, also a common ingredient in Greek cooking, followed by rows of peppers, eggplants, string beans, and the melons: watermelon, cantaloupe, and honeydew. Around the perimeter, we had herbs: mint, oregano, dill, amaranth, basil, and parsley.

My father had created a trough system that ran down the right side of the garden and branched off to each row so that he could water the plants efficiently. And while the trough system was ingenious, perhaps the *pièce de résistance* was the string-bean trellis made from an old swing set that my father had rigged, minus the swings, with two crossbeams and countless vertical poles. To my father, gardening wasn't a hobby. It meant sustenance and nourishment. It was the circle of life: birth, tending and growing, harvest, and a life-giving death when the fruits of the garden nourished family and friends.

Indeed, gardening was of vital importance to my whole extended family. We had the luxury of a yard, but some of my uncles did not. So they'd use every green space available to them. Outside their homes, tomatoes sprang up on the thin lane of soil that ran between the two cement tracks intended to be a driveway. They'd plant secret gardens in public parks, safely hidden from view behind bushes. They'd even seek out clearings beyond the trees that lined the Northern State Parkway, a four-lane highway with no shoulder. They'd just pull off onto the grass on the side of the highway, walk into the woods, and search until they found a hidden spot to plant that year's garden. To them, a tomato, cucumber, or watermelon meant life.

Every day I would wait for my father to return home from work, change into his old clothes, and step outside and into the garden. I would proudly show him that I was doing the things he had taught me. As a young boy that meant pulling the weeds and trying to screw the garden hose up to the trough by myself or, when I was older, tilling the soil and watering the plants in just the way he had shown me. I never viewed it as a chore. It was precious time alone with my father. Gardening was important to him, so it became important to me. It gave him peace, and in turn I found peace in it too.

And those vegetables! I can still remember the vivid tastes, smells, and textures. "Smell this," my father said as he held a ripe tomato under my nose. "What do you smell?"

"Dirt," I answered.

"Earth," he corrected me. "You smell the earth."

We'd eat from the garden on a daily basis. While my father and I were working in the yard—mowing the lawn, trimming the trees, weeding the garden—my mother would take the vegetables we had just picked and soak them in an ice water bath. When they were almost as cold as the ice itself, she would pull them out, peel and chop cucumber, red onion, and feta cheese in a bowl, liberally douse them with red wine vinegar, drizzle with olive oil, sprinkle with oregano and salt, and toss it all together. With great ceremony, my mother would bring the salad and a loaf of bread to our old beat-up picnic table outside and we would all gather around to savor the bounty that we had each had a part in creating.

The taste of that salad, after working in the hot sun, was reward enough. The crisp, icy, cold snap of those cucumbers and the sourness of the vinegar had me scrunching my face in a pucker, but, as soon as I recovered, I'd be back for more, the next time with a piece of bread to dip in the mélange of flavors that had collected in the dressing at the bottom of the bowl.

On weekends, while my father was tending the grill, he would peel cucumbers, quarter them, and sprinkle them with salt for us to grab with our fingers and eat as a *meze*. They were so crisp, their flavor enhanced by the salt, and they tasted and smelled like fresh air, like life.

Throughout the summer we had abundant harvests. What we didn't eat, we'd bring by the bagful to our cousins and friends. What they couldn't eat, we'd preserve, pickle, and dry for the winter. Nothing went to waste.

As summer drew to a close, we left a selection of each type of fruit and vegetable on the vine to grow to immensity. These would not be for eating, but for harvesting seeds to provide for next year's garden. When the zucchini were nearing two feet in length and as many as ten inches around, we would pick them, split them down the middle, and deposit them in the sun to dry out on our old picnic table. As the flesh of the zucchini dried, the seeds became more accessible and easier to harvest—the beginning of next year's garden. We did the same for everything that grew in our garden. To my father, part of providing for and nourishing his family each year entailed preparing his garden for the following year. He could not have had this year's garden without the last, and he would not have next year's garden without this one.

"You see these seeds?" my father would ask me as he held out a handful of tomato seeds he had carefully placed on a paper towel for me to examine. "Remember these seeds, because we're going to fold this up and use them for next year."

The recipes in this chapter are a taste of my childhood summers. I hope you'll delight in them as I did with my family then and still do today. You will make salads that can be served either as part of an array of side dishes, or as single accompaniments to almost any kind of protein, whether cooked fresh or left over. These dishes have a tremendous amount of flexibility. At my mom's table, we didn't plate the food. Everybody sat down at the dinner table and reached for whatever she had made—four or five dishes on the table at once. We were a family and we ate family-style. Welcome to my family!

WILD BITTER GREENS, ROASTED PEPPERS, GRILLED ONION, OIL-MARINATED DRIED TOMATO & KEFALOTIRI

AGRIA PIKRA HORTA ME PSITES PIPERIES, KREMMYDIA STIN SCHARA, LIASTES TOMATES, KEFALOTYRI

SERVES 4 TO 6 AS A SIDE DISH, OR MORE FAMILY-STYLE,
AS PART OF A LARGER SPREAD

Very, very simple. This is one of the most versatile salads I make. It goes well with any protein, and it functions like a vegetable and salad all in one. If you are doubling or tripling this dish—or any of my salads—for a large party, serve the dressing on the side, so that if there are any leftovers you can keep the greens fresh and bright. Once a salad is dressed, the vinegar begins to break down the greens and they'll wilt if not used in a very short time. If you know you'll eat all the salad right away, go ahead and toss with the dressing. If you use artisanal-quality oil-marinated roasted red peppers and artichokes from a jar, this recipe takes you almost no time at all and the result will be almost as good as if you made your own from scratch. Just be sure to buy premium European brands, and get the best greens possible. This is a fantastic side salad for grilled *souvlaki*. And by the way, *souvlaki*—shish kebab—doesn't have to be pork or chicken; it can be beef, or lamb, or swordfish, or scallops, or shrimp.

1 small head frisée

2 cups baby arugula leaves

1 recipe Grilled Onions (page 270)

1 large fire-roasted red bell pepper (page 270) home-roasted or store-bought, cut into strips

6 large sun-dried tomatoes, cut into thick strips

4 cloves Garlic Confit (page 264), optional

3 pieces Artichoke Confit (page 267), halved, or 6 halves oil-marinated artichokes from a jar, halved again

2 tablespoons small, picked sprigs parsley

2 tablespoons small, picked sprigs dill

6 leaves fresh mint

½ to ⅔ cup Red Wine–Black Pepper Vinaigrette (page 273)

2 ounces *kefalotiri* cheese, shaved with a vegetable peeler into large shards

Wash the frisée and arugula, spin dry, and wrap in clean towels. Chill.

Just before serving: In a large bowl, combine the grilled onions with all the ingredients, except the vinaigrette and half the *kefalotiri*, and toss gently with clean hands. Drizzle with about ½ cup of the vinaigrette, toss again gently but thoroughly, and taste. Season with salt and pepper, scatter with the remaining cheese, and serve immediately.

SWEET-&-SOUR EGGPLANT & ONION STEW
IMAM BAILDI

A classic sweet-and-sour eggplant dish, this works wonderfully as a side dish with any sort of gamey meat. Rabbit and venison would both be fantastic. The cinnamon here is very reminiscent of Middle Eastern flavors, a legacy of the centuries-long Turkish occupation of Greece. In fact, influences come not just from the Middle East, but also from Africa and Italy, because of cultural migrations over time. The Greeks took the flavor profiles from these different cultures and added them to the ingredients that they had naturally on hand, thereby creating dishes that have completely unique identities.

If you have any of this dish left over, pulse it briefly in a food processor to make a chutneylike spread that is fantastic as a topping for crostini. I like to stir in some raisins or tart cherries, spread on toasted bread, and then top with a little crumbled feta.

Because of the preservative qualities of the sugar and vinegar, this dish will last for up to one and a half weeks in the fridge.

15 small, whole cipolline onions
  or shallots
2 tablespoons extra-virgin olive oil
1 clove garlic, smashed
¼ cup red wine vinegar
2¼ cups water
¾ cup smooth tomato sauce,
  homemade or store-bought
1½ tablespoons tomato paste
2 cinnamon sticks

3 large sprigs thyme
1 teaspoon dry Greek oregano
1½ tablespoons granulated sugar
Kosher salt and cracked black pepper
Blended oil, for deep-frying (50 percent
  canola or sunflower, 50 percent extra-
  virgin olive)
1½ large eggplants, sliced crosswise 1 inch
  thick, then cut into 1-inch chunks

If the onions are large, cut them in half. Warm a large skillet over medium-high heat and add the oil. Add the cipolline and garlic, and pan-roast until slightly golden, shaking the pan. Deglaze the pan with the vinegar, then add the water, tomato sauce, tomato paste, cinnamon sticks, thyme, oregano, and sugar. Season generously with salt and pepper. Bring up to the boil and then reduce the heat. Partially cover the pan and braise gently until the onions are just fork-tender, up to 20 minutes. The juice will be quite thick. Reserve.

Prepare a pot of blended oil or deep fryer for deep-frying; heat the oil to 350°F to 375°F. Salt and pepper the eggplant, and deep-fry until nicely browned. Drain on paper towels to get rid of the excess oil; season again with salt.

Fold the fried eggplant into the onion mixture and taste for sugar and vinegar. Remove the remains of the thyme sprigs and the cinnamon sticks, if you like.

☼ If you prefer not to deep-fry the eggplant, you can sauté thick, round slices in olive oil until golden brown, then drain and quarter them into wedges.

MY DEEP-FRYING RULES

◉ Never fill the pot more than halfway with oil, to prevent boilovers.

◉ Be sure the oil is up to the correct temperature before you begin (if you have a fryer, be sure to maintain the temperature; if you don't have a fryer, it is critical to use a thermometer).

◉ Fry in small batches, so you don't crowd the pan (this lowers the temperature of the oil and the object being fried will become saturated and soggy rather than crisp and lightly fried).

◉ Between batches, return the oil to the correct temperature.

◉ If you do have an oil fire, smother it with a towel, *not* water.

CUCUMBER SALAD, CELERY, LEEK & TSAKISTES OLIVES WITH LEMON-DILL VINAIGRETTE

AGOUROSALATA, SELINO, PRASSO, TSAKISTES ELIES ME LADOXYDO LEMONIOU KAI ANITHOU

SERVES 4, OR MORE FAMILY-STYLE, AS PART OF A LARGER SPREAD

In the summertime, my dad always had a big garden. This recipe is something my mother used to throw together using the vegetables from his garden, and we would have it for lunch on a hot day when we were cutting the grass or doing other yard work. She'd put some feta cheese and some bread on the side, and we would open up a couple of cold beers and sit under a tree. It's a bright salad with the flavors of the Mediterranean. Very simple, very clean, very summer. Make sure all the vegetables are cold.

½ large leek, sliced and rinsed

⅓ cup small, picked sprigs dill

25 leaves fresh mint

½ cup small, picked sprigs parsley

1 cup cracked, brined green olives, such as *tsakistes,* pitted

1½ English cucumbers (chilled), halved lengthwise and thickly sliced

½ red onion, slivered lengthwise

3 stalks celery, sliced crosswise

½ to ⅔ cup Lemon-Dill Vinaigrette (page 271)

Sea salt and cracked black pepper

½ lemon

½ cup crumbled feta cheese (optional)

Prepare an ice water bath. In a pot of salted, boiling water, blanch the leeks until tender but not mushy, about 3 minutes. Plunge them into the ice water bath and swish around well to rinse out any dirt (this sets the nice bright color and keeps them crisp; they'll fall apart into rings). Drain and reserve.

Roughly chop the dill, mint, and parsley. Pull the olives into rough pieces. In a large bowl, combine the leeks, herbs, olives, cucumber, red onion, and celery. Toss well with clean hands and drizzle with ½ cup of the Lemon-Dill Vinaigrette. Season with sea salt and cracked pepper and toss again. Add a little more vinaigrette to taste. Squeeze a little lemon juice over the top. Top with feta, if you like.

☀ This salad would be tremendous with a big can of good albacore tuna flaked over the top and folded in. If you want it a little richer, you can fold in a tablespoon of mayonnaise (with or without the tuna), but I like to keep it clean. In this recipe, as with most others in this book, acidity is a critical element.

SHAVED FENNEL, CABBAGE, OLIVE, ONION & GRAVIERA SALAD WITH RED WINE–BLACK PEPPER VINAIGRETTE

MARATHO, LACHANO, ELIES, KREMMYDI KAI GRAVIERA ME LADOXYDO KOKKINOU KRASIOU KAI KOKKOUS MAVROU PIPERIOU

SERVES 4, OR MORE FAMILY-STYLE, AS PART OF A LARGER SPREAD

I think of this as a sort of Greek coleslaw, only much brighter in flavors and far more exciting.

1 bulb fennel, trimmed
2 tablespoons fresh lemon juice
¼ head savoy cabbage, cored
⅔ cup cracked, brined green olives, such as *tsakistes,* pitted
⅔ cup oil-cured Thássos olives, pitted
4 ounces *graviera* cheese, coarsely grated

¼ cup small, picked sprigs dill
8 leaves fresh mint
¼ cup small, picked sprigs parsley
¼ cup small, picked sprigs thyme
½ to ⅔ cup Red Wine–Black Pepper Vinaigrette (page 273)
Sea salt and cracked black pepper

With a mandoline or a very sharp knife, shave the whole bulb of fennel crosswise as thinly as possible (no need to remove the core). Transfer to a large bowl and drizzle with the lemon juice. Shave the cabbage lengthwise, and add. Pull the olives into rough pieces, and add them along with about two thirds of the cheese, dill, mint, parsley, and thyme.

Drizzle with about ½ cup of the vinaigrette and toss aggressively with clean hands until all the ingredients are nicely coated. Season generously with sea salt and pepper, taste, and add a little more vinaigrette if you like (never so much that it pools in the bottom of the bowl). Transfer to a platter and top with the remaining cheese and fresh herbs.

ACIDITY IN GREEK FOOD

One of the flavors that distinguishes Greek food and makes it bright and fresh is acidity, and often—but not always—it comes from lemon juice. You can serve things that are rich and slightly fatty—like one of the many wonderful confits—but in order to keep everyone's taste buds alive and interested, you've got to cut that fattiness with acidity.

STEWED ENGLISH PEAS & MUSHROOMS

ARAKAS LADEROS KAI MANITARIA

SERVES 4, OR MORE FAMILY-STYLE, AS PART OF A LARGER SPREAD

To keep the fresh summer peas really green, you need to blanch and shock them in ice water. If you have a pasta strainer insert, it's perfect for the peas because you can get them quickly into the ice water and keep that beautiful bright color and flavor and prevent them from becoming mushy. I prefer a light and fruity olive oil for this dish, rather than the full-bodied Greek olive oil I normally use.

If you make this dish in the winter, you can use it with frozen *petits pois* and even add a little tomato paste and cinnamon—a very different dish but perfect for cool weather.

8 ounces small button mushrooms

2 tablespoons extra-virgin olive oil, plus more for drizzling

1 large shallot, chopped

8 ounces whole pearl onions, peeled, or thawed frozen pearl onions

½ cup white wine

2 cups water (1 cup only if using frozen pearl onions)

1 large sprig thyme

10 ounces shelled English peas, blanched for 1 minute in boiling water, then shocked in an ice water bath, and drained

20 leaves fresh mint

¼ cup small, picked sprigs dill

2 whole scallions, thinly sliced

Kosher salt and cracked black pepper

Juice of 1 lemon

Rinse the mushrooms in a bowl of cold water, swishing them around. Immediately drain and spread on a towel. (If they're larger than bite-size, halve or quarter them.)

In a braising pan or large, heavy skillet, warm the olive oil. Add and sauté the shallot until just softened, then add the mushrooms and pan-roast until slightly golden, shaking the pan. Add the pearl onions and cook for a minute, then deglaze the pan with the white wine. Add the appropriate amount of water and the thyme, and bring to a boil. Reduce the heat, cover the pan, and simmer gently over low heat until the onions are soft, 15 to 20 minutes (5 to 10 minutes if using frozen pearl onions). Check occasionally and add a little more water if it's all evaporated. Season with kosher salt and pepper.

In a bowl, fold the peas and mushroom–pearl onion mixture together. Add the mint, dill, and scallions, and drizzle liberally with extra-virgin olive oil. Toss, season generously with sea salt and cracked pepper, and squeeze the lemon juice over the top. Toss again.

STEWED STRING BEANS, ZUCCHINI & POTATO

FASOLAKIA LADERA ME KOLOKYTHAKIA KAI PATATES

SERVES 4 TO 6 AS A SIDE DISH, OR MORE FAMILY-STYLE, AS PART OF A LARGER SPREAD

This is a one-pan dish that my mother would serve alongside any sort of red meat, especially in the early fall, when all these vegetables are at their best. Cook the quartered potatoes and quartered green zucchini in the tomato broth until they're soft, then add blanched and shocked string beans. You end up with another traditional vegetable side, in a reduced tomato-cinnamon broth, or sauce. This dish is suitable for Lent, because it is completely meatless—it's actually vegan.

2 tablespoons extra-virgin olive oil, plus more for drizzling
1 large Spanish or sweet onion, sliced into rounds
2 cloves garlic, smashed
1 pound Yukon gold potatoes, peeled, quartered lengthwise, and then halved crosswise
2 tablespoons tomato paste
2 cinnamon sticks

2 teaspoons dry Greek oregano
2 large sprigs thyme
1 (15-ounce) can plum tomatoes
4 cups water
2 small zucchini, quartered lengthwise, and then halved crosswise
Kosher salt and cracked black pepper
6 ounces fine French beans
1 tablespoon red wine vinegar
Sea salt

Warm the olive oil in a large skillet over medium heat. Add and sweat the onions and garlic until translucent. Add the potatoes and tomato paste and stir for 1 minute. Then add the cinnamon, oregano, thyme, canned tomatoes (squeeze them a little as you add to the pan) with about half their juices, and water. Add the zucchini quarters to the stew. Season generously with kosher salt and pepper and bring to a boil. Reduce the heat, partially cover the pan, and simmer gently for 10 minutes. Remove the cinnamon sticks.

While this is happening, prepare an ice water bath and bring a pot of generously salted water to a boil. Blanch the green beans for 2 to 3 minutes, depending on their size; then immediately plunge into the ice water bath. Drain well and reserve.

When the potatoes are fork-tender, add the blanched beans and let them warm through for a minute or two, folding together. Season with sea salt and pepper and drizzle with the red wine vinegar and a little more olive oil. Serve hot, warm, or at room temperature.

GRILLED SUMMER SQUASH, FETA & MINT SALAD

GLYKOKOLOKYTHA STIN SCHARA ME FETA KAI SALATA DYOSMOU

SERVES 4 TO 6, OR MORE FAMILY-STYLE, AS PART OF A LARGER SPREAD

Here's a great summer dish that is really versatile. It morphs into a wonderful pasta salad with the addition of some penne or rigatoni. Serve hot, warm, or at room temperature. Because of all the herbs and spices, you develop interesting flavors. For a beautifully simple and light spring or summer meal, serve this salad with a piece of grilled chicken or a lamb chop. It even can be served cold from the fridge, along with some arugula leaves.

1 Spanish or sweet onion, sliced into
¼-inch rounds
Extra-virgin olive oil
Kosher salt and cracked black pepper
2 green zucchini, cut ⅜ inch thick on
the diagonal
2 yellow squash, cut into ⅜-inch rounds
Tiny handful small, picked sprigs dill

10 leaves fresh mint
1 tablespoon crumbled feta cheese,
plus a little more for serving
⅓ to ½ cup White Wine Vinaigrette
(page 273)
1 teaspoon dry Greek oregano
Tiny handful small, picked sprigs thyme
Sea salt

Preheat a gas or charcoal grill, or ridged cast-iron griddle pan, until very hot. Brush the onion rings with a little olive oil and season with kosher salt and pepper. In a bowl, toss the zucchini and squash with olive oil, salt, and pepper. Grill all the vegetables until the onions are softened and the zucchini and squash are nicely char-marked.

While they're grilling, chop the dill and mint roughly, and whisk the feta into the White Wine Vinaigrette until creamy.

In a large bowl, combine all the grilled vegetables (pull the onions apart into rings), chopped dill and mint, oregano, and picked thyme. Toss with clean hands, then drizzle with about ⅓ cup of the vinaigrette. Season with a little sea salt and toss again. Scatter a little extra feta over the top.

GRILLED WATERMELON & GRILLED MANOURI

KARPOUZI KAI MANOURI STIN SCHARA

SERVES 4 AS A PLATED APPETIZER, OR MORE FAMILY-STYLE,
AS PART OF A LARGER SPREAD

This dish can be prepared on the grill or in a very well seasoned, ridged cast-iron grill pan. Just make sure the cheese is very cold and very firm. *Manouri* is a unique, semisoft Greek cheese, but if you can't find it, substitute a block of good Greek feta.

12 ounces *manouri,* very cold

1½ pounds seedless watermelon, in two
   1-inch-thick, center-cut slices

Extra-virgin olive oil

Kosher salt and cracked black pepper

20 leaves fresh mint

20 picked sprigs dill

Sea salt

Preheat a charcoal or gas grill until hot.

Cut the *manouri* into two 1-inch-thick circles. Trim the rind from the watermelon rounds and cut into large pie-shaped wedges, about 5 inches on the longer sides. Brush the watermelon and the *manouri* with a little olive oil and season with kosher salt and pepper.

Grill the watermelon wedges and the *manouri* rounds just until slightly char-marked on both sides. Transfer to a platter and cut the *manouri* into wedges about the same size as the watermelon. Drizzle with a little more olive oil. Scatter with the mint leaves, dill sprigs, and a little sea salt. Grind a little pepper over the top.

☀ For an extra bit of tanginess, scatter with a few drops of aged or reduced balsamic vinegar.

SUMMER AND GRILLING IN MY FATHER'S GARDEN

Whenever summer arrives, my father's garden comes to mind, and whenever my father's garden comes to my mind, it means outdoor backyard grilling. It was a focal point in our house. We had a big swimming pool, and when it was hot there were always people around swimming, eating, drinking—and grilling. In the summer, I still love to keep away from pots and pans and have everything happening on the grill. So take summer vegetables, from the garden if you are lucky enough to have one, and season them with salt and pepper, coat them with good olive oil, and put them on the grill. (Use a ridged grill pan, if you don't have access to a grill.)

FOUR CHEESE–STUFFED ZUCCHINI BLOSSOMS
YEMISTI KOLOKYNTHOANTHI ME TESSERA TYRIA

MAKES 12 STUFFED BLOSSOMS

This dish is a creative variation on something my mom loved to make in the summertime. Her *gemista* were vegetables stuffed with a rice-and-ground-meat mixture. But in the summer, zucchini blossoms are a rare treat. So instead of making my mom's traditional, heartier stuffing, I make a lighter stuffing and use it to fill these beautiful blossoms. Then I fry them in a light and crisp tempura batter.

These are wonderful canapés because they are one- or two-bite finger foods. They should be served within a minute or two after coming out of the oil, otherwise, they will get a little soggy. This dish has a very limited window of seasonality. With special things like this, it's worth giving them a little extra care. Please be sure to check out "My Deep-frying Rules" on page 23.

FOR THE TEMPURA BATTER
1¾ cups soda water, or as needed
1⅓ cups all-purpose flour
6 tablespoons cornstarch
3 teaspoons salt

FOR THE ZUCCHINI BLOSSOMS
12 zucchini blossoms, preferably with a
    length of stem still attached
⅔ cup very fresh whole-milk ricotta,
    drained

¼ cup finely grated *kefalotiri* cheese
¼ cup finely grated *mizithra* cheese
¼ cup crumbled *manouri* cheese
1 tablespoon small, picked sprigs dill,
    chopped
8 leaves fresh mint, chopped
Canola or safflower oil, for deep-frying
    (for even better flavor, use half extra-
    virgin olive oil)
Lemon wedges, for serving

For the tempura batter, pour the soda water into a bowl. In a sifter, combine the flour, cornstarch, and salt, and sift it into the soda water. Whisk until evenly blended. The batter should have the consistency of thin pancake batter. Add a little more soda water if necessary to thin it. Cover and refrigerate for 45 minutes.

For the zucchini blossoms, gently pull open the tops of the zucchini blossoms and pull out the dark orange pistils. Combine the four cheeses and the chopped herbs and season well; mix until smooth.

Use 1 to 1½ tablespoons of the filling to stuff each flower, pushing it as far down toward the base as you can.

Prepare a pot of oil or a deep fryer for deep-frying; heat the oil to 350°F. Gently twist the tops of the blossoms a bit, to hold in the filling. Dip and roll a blossom in the batter, making sure to coat it well. Using tongs, and using the stem as a handle, submerge it in the hot oil and hold for about 10 seconds before you let go (this seizes the batter and stops it from sticking). Proceed with dipping and frying the blossoms; as soon as one is golden brown, remove with a skimmer and drain briefly. Line a platter with a flattened brown-paper grocery bag, throw on some lemon wedges, and pass the blossoms as they are finished. This way, guests can squeeze a little lemon over each one *right* before they eat it. If you squeeze too early, the blossoms won't stay crisp. The filling will be very hot, so warn people before their first bite.

❁ Optional: Sweat a handful of spinach leaves and some sliced scallions in a little olive oil until very tender. Cool and squeeze out as much liquid as you can. Chop and add to the cheese filling, with one egg yolk to hold it all together. (Note: If you have a bounty of squash blossoms, chop some up and add them to the spinach-scallion mixture before adding to cheese.)

BULGUR SALAD WITH ROASTED PEPPERS, CAPERS, RAISINS, CELERY & ONION

SALATA ME PLIGOURI, PSITI PIPERIA, KAPARI, STAFIDES, SELINO KAI KREMMYDI

SERVES 4 TO 6 AS A SIDE DISH, OR MORE FAMILY-STYLE,
AS PART OF A LARGER SPREAD

Here, sweet and savory flavors combine with the bulgur, which gives a great chewy texture and nutty flavor. Traditionally, you might see this kind of mixture stuffed into a pepper, but I've made more of a simple salad and added the peppers in strips.

This dish is fantastic served with a loin of lamb, cooked medium-rare, and sliced tomatoes. It is also great with grilled giant shrimp or scallops. For another dimension of bright flavor, you can also fold in a tablespoon of strained or Greek yogurt. Serve this salad hot or at room temperature. It keeps nicely.

If you're going to a pool party and need to bring a salad, this one travels well because there's nothing that can wilt. And you might as well make twice as much, because the next day you can pick up some shellfish and sausage on the way home and turn the leftovers into a great dish for six people.

1 tablespoon extra-virgin olive oil, plus more for drizzling
¼ cup finely chopped Spanish or sweet onion
2 cloves garlic, crushed
1 cup coarse (no. 3) bulgur
3 cups water
Kosher salt and cracked black pepper
3 tablespoons capers
3 pale inner stalks celery, thickly sliced

½ cup golden raisins
20 leaves fresh mint
¼ cup small, picked sprigs dill
4 small fire-roasted red bell peppers (page 270), home-roasted or store-bought, cut into strips (see Note)
Small handful pale inner leaves from the celery heart
Sea salt
½ lemon

Put a saucepan over medium-low heat and add the olive oil. Add the onion and garlic, and sauté gently until tender. Add the bulgur and stir over the heat for 2 minutes to toast slightly without browning. Add the water and a generous amount of kosher salt and pepper. Bring to a boil, and remove from the heat. Cover and let stand for 1 hour.

Meanwhile, in a small pot of lightly salted boiling water, simmer the capers, celery, and raisins for 5 minutes. (This step hydrates the raisins, softens the celery, and soothes the strong briny flavor of the capers.) Drain and reserve. Roughly chop the herbs.

In a large bowl, combine the cooked bulgur, caper mixture, herbs, strips of pepper, and celery leaves. Season well with sea salt and cracked pepper and toss well with clean hands. Drizzle with a little olive oil and squeeze the lemon over. Toss again and taste.

Note: It's easy enough to roast red peppers, but to save even more time, you may substitute imported, fire-roasted peppers from a jar, packed in olive oil or brine. Whenever you use ingredients that are packed in a jar or a can, make sure they are of the highest quality. You don't want to destroy a dish you've worked on by compromising its integrity with inferior products.

☀ Here's a Greek paella, using mussels, clams, shrimp, and/or scallops: Open your shellfish in a hot pan over medium-high heat with a little white wine and garlic. Add this salad to the same pan, and toss everything together. To make it more like a traditional paella, you can render some sausage meat in the pan first, then add the shellfish, and deglaze the pan with the white wine. All of the flavor from the sausage gets incorporated into the liquid, which will permeate the toasted grains.

VEGETABLES AND THE LENTEN TRADITION

Because of the strong Lenten tradition and the relative poverty of so many of the Greek people over time, Greek food has a tremendous appeal to vegetarians and people who like to stay away from any sort of animal products. If they lived in the mountains, the Greeks were limited to what they could hunt, like quail and rabbits. Or, of course, if they lived near the sea, there were fish. But there was not a lot of protein for most people, so there is a long tradition of cooking vegetables, especially during the forty days of Lent, in which the Church says that you cannot eat anything that came from an animal with blood—no dairy, no eggs, no butter. But because the vegetables in these dishes are so substantial, they could easily make a main course with a hunk of bread.

ARTICHOKES & POTATO

AGINARES KAI PATATES

This recipe benefits hugely from the flavor of the Artichoke Confit. It's important to know that you are not just making Artichoke Confit here; you're also making a wonderful artichoke oil. Always keep the remaining oil for another use. You should use the leftover oil from the confit to make the *Ladolemono* used here, so nothing is wasted. This is a sturdy salad that can easily stay in the refrigerator for thirty minutes, or wait on the table for an hour.

If you double this recipe, the next day you can grill a piece of chicken and serve it atop some leftover salad. It's a simple dish that you can easily add a protein to: some leftover turkey, some pulled ham. All of a sudden, you have something you can pack into Tupperware and take to work.

1 pound fingerling potatoes, scrubbed

½ pound (about 1¼ cups) Artichoke Confit (page 267), with some of the oil (or 6 halves oil-marinated artichokes from a jar, halved again)

6 shallots, halved and thinly sliced lengthwise

4 stalks celery, thinly sliced crosswise

⅓ cup small, picked sprigs dill

12 leaves fresh mint

¼ cup small, picked sprigs thyme

½ to ⅔ cup *Ladolemono* (page 270)

Sea salt and cracked black pepper

½ lemon

½ cup feta or *manouri* cheese

Put the potatoes in a large pot of generously salted cold water and place over high heat. Bring to a boil, then reduce the heat and simmer gently until just crisp-tender, 7 to 8 minutes. Drain and spread out on a plate. Refrigerate for at least 30 minutes, until chilled, and up to overnight.

Cut the potatoes into rustic, bite-size chunks. In a large bowl, combine the potatoes, Artichoke Confit (with a tablespoon of the confit oil), shallots, celery, dill, mint, and thyme. Toss the mixture aggressively, with clean hands, and drizzle with ½ cup of *Ladolemono*.

Season with sea salt and pepper and toss again. Taste and add a little more *Ladolemono* if you like. Squeeze some lemon juice over the top. Finish with a sprinkle of feta or *manouri* cheese.

Left to right: Psilakis family boat, the Georgia; *family and friends, 1983; Costas Psilakis with his catch, a ten-pound bluefish, 1987*

open water

Just as I awaited my father's return from work on summer weekdays so we could tend the garden together, so too did I eagerly anticipate weekends spent on our boat.

Saturdays were full days on the boat, and we'd often have as many as fifteen people on board. The drill was always the same: mornings were spent fishing in peace, and the later part of the day was for swimming, cruising, and horsing around on the beach. Sundays were church days, so that meant only half a day on the boat. That was the day my mother would be most likely to join us, along with any aunts who wanted to come too. The women weren't interested in being on the boat for a whole day but still enjoyed our time on the water. My mother was and continues to be terrified of the water, but the boat meant so much to my father that everyone came on board at some point during the summer.

The boat was not an inexpensive hobby and, considering that my father had fled a war-torn island (on the heels of World War II) in search of a better life and that he had arrived in this country with so little, it was an *accomplishment*. This one simple possession represented, to him, that he had overcome hardship, provided for his immediate family and many members of our extended family as well, and still had enough left over to afford this luxury.

Our first boat, which we got when I was about ten, was a monster. It was an old, beat-up wooden boat we painted white. It was forty-three feet long, and a dozen people could easily lie down in the front to take in the sun. There was a fly bridge on top where my father could always be found when we were under way. I was always my father's first mate.

This behemoth had only one engine. That made docking in our narrow slip at the end of the day an adventure. My job was to leap, sometimes as far as five feet, to the dock with the rope in hand so I could manually pull the back end of the boat close enough to tie it up to the cleat. Then my father, done with the steering, would run down from the fly bridge to the front and throw me the other rope. I'd drag the front end in too and try to get the boat safely tied up to the dock without crashing into too many of the other boats nearby. If other people were with us, they'd stand along the sides of our boat with feet ready to push away from any other boat we were about to hit.

Some days my father would take just us kids out on the boat—my two younger sisters, Maria and Anna, and my brother, Peter, the baby of the family. After fishing, we'd motor out past Sands Point and in toward one of the area beaches. We'd jump in with nets and swim to shore, and there in the shallow water, as they swam around our feet, we'd scoop up nets full of whitebait (minnow-sized fish). My mother would later fry them and we'd pop them into our mouths whole.

It was the boat trips alone with my father that were most precious to me. It was about more than just getting his undivided attention; it was during those times that I had the opportunity to see a different aspect of the man he was on land. We would share those solitary and peaceful fishing hours in the mornings, when we would catch enough porgies to fill multiple tar buckets to overflowing. And it was here that my father taught me how special it was not only to have time with the people you love but also time alone with yourself.

My father was recognized as the head of our extended family. Not only were we children his dependents, but his brothers and brothers-in-law would often come to him for advice and financial assistance as well. While he was no doubt proud of the position he had achieved within the family, he had a tremendous amount of responsibility and pressure resting on his shoulders. On the boat, it was as if all of that were carried away by the wind. I don't think I ever saw my father more at peace.

My father wasn't big on reading instruction manuals. Early on during the second season with our boat, he forgot to check the oil before we headed out for the day. We had an oil leak, and by the time we got out into Long Island Sound our motor

was grinding. Of course, we learned all of this only after our engine exploded in the Atlantic Ocean and my father had to call the Coast Guard to tow us in.

Our second boat was a Silverton with twin diesel engines. This was an entirely different experience for me because, while I was still my father's first mate, having the twin engines took the chaos out of our boating excursions. Well, it eliminated *some* of the chaos. We Psilakises would never escape chaos altogether when boating.

We always came home with a bountiful catch. After spending hours scrubbing and washing the boat, my father and I would gut the fish. If it was bluefish, we'd scale it and hand it over to my mother to make *plaki*, a hearty peasant dish. She'd put the fish in a pan with tomatoes, onions, potatoes, white wine, lemon, and oregano, and bake it in the oven. If we caught porgy, which we often did, we wouldn't scale it. My father would put it on the grill, scales down. As the scales heated up they'd pull away from the skin and as the skin heated up it would naturally separate from the meat. The layer of fat between the skin and the meat would melt and essentially steam and baste the fish in its own fat. After he cooked the fish, my father would pile up the fish heads on a plate, and there was always someone who sat with that plate and sucked at the eyes and ate the cheek meat.

When I look back at my childhood summers, I think of fishing on our boat and the many happy times I shared with so many people—not just family, but friends as well. Nobody was overlooked; even our parish priest sometimes came along. Most of all, though, I remember what the boat meant to my father: the peace of mind it brought him.

The recipes in this section are, to me, a taste of the open water, a taste of freedom and tranquillity, a remembrance of time with my father.

OCTOPUS, SALAMI & APPLES
WITH ANCHOVY VINAIGRETTE
OCTAPODI, SALAMI KAI MILA ME LADOXYDO ANJOUYAS

SERVES 4

A few years ago, I was playing around with ways to incorporate fat into an octopus dish, and I happened to have an Italian hero sandwich. I realized that the fat molecules in the salami explode on your palate and resonate for a while. This was a revelation! While the fat remains on your palate, anything that follows benefits from its residual afterglow. Here, the texture of the octopus is faced with the crispness of the apple and the fat of the salami. Then, this tartly acidic vinaigrette makes for an amazing juxtaposition on the palate. Salt, acid, sweet, *fat*. It's an evolution that happens in your mouth and then telegraphs its message straight to the brain.

I always have an octopus dish on the menu, and this was the opening octopus dish at Onera, the restaurant that later became my flagship, Anthos. It got quite a lot of attention from the press!

4 legs of octopus, braised (as on page 218), at room temperature

1 small green apple, such as Granny Smith, peeled, quartered, cored, and cut into ¼-inch batons

4 ounces thickly sliced lountza (salami, such as Genoa, may be substituted) cut into ¼-inch batons

About ⅓ cup White Anchovy Vinaigrette (page 273)

Extra-virgin olive oil

Sea salt and cracked black pepper

Small handful picked fresh mint

Cut the octopus into rough chunks.

In a bowl, combine the octopus, apple, and salami. There should be roughly equal quantities of apple and salami. Drizzle the mixture with some of the chunky vinaigrette and toss to coat evenly.

Transfer to a platter or plates and drizzle with olive oil. Season with a little sea salt and cracked pepper and garnish with fresh mint.

ROASTED SKATE WITH WALNUT BAKLAVA, YOGURT & CANDIED QUINCE

*SELAHI ME BAKLAVA KARYDIOU,
YAOURTI KAI ZAHAROMENA KYDONIA*

SERVES 4 AS A PLATED APPETIZER, OR 2 TO 3 AS AN ENTRÉE

This dish is a little complicated, but if you take the time to make the candied quince, you will definitely also want to make my wonderful yogurt dessert on page 108. The fruit will keep for weeks in the refrigerator, as long as you sterilize the jar. Watch out for cross-contamination from the spoon you use to scoop it out (always use a perfectly clean one).

1 teaspoon ground cinnamon

¼ teaspoon ground cloves

Pinch of ground nutmeg

2 tablespoons sugar

2 tablespoons water

1 cup walnut halves

4 sheets phyllo dough, thawed

¼ cup clarified butter

2 tablespoons strained or Greek yogurt

1 tablespoon distilled white vinegar

Sea salt and cracked black pepper

1 tablespoon blended oil

1 tablespoon water

1¼ pounds boneless, skinless skate wings

All-purpose flour

½ cup Candied Quince (page 277)

1 teaspoon chopped dill

4 leaves fresh mint, slivered

2 scallions, green part only, thinly sliced

5 to 6 tablespoons unsalted butter

2 large leaves sage, slivered

1½ tablespoons capers

First, make the walnut baklava: in a small bowl, combine the cinnamon, cloves, and nutmeg. In a small nonstick skillet, combine the sugar and water and, over low heat, stir until the sugar has dissolved. Add the walnuts and toss to coat. Cook, stirring, until all the moisture has evaporated and the sugar begins to caramelize. Transfer to the bowl with the spices and toss. Cool on a piece of parchment. Chop fine. Use half the nuts for the walnut baklava and reserve the rest for serving.

Preheat the oven to 350°F. Lay 1 sheet of phyllo dough on a large, rimmed baking sheet. Brush with clarified butter and scatter evenly with a big pinch of the spiced nuts. Repeat with 2 more sheets of phyllo and finish with the last phyllo sheet. Brush it with butter, but do *not* scatter with nuts. Bake for about 15 minutes, until mottled golden and dark brown. Let cool, then break the walnut baklava into odd-shaped shards, and reserve.

In a bowl, whisk together the yogurt and vinegar. Season with salt and pepper. Reserve.

In a large skillet, warm the blended oil over medium heat. When it is very hot, season both sides of the skate pieces with salt and pepper, and dust one side generously with flour. Rub the flour in, then shake off the excess. Slide the pieces into the hot pan, flour-side down. Cook without disturbing for about 2 minutes, until golden. Turn over, and remove the pan from the heat, allowing residual heat to finish cooking the fish while you complete the dish.

Smear the plates or platter with some of the yogurt mixture. Alternate layers of skate and crushed baklava, showcasing the fish as much as possible. Scatter a few pieces of candied quince over and around, and throw the fresh dill and mint and scallion greens over all.

Add the butter, sage, and capers to another small pan over medium heat. Swirl the pan for a minute or two and, the instant the butter foam begins to go a little brown at the edges, remove from the heat. Immediately spoon the foamy brown butter over the top of the plated dish.

CLARIFYING BUTTER IN THE MICROWAVE

Cut the butter into chunks and put in a microwave-safe container. Heat (uncovered) for 30 seconds at a time, to avoid excessive foaming, just until separated. Skim off and discard the foam from the top. Pour off the clear yellow clarified butter, leaving behind the white solids at the bottom. Any leftover clarified butter can be reserved for future use.

GRILLED SARDINES WITH CHOPPED SALAD & SKORDALIA SOUP
SARDELES STIN SCHARA, SALATA PSILOKOMENI, SOUPA SKORDALIA

SERVES 4 AS A PLATED APPETIZER

In Greece, sardines are fried, sautéed, or grilled, and served with a wide array of accompaniments. The yogurt here is my own take.

FOR THE SKORDALIA
1 Idaho potato, peeled and quartered
3 cloves garlic, sliced
3 tablespoons distilled white vinegar
3 tablespoons extra-virgin olive oil
Kosher salt and cracked black pepper

FOR THE GRILLED SARDINES & SALAD
8 to 12 fresh sardines, scaled and
  gutted, heads off
1 tablespoon strained or Greek yogurt

1½ tablespoons distilled white vinegar
¼ recipe Greek Salad (page 213,
  see Note), roughly chopped
2 to 3 tablespoons Red Wine–Black
  Pepper Vinaigrette (page 273) or
  2 tablespoons extra-virgin olive oil
  and 1 tablespoon fresh lemon juice
Kosher salt and coarsely cracked
  black pepper
Pinch dry Greek oregano

continued

For the *Skordalia*, cook the potato in boiling salted water until very tender.

Meanwhile, in a small food processor, purée the garlic and vinegar until very smooth.

Put the potato through a ricer into a bowl and stir in the garlic-vinegar mixture. Stir in the olive oil, 1 teaspoon salt, and a generous grinding of pepper. The *Skordalia* should be the consistency of applesauce. Whisk the *Skordalia* with the yogurt and vinegar to a thick paste.

For the grilled sardines, open out each sardine's central cavity, as you would a book. Using your thumb, push out any of the innards that may remain. Then work your thumb in between the rib cage and the flesh, starting at the tail end and working your way down toward the head to release the rib cage and the spine. Repeat on the other side and remove the skeleton. With tweezers, pull out any pinbones that extend beyond the outside edges on either side. Leave the back fin in place. Dry the sardines well with paper towels and hold in the refrigerator on a rack, uncovered, until ready to grill.

Assemble and dress the little chopped Greek Salad (if using olive oil and lemon juice instead of the vinaigrette, be sure to season well). Place a nice big smear of the *Skordalia*-yogurt mixture on each of 4 plates.

Preheat a charcoal or gas grill, or ridged cast-iron grill pan, until very, very hot. Season the sardines on both sides with salt and pepper. Grill with the skin side down for 30 to 40 seconds, then turn over for 1 second only, and transfer to warm plates on top of the *Skordalia*. Top each sardine with a sprinkle of Greek oregano and a little of the chopped salad.

※ Try topping with a pinch of *paximadi* (toasted rustic bread crumbs) for texture.

※ Rather than make up the entire recipe for Greek Salad, thinly shave a little iceberg lettuce and fennel and toss with whatever you have in the refrigerator: pitted, halved olives; crumbled feta; capers and/or caperberries; diced roasted pepper. The greens are not as important as the sardines here, but you do want something crispy-briny as a garnish.

GRILLED CUTTLEFISH STUFFED WITH SPINACH

SOUPIA YEMISTI ME SPANAKI STIN SCHARA

SERVES 4 TO 6 AS A PLATED APPETIZER

The roasted tomatoes here make a fantastic garnish for almost any protein. I like them served either hot or at room temperature. They're also a great *meze*, or stand-up starter, with a sprinkle of feta and a sprig of dill or chive.

FOR THE ROASTED TOMATOES
2 tablespoons finely chopped leaves
    thyme
3 cloves garlic, smashed and finely
    chopped
Kosher salt and cracked black pepper
3 tablespoons extra-virgin olive oil
4 small, ripe tomatoes, halved crosswise

FOR THE SPINACH
1 tablespoon mild extra-virgin olive oil,
    plus more for grilling
1 whole scallion, sliced
1½ cups baby spinach leaves

1 shallot, finely chopped
2 teaspoons roughly chopped dill
Sea salt and cracked black pepper
1½ tablespoons crumbled feta cheese

4 whole baby cuttlefish (sepia) or
    2 large calamari, cleaned
½ bulb fennel, shaved paper-thin
½ teaspoon dry Greek oregano
2 teaspoons capers
About 10 cherry or grape tomatoes,
    halved (optional)
Fresh lemon juice

For the roasted tomatoes, preheat the oven to 325°F. Mix the thyme, garlic, ½ teaspoon salt, and a generous grinding of pepper with the olive oil. Spread this mixture on the cut sides of the tomatoes and roast uncovered for about 1 hour and 15 minutes, until slightly shrunken.

For the cuttlefish, warm the tablespoon of oil in a small skillet over medium-high heat. Add the scallion and spinach and wilt for 1½ minutes, stirring. Add the shallot and dill, season with a bit of salt and pepper, and remove from the heat. When this is cool, stir in the feta.

Stuff the bodies of the cuttlefish with the spinach mixture. Poke the head inside the top opening and secure with a toothpick.

Preheat a charcoal or gas grill, or ridged cast-iron grill pan, until very, very hot. Paint the cuttlefish with oil, and season with salt and pepper. Grill until slightly firm to the touch. (This will not take long, as the stuffing is cooked and the cuttlefish will cook through quickly. Do not overcook or they will get chewy.)

Toss the shaved fennel, oregano, capers, and cherry tomatoes with a little olive oil and lemon juice. Season with salt and pepper. Cut the cuttlefish in half crosswise and serve with 2 or 3 roasted tomato halves and a little of the fennel salad.

FRIED RED MULLET WITH LENTILS, LEMON & OIL

TIGANITO BARBOUNI, FAKES KAI LADOLEMONO

There is really no substitute for red mullet, but if you can't find it, this dish works with whiting. Ask your fishmonger to clean, scale, and fillet the fish, leaving the skin on. If you enjoy lentil soup, double the lentil recipe, and I guarantee you'll be delighted. It's my mother's recipe and one of my favorite cold-weather dishes.

1 tablespoon mild extra-virgin olive oil
1 onion, finely chopped
1 stalk celery, finely chopped
4 cloves garlic, finely chopped
1 small Idaho potato, peeled and finely chopped
1 large carrot, finely chopped
1 fresh bay leaf or 2 dried leaves
1 large sprig fresh thyme
½ pound brown lentils
½ cup red wine
2 tablespoons sherry vinegar
Kosher salt and cracked black pepper

Canola or safflower oil, for deep-frying (or use half extra-virgin olive oil)
4 to 6 small red mullet, filleted and pinbones removed (skin on)
About 1 tablespoon Garlic Purée (page 264)
About 1 tablespoon Dijon mustard
6 to 8 large leaves sage, trimmed to the length of the mullet fillets
All-purpose flour
Ladolemono (page 270) or extra-virgin olive oil and lemon juice
Small handful picked fresh herbs, such as parsley, dill, and/or mint
Sea salt

First, braise the lentils: in a large, heavy-bottomed braising pan, warm the olive oil over medium-high heat. Add all the vegetables, bay leaf, and thyme sprig, and cook for 3 to 5 minutes, to soften without browning. Add the lentils and stir for 2 minutes, then deglaze the pan with the red wine and sherry vinegar. Simmer until the wine is completely evaporated, then add enough water to cover everything by a good inch. Bring to a boil and season with salt and pepper. Reduce the heat, cover, and simmer for 20 to 25 minutes, until the lentils are just tender. Strain, reserving all the liquid in a large measuring jug. Return the drained lentils to the empty cooking pot.

In a food processor, purée ¼ cup of the lentils with about ½ cup of the braising liquid. Add this into the drained lentils and adjust with remaining liquid to form a "soupy" consistency. Taste for seasoning and reserve.

In a large, heavy pot no more than half filled with oil or in a deep fryer, heat the canola oil to 375°F. Dry the fillets well with paper towels. Season both sides of the fillets with salt and pepper. Smear the flesh side with a film of both Garlic Purée and mustard.

Make a sandwich with the sage leaves in the middle and the mullet, skin sides out. Push onto long bamboo skewers, back and forth, as you would for a satay. Dredge in flour, shaking off the excess. Fry in the hot oil until golden brown, 2 to 3 minutes.

Spoon some of the lentil mixture onto warm plates and top with one fish satay, pulling out the skewers. Drizzle with a little *Ladolemono*, a few grains of sea salt, and a sprinkle of fresh herbs.

OUZO & ORANGE–BRAISED SNAILS

SALIGARIA SIGOVRASMENA SE OUZO KAI PORTOKALI

SERVES 4 TO 6 AS AN APPETIZER, OR MORE FAMILY-STYLE,
AS PART OF A LARGER SPREAD

This is a butter braise, my own elegant take on snails, which are a popular and traditional Greek dish from the islands (especially Crete). More often, snails are braised in a tomatoey broth. Just like mussels in white wine, there are lots of delicious buttery juices here, which should be mopped up with hunks of crusty bread. For an entrée, add some orzo or flat pasta, like *hilopites* or pappardelle.

1 tablespoon mild extra-virgin olive oil

½ Spanish or sweet onion, finely chopped

½ bulb fennel, finely chopped

1 stalk celery, finely chopped

¼ cup ouzo

1 cup white wine

1 (28-ounce) can Helix snails, thoroughly rinsed and drained

1 cinnamon stick

1 quart water

Zest and juice from 1 orange

2 tablespoons fresh lemon juice, plus more for serving

8 ounces unsalted butter

Kosher salt and cracked black pepper

Large handful torn fresh herbs, such as dill, mint, parsley, and/or chives

Hunks of crusty bread

In a large skillet, warm the olive oil over medium-high heat. Add the vegetables and wilt for 3 to 5 minutes without browning. Deglaze the pan with the ouzo and white wine and immediately add the snails, cinnamon, water, zest and juice of the orange, lemon juice, and butter. Season with salt and pepper. Bring to a boil and reduce the heat slightly. Simmer briskly, uncovered, until the snails are tender and the juices are creamy, about 35 to 40 minutes.

Throw in the fresh herbs and remove from the heat. Taste for seasoning and add more lemon juice if needed. Serve in large, warm bowls with hunks of bread.

GRILLED SWORDFISH WITH TOMATO-BRAISED CAULIFLOWER
KSIFIAS STIN SCHARA, KOUNOUPIDI KOKKINISTO

SERVES 4

Here is an excellent example of pronounced cinnamon flavor in a savory dish. The cauliflower here is a terrific side dish on its own.

2 tablespoons extra-virgin olive oil
1 medium head cauliflower, broken
  into florets
Kosher salt and cracked black pepper
Large pinch ground cinnamon
½ large Spanish or sweet onion, thinly
  sliced
1 fresh bay leaf or 2 dried leaves

2 cinnamon sticks
1 tablespoon tomato paste
2 tablespoons red wine vinegar
1½ cups water
2 whole sprigs thyme
2 teaspoons Dijon mustard
4 swordfish steaks, about 5 ounces each
Sea salt

In a large, heavy pot over medium-high heat, warm the oil until it is very hot. Add the cauliflower florets. Season with kosher salt and pepper, and dust with the cinnamon. Shake the pan for 2 to 3 minutes, until nicely golden. Add the onion, bay leaves, and cinnamon sticks. Stir in the tomato paste and cook for 1 minute. Deglaze the pan with the vinegar. Add the water, thyme sprigs, and mustard. Partially cover the pan and braise over low heat until the cauliflower is tender. Remove from the heat and discard the bay leaves and cinnamon sticks. (Make ahead and rewarm before serving, if you like.)

Preheat a charcoal or gas grill, or ridged cast-iron grill pan or cast-iron skillet, until very hot. Season both sides of the swordfish steaks with kosher salt and pepper. Grill for 1½ to 2 minutes on each side. Rest the steaks for a couple of minutes and serve with the braised cauliflower. Finish with a pinch of sea salt.

Note: Swordfish should be cooked to the same temperature as you would enjoy a piece of tuna (if immune deficiencies are not an issue). Overcooking will dry out the fish and make it chewy.

※ For a sweet-and-sour dish, add a handful of raisins, dates, dried apricots, or dried cherries, and some pine nuts, caperberries, and *tsakistes* green olives.

※ If you have some Garlic Purée (page 264), stir a tablespoon into the braised cauliflower.

CRETAN SPICED TUNA WITH BULGUR SALAD

TONOS KARYKEVMENOS ME KRITIKA BACHARIKA, SALATA ME PLIGOURI

SERVES 4 AS A PLATED ENTRÉE

Bulgur wheat comes in various sizes, and each one requires different cooking and/
or soaking times. If you are unable to find precooked coarse (no. 3) bulgur, prepare it
according to the instructions on the package.

1 tablespoon extra-virgin olive oil, plus
    more for drizzling
¼ cup minced Spanish or sweet onion
2 cloves garlic, crushed and chopped
1 cup coarse (no. 3) bulgur
3 cups water
Kosher salt and cracked black pepper
8 large sun-dried tomatoes, slivered
1 cup golden raisins
1 cup pine nuts
¼ cup capers
24 oil-cured Thássos olives (or Moroc-
    can black olives), pitted and chopped
½ cup strained or Greek yogurt

¼ cup distilled white vinegar
Large pinch sweet paprika
2 tablespoons blended oil (90 percent
    canola, 10 percent extra-virgin olive)
1½ to 1¾ pounds ahi tuna loin, cut
    into 4 steaks
Cretan Spice Mix (page 270)
⅓ to ½ cup Red Wine–Black Pepper
    Vinaigrette (page 273)
¼ cup roughly chopped fresh herbs,
    such as parsley and/or dill
Fresh lemon juice
Sea salt

In a saucepan, warm the olive oil over medium-low heat. Add the onion and garlic and
sauté gently until tender. Add the bulgur and stir over the heat for 2 minutes, to toast
slightly. Add the water and a generous amount of kosher salt and pepper. Bring to a
boil and remove from the heat. Cover and let stand for 1 hour.

Combine the cooked bulgur, sun-dried tomatoes, raisins, pine nuts, capers, and olives.
Reserve. Whisk together the yogurt, vinegar, and paprika. Season with salt and pepper.

In a large skillet, warm the blended oil over medium-high heat. Season the tuna on
both sides with salt and pepper. Dust all sides generously with the Cretan Spice Mix.

Sear the tuna for about 2 minutes, then turn over, reduce the heat, and cook for 1½ to
2 minutes more, depending on how you like to serve tuna.

Add just enough vinaigrette to dress the bulgur salad lightly. Season with salt and
pepper, sprinkle with fresh herbs, and toss.

Smear a large spoonful of the yogurt mixture on each of 4 dinner plates. Top with bulgur
salad. Cut the tuna steaks into thick slices and place on top of the salad. Drizzle with lemon
juice and olive oil. Finish with sea salt and cracked pepper.

ROASTED SCALLOPS WITH CAULIFLOWER, TART DRIED CHERRIES & CAPERS IN BROWN BUTTER SAUCE

KTENIA PSITA, KOUNOUPIDI, APOXYRAMENA KERASSIA, KAPARI, SALTSA VOUTYROU

SERVES 4 AS AN APPETIZER

This is a superquick pan-roast, so get everything ready before you begin. Then go straight to the table as soon as it's done.

Florets from 1 small head cauliflower, roughly chopped
Kosher salt and cracked black pepper
1½ tablespoons olive oil, divided
12 (U-10) diver-caught scallops, side adductor muscle removed
Good pinch ground cinnamon

1 large shallot, finely chopped, divided
2 cups (about 2 ounces) triple-washed spinach leaves
⅓ cup unsalted butter
2 large leaves sage, slivered
1½ tablespoons capers
½ cup tart dried cherries

In a saucepan, cover the cauliflower with cold water, season with salt, and bring to a boil. Prepare an ice water bath. When cauliflower is tender, shock immediately and reserve. (You may do this step an hour or two ahead of time, if you like.)

In a sauté pan, heat half the olive oil over high heat until very hot. Season the scallops with salt and pepper and place them in the hot pan. Do not move them for 2½ to 3 minutes, until the bottoms are crusty and golden. Flip the scallops and remove the pan from heat, leaving scallops in pan.

In another pan, warm the remaining olive oil over medium-high heat. When it is very hot, add the cauliflower and dust with cinnamon. Sauté the mixture for a minute or two, shaking the pan, until nicely caramelized. Add half the shallot and cook for a few seconds. Add the spinach and let it wilt slightly. Remove from the heat so the spinach keeps its color and body. Divide this mixture among 4 plates.

Wipe the pan with a paper towel, return to high heat, and add the butter, sage, and capers. Season with salt and pepper. Swirl the pan for a minute or two, and the instant the butter foam begins to go a little brown at the edges add the cherries and remaining shallot. Swirl for 10 seconds more and remove from the heat. Transfer the scallops to warm plates on top of the cauliflower and immediately spoon the foamy top of the brown butter right over the scallops. Scatter the cherries over the top and serve.

ROASTED JOHN DORY WITH CRAB-YOGURT-ORZO SALAD & BUTTERNUT SOUP

PSITO HRISTOPSARO, KAVOUROSALATA ME YAOURTI KAI KRITHARAKI, SOUPA APO KOLOKYTHA

SERVES 4 AS A PLATED ENTRÉE

This is my little pun on the Greek diner standard, whole fish stuffed with crab. Except that diners don't use yogurt. Or squash. In my version, you get bright acidity from the sheep's milk yogurt, sweetness from the squash, and a crisp-brininess from the fish. You may freeze the leftover butternut soup and serve it alone, or add cinnamon-dusted cauliflower, a dollop of yogurt, and a generous drizzle of sage brown butter for a startlingly good upgrade.

FOR THE BUTTERNUT SOUP
1 small butternut squash, halved lengthwise, seeded but unpeeled
2 tablespoons extra-virgin olive oil
Kosher salt and cracked black pepper
6 sprigs thyme
1 onion, finely chopped
1 cup white wine
1½ quarts water
1 cup heavy cream
½ teaspoon ground cinnamon
Pinch ground cloves
Pinch ground nutmeg
1 tablespoon honey, preferably thyme

FOR THE ORZO SALAD
¾ cup orzo
2 tablespoons strained or Greek yogurt

1 tablespoon distilled white vinegar
1 tablespoon water
1 teaspoon chopped dill
4 leaves fresh mint, slivered
2 scallions, green part only, thinly sliced
Kosher salt and cracked black pepper
1 pound peekytoe or other lump crabmeat, picked over

FOR THE JOHN DORY
1½ pounds John Dory fillets (or flounder)
Sea salt and cracked black pepper
All-purpose flour
1 tablespoon blended oil (90 percent canola, 10 percent extra-virgin olive)

For the butternut soup, preheat the oven to 375°F. Paint the cut side of the two squash halves with 1 tablespoon olive oil, season with salt and pepper, stuff the cavities with thyme, and wrap each in aluminum foil. Roast for 45 to 60 minutes, until very tender. Cool, discard the thyme sprigs, and scoop out the flesh. In a heavy pot, warm the remaining tablespoon of olive oil over medium heat. Add the onion and wilt for 4 to 6 minutes, until very tender. Deglaze the pot with the white wine and let it evaporate completely. Stir in the squash pulp and add the water, cream, cinnamon, cloves, nutmeg, and honey. Season with salt and pepper. Bring to a boil and cook for 2 minutes, then remove from the heat. With an immersion blender—or in a blender, in batches—purée until smooth. If you prefer a really smooth soup, press through a fine sieve. It should be a juicy (not too thick) soup consistency.

For the orzo salad, cook the orzo in boiling salted water for 9 minutes, or according to the package instructions. While it is cooking, in a large bowl, stir together the yogurt, vinegar, water, dill, mint, and scallions. Drain the orzo, rinse well, and shake dry. Transfer to the yogurt mixture and season with salt and pepper; mix well. Fold in the crab.

For the John Dory, cut each of the John Dory fillets into 3 smaller pieces, according to the natural contours of the fish. Season with salt and pepper and dust *one side only* generously with flour (the flour helps prevent the fish from sticking to the pan). Shake off the excess flour.

In a large skillet, warm the blended oil over medium-high heat. Add the fillets, flour-side down. Sauté just until the edges begin to turn white and the floured side is browned. Turn the fillets over and immediately remove the pan from the heat.

Quarter the orzo-crab mixture and mound in the center of 4 large shallow bowls. Place one or two small pieces of John Dory over the orzo-crab mixture and drizzle the warm butternut soup around the edges.

❄ Make a little frisée salad as an extra garnish: Toss ¼ head of frisée and a pinch of long-cut chives with a few fried shallot rings (see *Manti* recipe, page 77). Toss with a drizzle each of lemon juice and extra-virgin olive oil. Place just a pinch of this in between the pieces of sautéed John Dory and then balance a pinch on top, as a garnish. It will raise the dish to a new height.

HALIBUT, FENNEL, CLAMS & SAUSAGE WITH FENNEL BROTH
HIPPOGLOSSOS, MARATHO, STRIDIA KAI LOUKANIKO ME ZOMO MARATHOU

SERVES 4 AS A PLATED ENTRÉE OR FAMILY-STYLE

This is a rustic yet elegant dish that requires a bit of dexterity at the last minute. Having all of your ingredients lined up and ready to go is critical, because to finish this dish without burning anything, you have to work fast and furiously. I suggest you begin warming pan number two for the cockles and confit when you put the halibut into pan number one. *Loukanika* is a fresh, partially dried Greek pork sausage that often contains fennel and orange. It's similar in consistency to fresh chorizo, but far milder. Chinese sausages are smaller, but closer in flavor profile than chorizo (which would alter the flavor profiles of this dish).

2 whole pieces Leek Confit (page 268), plus a little bit of the confit oil
1 cup drained Fennel Confit (page 266)
1½ to 1¾ pounds halibut or cod steaks
Kosher salt and cracked black pepper
2 tablespoons blended oil (90 percent canola, 10 percent extra-virgin olive)
4 to 5 ounces fresh *loukanika,* sliced ½ inch thick on a diagonal

16 live cockles
3 large shallots, finely chopped
¾ cup water
¼ cup Garlic Purée (page 264, optional) or cold, unsalted butter
1 tablespoon dill, chopped
Extra-virgin olive oil
Sea salt

Line up all your ingredients so you can work quickly while the halibut finishes cooking in the oven.

Preheat the oven to 375°F. Season both sides of the halibut with kosher salt and pepper. In a large ovenproof skillet, warm the blended oil over medium heat. Add the fish and sear on one side for about 1½ minutes. Transfer the pan to the oven to finish cooking for 3 to 4 minutes, while you quickly make the garnish in the next step.

Warm another large skillet over medium-high heat and drizzle in a little of the oil from the Leek Confit. Add *loukanika* to cook for 2 minutes. Add the cockles, shallots, Fennel Confit, and Leek Confit, pulling the leek pieces apart. Sauté for a minute, deglaze the pan with the water, and reduce by half. Swirl in the Garlic Purée or mount with butter, and remove from the heat. Add dill and season with kosher salt and pepper. Divide the halibut among 4 dinner plates (or serve on a platter) and top with the cockle-vegetable mixture. Drizzle with the pan juices. Finish with extra-virgin olive oil and sea salt.

❀ Add some diced Candied Orange Peel (page 279) to the final garnish, or make an avgolemono with the pan broth, to send the dish to new heights.

Left to right: Thanksgiving dinner, Long Island, 1993; George Kostaras and friends, Kalamata

dinner, family style

To say that food was sacred in our home when I was growing up would not be an exaggeration. The food—the dishes that my mother created—was not simply nourishment but also an expression of our culture, where my parents came from, and, most of all, love. Family dinners particularly were always a special time of day in my mother's home.

My mother was a housewife. Her role in our household was to care for her family, like many other women of her generation. She cleaned, she cooked, she raised four successful children, and she cared for and loved her husband until the day he died. It all sounds pretty straightforward and in some sense it might have been. But it was the care and pride with which she executed these things that made her, and what she did for us, so meaningful.

In the same way my father's single objective in life was to provide for his family, my mother's mission was to nurture and feed her family—both literally and figuratively—so that when we sat down to our table as a family each and every night of the week, each and every day of the year, she was feeding our bodies, our hearts, and our minds to keep us together, to reinforce the value of family and our interconnectedness.

My mother was a perfectionist, and it was her passion for food and cooking that enabled her to bring and hold us all together. Whether it was at our family dinners or the countless family parties and celebrations that we hosted in our home, my mother would cook for hours, and sometimes for days, to feed everyone with the very best she could make. This was *her* arena, and while my father's role as provider defined him in our family, to a certain extent these family dinners defined my mother's role as the matriarch of our family.

Dinner was the one time each day it was *guaranteed* that the whole family would be together. It did not matter what time my father got home from work. We *always* waited for him so that we could sit down to eat as a family. While as a child I didn't understand them as such, I now know that these dinners were my mother's gift to us. The time, energy, and passion she put into them defined us as a family.

It was clear to me that missing one night of family dinner would not make my mother angry, but, far worse, it would wound her in a way that would cause her pain in the depths of her soul. To miss one of those dinners would signify to her that whatever else I was doing was more important than she was, more important than my family, and more important than her singular wish to keep us together.

Even at the worst of times, when I was a rebellious teenager with a Mohawk haircut, multiple earrings, and an attitude to match the look, despite a strong desire to do otherwise, I respected and honored my mother by showing up at her table. Through good times and bad, the conversations ranged from lively and animated to all-out shouting matches, but we were all there, together. To my mother, that was what mattered. We would weather the storms and emerge the way she intended: as a family.

I can say without a doubt that my passion for food comes from my mother. I can remember, when I was a young boy of about four, my mother sitting me at our kitchen table in front of a sea of foot-long strips of phyllo dough and a bowl of cheese filling and enlisting me to help her with the *tiropitas* (little filled triangles). Not big enough to see over the table from a seated position, I would kneel on a chair to gain enough altitude to do my job. One by one, I would spoon a scoop of cheese at the end of each two-inch-wide strip and fold the phyllo over into a triangle, flip-flopping from one side of the phyllo rectangle to another, very similar to the paper football triangles I would later fold during class in grammar school, (mostly) escaping the detection of watchful teachers. After folding each strip until there was no dough left, I would place each *tiropita* on a tray and start again on the next one, until I had folded each of the dozens of strips that had once obscured the entire table.

The meatballs we made as children might have been a way for my mother to occupy some of her energetic brood while she cooked, but at the same time she was teaching us and sharing her passion for cooking with us. I felt proud when I stood by my mother's side and rolled those meatballs and prouder still when my meatballs were good enough to go into the pot. But they were not good enough to be indistinguishable from my mother's. When we sat down to dinner with my father, I would always try to find mine in the pot so I could show him what I had done, how well I had done it—what I had learned from my mother.

I think the best illustration of my mother's passion for her cooking, her level of dedication to feed her family to the best of her ability, and the pride she took in cooking even the smallest, most inconsequential dish, would be her preserved cherries. At the time, there was no such thing as a tool for pitting cherries. Cherries had to be pitted by hand with whatever tool the pitter found most successful and expeditious. When my mother preserved cherries, she would buy eighty pounds of them, plop them down on our kitchen table, and pit them by hand, one by one, *with a bobby pin*. Eighty pounds of cherries, two days of work.

When we were old enough, we were enlisted to help, and my mother lectured us, so we were careful to keep the cherry intact.

"Only one hole," she would remind us.

But we knew. My mother wanted the cherries to stay round and full, and if we made two holes, one at the top and one at the bottom, the cherry would collapse in on itself, lose its integrity, and lose some of its flavor—and it would look ugly—when she put it into the syrup in which she would preserve it. If we made only one hole, the cherries would be plump and round and fill up with syrup and, when they were extracted from the syrup weeks or months later, they would look as if they just came off the tree.

The attention to detail my mother paid to these spoon fruit cherries was exhibited in everything she did, especially in her kitchen. And when we sat down to her table, night after night and year after year, she was giving us not only the gift of a sumptuous meal, but the gift of her time, her passion, and her love for and commitment to our family.

These are the recipes my mother made for our family table on a regular basis. I hope you'll use some of them to join your family and friends together too.

Christmas dinner, 1985

STEAK WITH BONE MARROW HTIPITI

BRIZOLA ME HTIPITI APO MEDOULI

SERVES 4

Here's something steak houses don't tell you: at most of them, there is a pot of rendered beef fat (all the trimmings and fat from the dry-aged beef). The cooks dip a steak into this fat before it's cooked at superhigh heat, and then again afterward. Mmmmm. If you want to go the extra mile, render down some fat trimmings over really low heat, then cool and mix into my tremendously rich and tasty take on *htipiti*, here. (*Htipiti* is usually made with feta cheese and roasted pepper, herbs, and garlic.) For a true Greek steak house plate, serve with Tomato and String Bean Salad (page 104) and Greek Creamed Spinach, as here. Of course, dry-aged steaks will make the menu even more of a standout.

FOR THE STEAK

3 (2- to 3-inch) marrow bones, very cold, soaked in water to cover, overnight
½ cup (4 ounces) unsalted butter, at room temperature
1 shallot, roughly chopped
2 teaspoons dry Greek oregano
3 small, picked sprigs thyme, finely chopped
Spine from 1 small sprig rosemary, finely chopped
6 cloves Garlic Confit (page 264) or 1½ tablespoons Garlic Purée (page 264)
About 1 teaspoon grated lemon zest
Kosher salt and cracked black pepper
2 (10- to 11-ounce) sirloin steaks, about 2 inches thick, preferably dry-aged, at room temperature

Extra-virgin olive oil
½ lemon
Sea salt

FOR THE GREEK CREAMED SPINACH

1 tablespoon olive oil
3 tablespoons very finely chopped shallot
4 whole scallions, sliced ½ inch thick on a diagonal
8 ounces baby spinach leaves, roughly chopped
Kosher salt and cracked black pepper
1 cup Greek Béchamel Sauce Without Eggs (page 276)
3 tablespoons roughly chopped dill

For the steak, preheat the oven to 400°F. In a small roasting pan, roast the marrow bones for about 10 minutes, until the marrow is softened but not melted. When cool enough to handle, scoop the marrow out into a food processor and add any pan drippings. Add the butter, shallot, 1 teaspoon of the oregano, the thyme, rosemary, Garlic Confit, lemon zest, 2 teaspoons kosher salt, and a generous grinding of pepper. Pulse until smooth and scoopable.

Brush the steak on both sides with olive oil, then season aggressively on both sides with kosher salt and pepper—if you think there's too much salt, add more.

Preheat a charcoal or gas grill, or ridged cast-iron grill pan, until hot. Grill the steaks for 6 to 8 minutes on both sides (see "When Is It Done?"). Transfer to a rack in a roasting pan (or the back side of a plate) to rest for at least 10 minutes (see "Why the Rest?").

After resting, transfer steaks to oven for 2 minutes, to warm up the outside without cooking any further. Smear the *htipiti* nice and thick on top of each steak, then cut lovely thick slices; divide among 4 dinner plates. Squeeze the lemon over the top and scatter with a little sea salt and the remaining oregano.

For the Greek Creamed Spinach, in a large skillet, warm the oil over medium heat. When it is hot, add the shallot and scallion and cook for 2 to 3 minutes, to soften slightly. Add the spinach and cover the pan for a minute, just to begin cooking the spinach. Toss for a few minutes, to wilt without collapsing. Season well with salt and pepper and thoroughly stir in the Greek Béchamel Sauce and dill. Remove from the heat.

WHEN IS IT DONE?

I like to use a cake tester or small metal skewer to gauge the doneness of any kind of protein. Pierce the steak through to the center and leave the skewer in place for a few seconds. Then press it gently against your lower lip. If it's not warm at all, that's steak *au bleu*, as they say in France. The hotter the skewer, the more done the steak. For me, when it's warm, that's medium-rare. If it's really hot, you're way overdone. You can also use the touch test: pinch the steak on its side between your index finger and thumb; if it gives easily, that's rare. The more it bounces, the more done it is. If the meat springs back quickly like a rubber ball, it's overdone. Medium-rare is about a third of the way between soft and really firm.

WHY THE REST?

I guarantee you that some people spend a fortune on a steak, then—when they think it's done—put it on a plate and run to the table. Resist this urge. When you cut into a steak right away, all the tasty juices run onto the plate. When protein is exposed to heat, it reacts violently and sends all the blood and juices into the center. During the resting process the meat relaxes, and juices gradually make their way out to the edges again so that by the time you slice, the meat is equally pink all the way through and there should be almost no escaping juice. Also be sure to rest it on a rack to allow air circulation around the entire piece of meat. Hot meat resting directly on a surface will not cool evenly, as the heat will be transferred back and forth from the steak to the surface it is resting on. Here, I return the steaks to a very hot oven, just briefly, right before serving, so the surface of the meat will be hot enough to melt the *htipiti*.

BEEF STEW WITH LEEKS
BODINO STIFADO ME PRASO

❖——❖

SERVES 4 TO 6 FAMILY-STYLE, WITH POTATOES, RICE, OR ORZO

Braises like this are perfect for meat with tough muscle tissue and tendons (which come from the part of the animal that works hard), a great example of poverty cooking. This less expensive cut of meat develops its own natural and luscious sauce as it cooks. You want a little marbling in the meat, because it melts down as you cook and adds a lot of flavor to the sauce. You can use brisket, shanks, shoulder—all fairly tough meats—but save the filet mignon for the grill or a pan. It takes a little time to cook and become tender, but it's a relatively easy setup, and once you get it onto the stove you don't have to worry about it for about an hour. So you can do your laundry, or walk the dog, or make a salad.

A couple of days later, if you have any leftovers, you can shred the meat, then return the meat to the sauce and add your favorite pasta. The resulting dish is a Greek version of beef Stroganoff.

The herbs are very important to the flavor development here, since I'm using water instead of stock, so use fresh herbs if possible.

3 tablespoons blended oil (90 percent canola, 10 percent extra-virgin olive)

2 pounds beef stew meat, cut into 1½-inch chunks

Kosher salt and cracked black pepper

½ large Spanish or sweet onion, finely chopped

1 carrot, finely chopped

1 stalk celery, finely chopped

1 large leek, cut into thick rounds, washed well in cold water, drained

2 tablespoons tomato paste

½ cup red wine

2 tablespoons red wine vinegar

3 to 5 cups water

1 fresh bay leaf or 2 dried leaves

1 large sprig rosemary

1 sprig thyme

1 sprig sage

2 cinnamon sticks

Extra-virgin olive oil

Grated orange zest

1 tablespoon roughly chopped parsley

Place a large, heavy pot or Dutch oven over medium-high heat and add the blended oil. Season the beef aggressively with kosher salt and pepper. When the oil is hot, add the beef and sear on all sides, 5 to 6 minutes. Add all the chopped vegetables to the pan with the beef and sauté for 2 minutes. Add the tomato paste and stir for 1 minute. Deglaze the pan with the red wine and red wine vinegar, and let them reduce completely away.

Add 3 cups of the water, 2 teaspoons salt and a generous grinding of pepper, the bay leaves, rosemary, thyme, sage, and cinnamon. Bring to a boil, then reduce the heat to low and partially cover the pan. Simmer gently for about an hour. Check and, if the mixture is dry, add another cup or two of water. Keep simmering for 15 to 40 minutes more, until the meat is tender and the braising liquid has reduced to a saucy consistency. Remove the bay leaves and cinnamon sticks. Transfer to a platter and drizzle with a little extra-virgin olive oil, and scatter with a little orange zest and the parsley.

Photos: page 68, Creamed Spinach; page 69, Beef Stew; above, browned beef and aromatics

PORK SOFFRITO WITH SPICY PEPPERS & CABBAGE

HIRINO SOFFRITO ME KAFTERES PIPERIES KAI LAHANO

SERVES 2

This is a quick sauté that combines fruit, crisp greens, tender pork, and flavorful pan juices. It's fast and furious, so get your *mise-en-place* together before you start. If you don't like the heat of pepperoncini, tame it (see "Taming the Brine" at right) or leave it out—but be sure to replace the acidity with a little white wine vinegar or lemon juice. Since you need so much pan space, I've given the recipe for two people, but if you have two really big (12-inch) skillets, go ahead and double the recipe. Here, the Garlic Purée acts as an emulsifier to finish the pan sauce, but if you don't have it, finish the sauce with a little butter.

½ pound pork tenderloin, cut into 1-inch rounds

¼ cup cracked, brined *tsakistes* green olives, pitted and pulled into pieces

¼ small head savoy cabbage, sliced paper-thin

½ bulb fennel, sliced paper-thin

¼ of a red onion, sliced paper-thin

1 orange, peeled with a knife and separated into pith-free segments

1 tablespoon roughly chopped parsley

2 tablespoons chopped dill

Vinaigrette of your choice, or extra-virgin olive oil and fresh lemon juice

Sea salt, kosher salt, and cracked black pepper

All-purpose flour

2 tablespoons extra-virgin olive oil

1 shallot, finely chopped

1 tablespoon capers

1 pepperoncini (pickled yellow pepper), sliced

½ cup white wine

1 tablespoon fresh lemon juice

1½ tablespoons Garlic Purée (page 264) or cold, unsalted butter

Caperberries, for garnish (optional)

1 tablespoon chopped dill

Pound each slice of pork between two sheets of plastic wrap to an even thickness of less than ¼ inch.

In a large mixing bowl, combine the next seven ingredients (olives through 1 tablespoon of the dill), for the salad. Toss with about ¼ cup vinaigrette, or 3 tablespoons extra-virgin olive oil and 1½ tablespoons fresh lemon juice. Season with sea salt and pepper and toss well with clean hands.

Season both sides of the tenderloins generously with kosher salt and pepper and dust lightly with flour. Place your largest skillet over medium-high heat and add the 2 tablespoons olive oil. When it is hot, add the pork to the pan and sauté for just under 1 minute on each side, until pale golden. Transfer to a platter and reserve. Reduce the heat a little and add the shallot, capers, and pepperoncini and cook until slightly softened.

Deglaze the pan with the white wine; reduce to a simmer and add the 1 tablespoon lemon juice. Reduce liquid by two thirds. Add the Garlic Purée or butter and swirl to melt into the juice. Add the remaining dill and season with sea salt and pepper. Return the pork to the pan and remove from the heat. Swirl the pan to coat the pork with the sauce. Transfer to a platter with all the juices and goodies from the pan, and pile the tossed salad on the top.

TAMING THE BRINE

I love salty food, and Greek cooking is full of briny influences. But some people are put off by strong salty-briny flavors. If you're one of them, simmer brined or salt-cured olives, capers, and/or pepperoncini in boiling water for 5 minutes, then drain and proceed with the recipe. This way, you still get the fruity flavors and body from the ingredients rather than the brine/salt.

SOUVLAKI: CHICKEN & PORK SHISH KEBAB
KOTOPOULO SOUVLAKI KAI HIRINO SOUVLAKI

SERVES 4

I can't emphasize enough the importance of brining lean meats and poultry. With meat that does not have a lot of fat to function as internal basting, we brine to make it tender and juicy. The molecular structure of protein is such that tendons and proteins are coiled. In a brine, the proteins start to uncoil, and we have a chance to get flavor and moisture in there, allowing us to cook the meat and still keep it juicy, juicy, juicy. With meats that are fatty on the outside and well marbled inside, and that will braise for a very long time, there is no need to brine because the natural juices will come out as the fat breaks down. Yes, you have to plan ahead (at least overnight), but the payoff is truly fantastic. I'd prefer if you give the *Souvlaki* 12 hours in the brine and then 12 hours in the marinade, but if you have to choose one, brining is the more important step. Note that if you need more brine to cover the meat, increase the quantity while keeping the ratios the same, 1 quart water to ¼ cup of salt.

1 pound pork tenderloin or 1 pound boneless, skinless chicken breast (about 4 single breasts)

FOR THE BRINE
1 quart cold water
¼ cup kosher salt
¼ cup granulated sugar
1 cup distilled white vinegar

FOR THE MARINADE
1 cup extra-virgin olive oil
3 cloves garlic, smashed and chopped

3 to 4 sprigs thyme
1 fresh bay leaf or 2 dried leaves
2 sprigs rosemary
2 shallots, sliced
Kosher salt and cracked black pepper

¼ recipe Greek Salad (page 213) with the vinaigrette on the side
Sea salt and cracked black pepper
½ cup *Ladolemono* (page 270)
4 rounds pita bread
Extra-virgin olive oil
⅔ cup *Tsatziki* (page 189), for serving

Carefully trim off the thin white membrane (silverskin) that runs down one side of the tenderloin.

In a plastic or ceramic bowl or crock, stir the brine ingredients together until the salt and sugar have dissolved (this will take a few minutes). Cut the pork tenderloin crosswise into generous 1-inch-thick slices (or, cut the chicken into very large chunks). Immerse in the brine and refrigerate overnight.

Remove the meat from the brine and rinse under cool running water. Pat dry with a towel. In a deep baking dish or roasting pan, combine the olive oil, garlic, thyme, bay leaves, rosemary, shallots, and a little salt and pepper. Thread the pieces of meat onto 4 wooden skewers and immerse the skewers in the marinade. Cover with plastic wrap, pressing the plastic right down onto the meat to exclude any air. Refrigerate for at least 4 hours; overnight is even better, though not essential.

Remove the skewers from the refrigerator and let stand at room temperature for 20 to 30 minutes while you preheat a charcoal or gas grill, or ridged cast-iron grill pan, until hot.

In a bowl, combine all ingredients for Greek Salad and reserve. (Do not dress!)

Season the *Souvlaki* lightly with salt and pepper and grill until firm and char-marked on all sides. Pork will take about 8 minutes total, chicken about 6 minutes. Transfer to a resting platter and dress with *Ladolemono*.

Paint the pita with extra-virgin olive oil, season with salt and pepper, and grill until firm and char-marked on all sides. Smear some *Tsatziki* in the center of each pita round. Push the meat off the skewer on top of the *Tsatziki.* Top with some Greek Salad. Pull the sides of the pita up to meet in the center, like a taco. Serve like a hand roll, or wrap and secure with a wide strip of parchment. Messy and great.

※ Instead of making pita sandwiches, serve the *Souvlaki* with double the portion of Greek Salad called for here, or Spinach Rice (page 167).

MANTI: RAVIOLI OF FOUR CHEESES WITH CRISPY SHALLOTS, BROWN BUTTER & SAGE

RAVIOLIA ME TESSERA TYRIA, TIGANITA KREMMYDAKIA, VOUTYRO, FASKOMILO

SERVES 4 TO 6

The *Manti* may be frozen in the same way as the dumplings on page 80. If frozen, you'll have to increase the cooking time a bit—but either way, when they rise to the surface they're done.

FOR THE HILOPITES PASTA
2 cups cake flour
½ cup all-purpose flour, plus more
   for dusting
1 tablespoon kosher salt
4 large eggs, separated
½ cup plus 2 tablespoons extra-virgin
   olive oil
10 tablespoons tepid water
Semolina, for dusting

FOR THE MANTI
3 large shallots
Milk for soaking
⅔ cup fresh, whole-milk ricotta cheese
⅓ cup grated *graviera* cheese

⅓ cup grated *mizithra* cheese
⅓ cup crumbled *manouri* cheese
1 large egg, beaten
Pinch of nutmeg, preferably freshly
   grated
Kosher salt and cracked black pepper
All-purpose flour and semolina (50/50
   mixture), plus more all-purpose flour
   for dredging
Blended oil (90 percent canola,
   10 percent extra-virgin olive) for frying, as needed
⅓ cup unsalted butter
12 leaves sage, cut into thick strips
1 large shallot, finely chopped

For the *Hilopites* Pasta, in a food processor fitted with a dough blade, combine the cake flour, all-purpose flour, and salt. Pulse to blend. Add the egg yolks, olive oil, and water and process on and off until the dough clumps up on the center stem. You may have to add a little more water to make the dough come together or add a bit more all-purpose flour if the dough is too wet. When the dough forms a cylinder on the stem, process for about 1 additional minute until smooth and elastic, not tacky. (Add a little more flour or water to adjust the consistency if needed.)

Turn the dough out of the processor onto a clean work surface and give a quick knead to form into a smooth, round ball. Sprinkle with more flour if the dough sticks to the surface and continue to knead until the additional flour is fully incorporated. Wrap with plastic wrap and refrigerate for at least 1 hour, preferably overnight. (The colder the dough, the easier it will be to roll out.)

Starting with the largest setting put the dough through a pasta machine and continue feeding, lowering the settings by two after each pass (to no. 9 or no. 10), and roll until the dough is almost translucent. Scatter with flour only if the dough threatens to stick.

Keep rolling until the dough is silky and flexible and, again, not at all tacky.

For the *Manti*, slice 2 of the shallots thinly into rings and soak in milk to cover. Refrigerate.

In a bowl, stir the ricotta and the other three cheeses until smooth. Stir in about half the beaten egg (reserve the rest) and the nutmeg; season liberally with kosher salt and pepper and stir again.

Dust a large, rimmed baking sheet very generously with all-purpose flour and semolina. Cut the pasta dough into about forty-eight 2 x 2-inch squares. Add a little water to the remaining egg and brush all four outside edges of the pasta squares. Place the cheese filling into a piping bag and pipe or use 2 small teaspoons to mound about 1 generous teaspoon into the center of each square. Bring two opposite corners up to meet in the center and press together firmly to make a fat triangle, pointed side up. Bring the remaining corners together to meet in the front and press together to make an agnolotti shape. Transfer to the baking sheet as you work.

Put a pot with (well-salted) water on to boil for the pasta. While you wait for the water, remove sliced shallots from milk. Dredge them in all-purpose flour and shake off the excess. Fry in a pot *half full* of blended oil at 350°F, until golden. Season with salt and pepper and reserve on absorbent paper in a warm place.

When the pasta water is boiling, lower the *Manti* into the water and cook until they rise to the surface. Meanwhile, finely chop the remaining shallot. Warm a very large skillet over medium-high heat. Add the butter and sage, swirling the pan until melted. Add the chopped shallot to the skillet. Retrieve the *Manti* with a skimmer, gently shaking off as much water as you can, and add them to the skillet. Season with salt and pepper. Swirl and cook just until the butter begins to turn golden and smell slightly nutty, a minute or so. Spoon some *Manti*, along with some of the butter mixture, onto warm plates. Top each with a few fried shallot rings.

RICOTTA

If you can find fresh ricotta, it will work much, much better than drained supermarket ricotta (fresh sheep's milk ricotta is the very best). And don't even bother with part skim. Sometimes you have to commit to a certain level of fat, and this is one of those times.

The difference between fresh and supermarket is even more crucial for ricotta than it is for yogurt. Draining yogurt overnight removes a great deal of water, but the process doesn't work as well with ricotta, even if it's drained for 24 hours. The dumplings will still work, but the dough will be quite wet, so you'll have to add much more flour to create dumplings strong enough to hold up to cooking, and they'll be floury and glutinous.

SHELLFISH YOUVETSI

YOUVETSI ME OSTRAKA

A *youvetsi* is a clay pot used to cook lamb by herdsmen in the mountains of Greece. They typically dug a hole, made a fire in the hole, and then allowed it to burn to embers. They placed the clay pot on top of the embers and then buried it. The herdsmen then tended to their flock and revisited the makeshift oven several hours later for dinner. Here I played around with tradition by using shellfish for a lighter, quicker version of this classic.

In this paella-like dish, add the longer-cooking shellfish first and those that require very little cooking, such as the shrimp and the razor clams, toward the very end, so that they are all done at the same time. My version is dominated by the mussels, mostly because they are less expensive than the other shellfish. Feel free to vary the ratio of shellfish any way you like. Sometimes I like to add some sliced spicy lamb sausage (*merguez*) at the beginning, with the vegetables.

3 tablespoons extra-virgin olive oil

1 Spanish or sweet onion, chopped

1 bulb fennel, quartered, cored, and roughly chopped

6 whole scallions, sliced

5 cloves garlic, smashed

4 stalks celery, roughly chopped

Kosher salt and cracked black pepper

Large pinch of saffron threads

6 littleneck clams

30 mussels, beards pulled away

2 cups dry white wine

2 tablespoons ouzo (optional)

4 razor clams

1 cup orzo, cooked and drained

6 U-10 shrimp, peeled

4 tablespoons unsalted butter (optional)

Small handful picked sprigs parsley, chopped

Small handful picked sprigs dill, chopped

15 leaves fresh mint, chopped

4 small lemons, halved

In a large, deep skillet, warm the olive oil over medium-low heat. Add the onion, fennel, scallions, garlic, and celery. Cook, stirring, until nicely softened but not browned. Season generously with salt and pepper and stir in the saffron. Add the clams and cook for a couple of minutes. Add the mussels next, and let them warm for about a minute. Then add the white wine and ouzo; bring quickly to a simmer. Add the razor clams and cover the pan.

Keep an eye on the shellfish; when they are all at least a little bit open, add the orzo. Finally, add the shrimp and cook until they are bright pink. Discard any shellfish that remain tightly closed. Swirl in the butter until it's all melted, and remove the skillet from the heat. Add herbs. Squeeze all the lemon halves over the top. Toss well and serve.

DUMPLINGS WITH SAUSAGE, DANDELION GREENS, SUN-DRIED TOMATO & PINE NUTS

ZYMARIKA, LOUKANIKO, AGRIA RADIKIA, LIASTES TOMATES, KOUKOUNARI

MAKES 90 DUMPLINGS

SERVES 8 NOW *OR* 4 NOW AND 4 AGAIN, UP TO FOUR WEEKS LATER

These delicate dumplings are worth the effort and care involved to make them light and airy. And this is important: Once you begin the process, there is no answering the phone or running to the bathroom. You must keep working until they are finished. The dumplings can be frozen for up to 4 weeks, so you can serve half of them right away and freeze the other half for a future, fantastic, stress-free meal. Ingredients for final serving make four portions. If you'd like to serve all 90 dumplings at once, double the serving ingredients and use two very large skillets. This recipe was *Bon Appétit*'s Dish of the Year for 2006.

1 small bunch dandelion greens, tough stems removed

3 tablespoons extra-virgin olive oil

4 shallots, finely chopped

3 cloves garlic, smashed and chopped

7 ounces spicy lamb sausage (such as *merguez*), sliced

¾ cup thick tomato sauce, homemade or store-bought

8 large sun-dried tomatoes

1 cup pine nuts

¼ cup Garlic Purée (page 264, optional)

½ recipe (about 45) Dumplings (recipe follows)

¼ cup crumbled feta cheese

½ cup small, picked sprigs parsley

½ cup small, picked sprigs dill

FOR THE DUMPLINGS

1 pound fresh, whole-milk ricotta, very cold (see "Ricotta," page xii)

All-purpose flour, as necessary, chilled for at least 2 hours

3 large eggs, cold, well beaten

1½ cups grated *graviera* cheese

2 teaspoons kosher salt

1½ teaspoons freshly ground black pepper

Semolina flour, for the baking sheet

Prepare an ice water bath. In a large pot of well-salted boiling water, cook the dandelion greens until tender (about 5 minutes), then retrieve with a skimmer (reserving the boiling water for cooking the dumplings). Shock the greens in the ice water bath. Drain, squeeze dry, and chop coarsely. Reserve.

Get all of your remaining ingredients together. Bring the dandelion-cooking water to a boil in a wide sauté pan so you will be able to work quickly.

In a very large skillet, warm the olive oil over medium heat. Add the shallots and cook for 2 minutes, to soften. Add the garlic and sliced sausage. Sauté for 2 minutes, then stir in the tomato sauce, a cup or so of the dandelion-cooking water, the sun-dried tomatoes, dandelion greens, pine nuts, and Garlic Purée. Reduce to a simmer and cook until sauce is the thickness of a marinara.

In the boiling water, cook the dumplings just until they rise to the surface; then retrieve with a skimmer. Shake gently and add to the other skillet, along with the feta and herbs. Toss to coat the pillowy dumplings with the chunky-saucy mixture.

❈ For the dumplings, *unless you have a source for very fresh, dry ricotta:* line a colander with a doubled layer of cheesecloth and place over a bowl. Turn the ricotta into the colander and leave to drain overnight in the refrigerator. (If you skip this step, your dumplings will require much more flour and will not be light and airy.)

Assemble all your well-chilled ingredients, clear your schedule, and turn off the phone. Generously dust a large board or marble slab with flour. In a large metal bowl, combine the ricotta, beaten eggs, *graviera*, salt, and pepper. Mix well with a large rubber spatula, breaking up the ricotta. Scatter two large handfuls all-purpose flour around the edges of the bowl. Using a spatula, gently lift the dough, working your way around the edges, only to cover the dough so it doesn't stick to the bottom of the bowl. There should be a substantial amount of flour on the outside of the mass, as you get underneath to coat. Scatter two large handfuls of flour on a clean work surface and turn out dough. Scoop from the bottom and fold it over gently toward the center, keeping the dough in a large, tall mass, always using a light and gentle hand. Add more flour by the handful, scattering it over the dough and the work surface and lightly working—not "kneading"—the dough just until it is no longer sticky or tacky. The quantity of flour depends on how wet the ricotta is; the idea is to add no more than is necessary to prevent sticking and make the dough stiff enough to maintain its shape and yet remain very delicate and tender. Cut off a quarter of the dough and gingerly pat with your fingertips, barely touching it as you roll out a rope about 4 feet long, rolling back and forth to about 1½ inches in diameter. Add more flour only if the dough begins to stick.

Cut off 1-inch cylinders and transfer them to a large rimmed baking sheet on a generous bed of half flour and half semolina. The dumplings will look a bit like marshmallows. Repeat with the remaining dough and chill the dumplings for 1 hour before cooking.

Note: To freeze all or half the dumplings, freeze on flour-lined baking sheets, without covering, for 6 hours; then transfer to large zipper-lock bags, 14 at a time. If the dumplings stick together during the freezing process, you can break them apart before bagging. The frozen dumplings will take a bit longer to cook.

my first recipes

I f I had to pinpoint one moment that put me on the path to where I am now—to being a chef—it would be the time I first made breakfast in bed for my parents. It was in honor of my mother's thirty-seventh birthday.

As a child, I was limited in what I could do to acknowledge my mother's birthday. I was only about eleven and not yet working, so I had no money of my own to buy her a gift or flowers. So I spent the days before her birthday hatching a plan to celebrate her special day in a way I thought represented what she deserved—and that would bring my parents joy and make them feel proud. I was going to cook my first meal.

Our refrigerator was always overflowing. Regardless of the day of the week or time of the year, when I opened the door, I was always ready to catch whatever might fall out. So I knew I wouldn't have much trouble secreting away some key ingredients for a few days by utilizing the most remote corners and spaces of our fridge. No casual user was likely explore that far back.

In my excitement, and perhaps on account of a little paranoia, I wanted to be sure that by Sunday our refrigerator would still be stocked with the ingredients I would need to prepare my menu. When no one was around, I dug the English muffins out of the fridge and wrapped two up in aluminum foil, replaced the original package of English muffins, and hid the ones I had claimed in the back. I did similar recon with eggs, blueberries, and any other items I thought I might need for the big day. I wanted to keep this quiet and, in our large family, simply finding opportunities to pull this off—without anyone else inadvertently walking in on the preparations—was part of the adventure.

On my mother's birthday, I was so excited that I was up long before the sun. My preperformance jitters were serving me well because, having no alarm clock, I had to rely on my internal clock. And I would need plenty of time to pull off this caper before my parents woke up and came downstairs.

I awakened Maria first. As the next oldest in line, she would be able to help me the most. Then I roused Anna and then Peter, who was only about three years old at the time. I enlisted them all to help me execute my plan, if only to be there to share in the excitement that was building as the clock ticked on.

I told Maria to take out the pots and pans I would need and started with four eggs sunny-side up. It was a good thing I started on these early because I broke so many yolks along the way that it took me hours to get them just right. Next I made blueberry muffins, sausage, and toast, with an English muffin for my father. I sent Maria to the garden to cut some flowers, which I put in two small vases that would adorn the breakfast trays. I finished with two bowls of yogurt topped with my mother's preserved fruits and a glass of juice for each tray.

I carried both trays to the top of the stairs and placed them outside my parents' door. I hurried Maria, Anna, and Peter up the stairs. I placed one tray in Anna's hands and another in Peter's hands (which weren't quite steady enough, so Maria helped him with his tray). In a burst, we pushed the door open, shouted "Happy birthday!" and placed one tray in bed on my mother's lap and the other on my father's.

Hugs and kisses were exchanged all around and then I shuttled my siblings downstairs to complete the surprise for my mother by making my sisters and brother breakfast too. For us, I made scrambled eggs (for which yolks didn't have to be whole!) and toast, and we shared in some of the blueberry muffins I had baked for my parents.

While I don't specifically remember cleaning up, I do remember the way I felt planning, preparing, and presenting that meal. I knew I wanted to experience that feeling as much and as often as possible. I'd always vaguely understood that there was something far more important in my mother's cooking than the ingredients in her recipes. But after planning and cooking this meal, I really understood: it was the love and passion with which she cooked each thing that made it so special. I felt the joy of presenting something I myself had created to the people I loved in the form of this gift—and giving that gift gave back tenfold to me. I had seen the joy on my parents' faces when we delivered those overflowing trays and I knew I had made them proud, and that in turn filled me with joy. I was proud of what I had created.

I had been raised to do what I had just done. As the oldest son, I had taken charge, executed a plan, looked after and included all of my siblings, and directed them in what to do. Little did I know it then, but in cooking and presenting that first meal I was preparing myself for a career in the kitchen.

From that day on, and for many months to come, I would run home after school so I could watch television. Unlike my peers, I wasn't trying to catch *Scooby-Doo*, but rather *Julia Child and Company*. My mother had only one cookbook to her name, *From Julia Child's Kitchen*, but she never actually cooked from that book or any other. I distinctly remember the orange spine of that cookbook, and I remember Julia cooking on TV. It was from that book and show that I cooked my first recipes, my first roast chicken and my first pork chops. I was on my way to becoming a chef, all thanks to that first meal of breakfast in bed.

The recipes that follow are a selection of the first recipes I ever cooked, those that I hold especially dear. They are not only the recipes that I learned from my mother, but also the recipes that set me on my path to becoming a chef. If you try only one recipe from this entire book (although my wish is that you'll try many more), I hope it will be from this section. These recipes are a window into my childhood and the springboard into my life in the kitchen.

WHOLE CHICKEN SOUP WITH AVGOLEMONO & ORZO
SOUPA AVGOLEMONO

SERVES 4 TO 6

This is a hearty, traditional Greek dish. It's more economical to buy whole chickens rather than chicken pieces, so you may remove four breasts from two whole chickens and freeze them for *souvlaki*, or grilled chicken for one of the salad recipes. The bones of the chicken add great body and flavor to this broth.

2 (3½-pound) chickens
Kosher salt and cracked black pepper
2 tablespoons blended oil (90 percent canola, 10 percent extra-virgin olive)
1 carrot, finely chopped
4 cloves garlic, smashed and chopped
1½ stalks celery, finely chopped
½ Spanish or sweet onion, finely chopped
2 fresh bay leaves or 3 dried leaves

3 large sprigs thyme
1 cup white wine
Water as needed
1 cup orzo

FOR THE AVGOLEMONO

3 large eggs, at room temperature, separated
4 tablespoons lemon juice
½ cup small, picked sprigs dill
Kosher salt and cracked black pepper

Preheat the oven to 325°F. Remove the breasts from both chickens and double-wrap in plastic wrap. Place inside a zipper-lock bag, label, and freeze for the next time you make *souvlaki*. Remove the leg-thigh joints from the chicken, pull off the skin, and discard. Set aside.

Place the chickens in a large roasting pan, season with kosher salt and pepper, and roast for 1 hour, until golden.

In a large, heavy pot, warm the blended oil over medium-high heat. Add all the vegetables and cook until softened but not browned, about 3 to 5 minutes. Add the bay leaves and thyme, then deglaze the pot with the white wine and cook until it completely evaporates. Add the roasted chicken carcasses. Season liberally with kosher salt and pepper. Cover with water by about 2 inches. Bring to a boil, then reduce the heat, cover, and simmer gently for 1 hour. Add 4 leg-thigh pieces and continue to simmer for another 40 to 45 minutes, until the chicken is tender. Skim off the scum that rises at the beginning. Lift out the leg-thigh joints and, when cool enough to handle, pull off and reserve the meat. Discard the carcasses and any stray bones, and skim a little fat from the soup if you like. Bring soup to a boil, add the orzo, and cook for another 8 to 10 minutes.

While the orzo is cooking, make the *Avgolemono*. Get everything together so you can work quickly. Draw off 2 cups of the chicken broth, without any of the vegetables (or orzo), and return the picked chicken meat to the soup. Slowly drizzle the warm chicken broth into the egg yolks, whisking all the time. Place the egg whites in a food processor and turn it on. When the whites begin to froth, after about 30 seconds, add the lemon juice, keeping the motor running all the time. When the whites are very frothy and thick, another 45 to 60 seconds, add the dill, and process for 10 to 15 seconds more while you season liberally with salt and pepper. Pour in the egg yolk mixture and immediately turn the machine off. Pour the *Avgolemono* over the soup and serve at once, as it will quickly start to deflate.

☀ If you will not be serving the soup right away, cook the orzo separately, cool down, and then add, and warm through, just before topping with the *Avgolemono*.

☀ For a lighter soup, skip the roasting of the chickens and simply simmer the chicken until tender.

LENTIL SOUP

FAKES

SERVES 4 TO 6

Like all starch-based soups, this one will thicken as it cools. If you make it the day before, hold on to any reserved cooking liquid so you can thin the soup when you reheat, if it's too thick. You can always use the liquid in another soup or a braise, as it's really a lentil stock, full of flavor from all the vegetables and aromatics.

2 smoked ham hocks

Water, as needed

2 tablespoons blended oil (90 percent canola, 10 percent extra-virgin olive)

2 Spanish or sweet onions, finely chopped

2 stalks celery, finely chopped

1 Idaho potato, peeled and finely chopped

2 large carrots, finely chopped

8 cloves garlic, smashed and finely chopped

2 fresh bay leaves or 3 dried leaves

3 large sprigs fresh thyme

1 pound brown lentils

1 cup red wine

2 tablespoons sherry vinegar

Kosher salt and cracked black pepper

⅓ cup grated *kefalotiri* cheese

2 scallions, green part only, sliced on the diagonal

Extra-virgin olive oil

In a large pot, cover the ham hocks with water. Bring to a boil and simmer for 5 minutes. Drain and set aside, discarding the water.

In a large pot, warm the blended oil over medium-high heat. Add all the vegetables, including the garlic, as well as the bay leaves, and thyme, and cook for 3 to 5 minutes to soften without browning. Add the lentils and stir for 1 minute, then deglaze the pot with the red wine and sherry vinegar. Simmer until the wine is completely evaporated; then add the ham hocks and enough water to cover everything by a good inch. Bring to a boil and season with salt and pepper. Reduce the heat, cover, and simmer for about 30 minutes, until the lentils are tender. Drain the lentils and vegetables, reserving all the liquid in a large measuring jug. Return the solids to the empty cooking pot.

In a food processor, combine about a third of the lentil mixture with 2 cups of the cooking liquid. Purée until completely smooth. Return this puréed mixture to the pot with the remaining lentils and mix. Add enough of the cooking liquid to get the desired consistency—again, I am partial to a hearty style but you may prefer it with a little more liquid. Taste for seasoning.

Ladle into bowls and top with a big pinch of *kefalotiri*, some sliced scallion greens, and a drizzle of extra-virgin olive oil.

☀ If you want the meat from the ham hock in the soup, you'll have to simmer it far longer than it takes the lentils to cook: Sauté a mirepoix of 1 carrot, 3 stalks celery, 1 large onion, 2 fresh bay leaves, and 6 smashed cloves of garlic until tender. Add the ham hocks, cover with water, and bring to a boil. Simmer for 1 to 1½ hours, until the meat is tender. Pull out the ham hocks. Strain the braising liquid, discarding the vegetables and bay leaves. Reserve the liquid and use for cooking the lentils, instead of the water. Pick off the meat from the ham hocks, discarding bones and tough cartilage. Add the meat with the puréed lentils.

☀ Cook ½ cup of orzo according to the package instructions and stir in just before serving.

☀ Serve with slices of day-old baguette, toasted and drizzled with olive oil.

☀ Use any lentils of your choice; French green lentils and black beluga lentils will take a bit longer to cook.

☀ Reduce the soup until it is very thick; then use it as a bed under a nice piece of fried fish. If you prefer it smooth rather than chunky, purée all the lentils. It will be almost like refried beans. Top this with a little strained Greek yogurt for coolness and tang; then throw on some torn fresh green herbs.

☀ For extra pork flavor without cooking the ham hock ahead of time, as above, sauté a few ounces of finely diced smoked slab bacon with the mirepoix.

WHITE BEAN SOUP

FASOLADA

Here, I use a white mirepoix—one without carrot—for a faintly licorice flavor that is very different from the other soups in this book. If you don't have a parsnip, use a small potato. As with all pulses and legumes, cooking time can vary enormously, depending on the age of the beans. Buy your beans from a supplier with good turnover, so you will know the beans are not too old. If you have any homemade stock around, go ahead and use it instead of the water.

2 tablespoons blended oil (90 percent canola, 10 percent extra-virgin olive)

1 parsnip, peeled and roughly chopped

1½ stalks celery, roughly chopped

½ bulb fennel, cored and roughly chopped

1 Spanish or sweet onion, roughly chopped

2 fresh bay leaves or 3 dried leaves

1 cup white wine

1 pound dry cannellini beans, soaked overnight and drained

1 leek, white part only, halved lengthwise and then sliced crosswise

Water, as needed

Kosher salt and cracked black pepper

¼ cup fresh lemon juice

3 tablespoons Garlic Purée (page 264, optional)

3 tablespoons chopped dill, plus a few more small, picked sprigs

½ cup crumbled feta cheese

Extra-virgin olive oil

In a large pot, warm the blended oil over medium-high heat. Add all the vegetables (except the leek) and the bay leaves and cook for 3 to 5 minutes, to soften without browning. Deglaze with the white wine; simmer until the wine is completely evaporated. Add the beans and leek, plus enough water to cover everything by a good 1½ inches. Bring to a boil and season liberally with salt and pepper. Reduce the heat, partially cover, and simmer for 45 minutes to 2 hours, until the beans are very soft but not falling apart. Add water if the level drops more than half an inch.

Strain the solids, reserving all the liquid in a large measuring jug. Return the beans and vegetables to the empty cooking pot. Discard the bay leaves. In a food processor, combine about a third of the bean mixture with 2 cups of the cooking liquid and purée until completely smooth. Return this puréed mixture to the pot with the remaining solids.

Add enough of the reserved cooking liquid to get the desired consistency; I like it thick and hearty, but you may prefer a thinner soup. Stir in the lemon juice, Garlic Purée, and chopped dill. Taste for seasoning. Ladle into bowls and top with some crumbled feta, a few sprigs of dill, and a drizzle of extra-virgin olive oil.

PASTA WITH KIMA

MAKARONIA ME KIMA

SERVES 4 TO 6 AS A PLATED ENTREÉ OR FAMILY-STYLE

This is a classic Greek meat sauce, but a little different from an Italian Bolognese, because there are no carrots or celery and you have the traditional Greek flavors of cinnamon, nutmeg, and cloves. You can serve it with any kind of pasta. Once you have this sauce, you can re-create anything that calls for classic braised ground meat with a new Greek flavor identity—tacos, meaty mac and cheese, chili. You can really play around with it, and it's very easy to make. Ten minutes to set it up, and then it's cooking by itself. Start the pasta ten minutes before the *Kima* is done, throw it into your sauce, and you're done. *Plus*, it's even better if you make it the night before.

3 tablespoons blended oil (90 percent canola, 10 percent extra-virgin olive)
1 Spanish or sweet onion, finely chopped
1 fresh bay leaf or 2 dried leaves
2 cinnamon sticks
1½ pounds ground beef
1 teaspoon ground cinnamon
Pinch ground nutmeg
Pinch ground cloves (optional)
3 tablespoons tomato paste
2 quarts water

1 (28-ounce) can plum tomatoes, crushed slightly, with all the juices
1 tablespoon red wine vinegar
1 teaspoon sugar
Kosher salt and cracked black pepper
1 pound rigatoni, perciatelli, bucatini, or pappardelle, for serving
⅓ cup grated *graviera* cheese
Small handful torn fresh herbs, such as dill, mint, and/or parsley
Extra-virgin olive oil

Warm a large, heavy pot over medium-high heat and add the blended oil. Wilt the onion with the bay leaves and cinnamon sticks for 3 to 5 minutes without browning. Add the ground beef and brown thoroughly. Add the spices and tomato paste; stir for a minute or two. Add the water, tomatoes, vinegar, sugar, 2 tablespoons salt, and a generous grinding of pepper. Bring to a boil.

Reduce the heat, partially cover, and simmer for 60 to 65 minutes. Skim off any scum that rises at the beginning. Later on, skim off the fat once or twice. Remove the bay leaves and cinnamon sticks. The sauce should be meaty with lots of juice.

Cook the pasta, drain, and toss with *Kima* (meat sauce). Scatter with *graviera* and fresh herbs, and drizzle with a little olive oil.

WHOLE GRILLED LOUP DE MER

LAVRAKI STIN SCHARA

SERVES 4

This recipe is my take on "whole grilled fish." It's the only dish that has not changed on the Anthos menu. The butchering here is a little difficult, but the result is simple grilled fish with no bones, as juicy and texturally sound as its fully bone-in counterpart. Additionally, the black olive compound butter internally bastes the fish while grilling. The results are spectacular. The caul fat, which melts away when grilling, reinforces the structural integrity of the boneless fish while sealing the compound butter in its cavity. If you are against the use of butter, this technique will allow you to stuff the fish with anything that excites you. My personal favorite is sun-dried tomato purée used to stuff the Roasted Leg of Lamb (page 142). This dish will not really achieve its potential without *Ladolemono*, so take a moment to make it. Here, we serve two fish for four people, but big eaters should feel free to double the compound butter and serve one fish per person.

½ teaspoon Dried Lemon Zest
   (page 270) or ¼ teaspoon fresh
4 cloves Garlic Confit (page 264) or
   1 tablespoon Garlic Purée (page 264)
½ scallion, green part only, roughly
   chopped
Kosher salt
2 oil-cured black olives, pitted and torn
3 ounces unsalted butter, at room
   temperature

Cracked black pepper
2 whole loup de mer or branzino,
   about 1 pound each
About 3 ounces pork caul fat
   (see option at right)
Extra-virgin olive oil
Ladolemono (page 270)
Small handful torn fresh herbs, such
   as dill, parsley, and/or chives
Sea salt

In a food processor, combine the Dried Lemon Zest, Garlic Confit, scallion, 1 teaspoon salt, and the olives. Process until smooth and add the butter and a generous grinding of pepper. Pulse until evenly blended.

Turn the butter out onto the bottom end of a large piece of parchment paper and fold the top down to cover. Smooth with your fingers until the layer of butter is ¼ inch thick. Freeze on a baking sheet for at least 2 hours, or overnight.

Place the fish on a cutting board positioned perpendicularly to your body and cut down on either side of the spine all the way through. Snip the spine just below the head and just above the tail and remove the skeleton in one piece. Using a pair of tweezers, remove any residual bones on both fillets. Break off a long piece of frozen butter and place inside each fish. Wrap each fish in a single layer of caul fat, trimming any overlapping bits with scissors.

Brush with olive oil and season with kosher salt and pepper. On a very hot charcoal or gas grill with wood chips (not a ridged griddle pan), grill for about 10 minutes total, turning over once, until beautifully charred. Immediately transfer to a platter, to catch the butter and juices. Drizzle with a liberal amount of *Ladolemono*, a handful of picked herbs, and a sprinkle of sea salt.

※ If you can't find caul fat, or are opposed to pork products, you may tie the fish up with fine kitchen twine.

※ Serve on a big platter in the middle of the table with Artichokes & Potato (page 36), but serve the side dish hot from the pan instead of at room temperature.

COD SKORDALIA WITH PICKLED BEETS

BACALIAROS ME SKORDALIA KAI PANTZARIA TOURSI

SERVES 4 AS A PLATED APPETIZER

Back before refrigeration, people developed ways of preserving food, such as salting and drying fish. Salt cod takes a little preparation, so you have to start it the night before. *Skordalia*, although traditionally served with *bacaliaros*, is a fantastic nondairy potato purée that has a feisty acid and raw garlic pop. It's great served with steak or any protein. Make the *Skordalia* while the oil is coming up to temperature for frying the cod, so it will be warm.

FOR THE PICKLED BEETS
1 quart distilled white vinegar
1½ tablespoons kosher salt
1½ tablespoons sugar
4 small beets

FOR THE COD
6 to 8 ounces dried salt cod
Milk
Kosher salt and cracked black pepper

FOR THE TEMPURA BATTER
¾ cup plus 2 tablespoons soda water, or
   as needed
⅔ cup all-purpose flour
3 tablespoons cornstarch
1½ teaspoons salt

FOR THE SKORDALIA
3 large Idaho potatoes, peeled and
   quartered
8 cloves garlic, sliced
¾ cup distilled white vinegar
¾ cup extra-virgin olive oil
Kosher salt and cracked black pepper

TO ASSEMBLE
Canola or safflower oil, for deep-frying
   (for even better flavor, use half
   extra-virgin olive oil)
¼ red onion, very thinly sliced
Small handful torn fresh herbs, such as
   parsley and dill
Extra-virgin olive oil
Lemon wedges, for serving

For the pickled beets, in a refrigerator-proof container, combine the vinegar, salt, and sugar. Stir until the salt and sugar dissolve.

In a pot of boiling water, cook the beets until tender, 25 to 40 minutes. Cool, peel, and cut in wedges. Immerse in the vinegar mixture and refrigerate overnight.

For the cod, the day before, cover the salt cod with water and soak in the refrigerator for 1 hour. Drain, then repeat, soaking for 2 hours. Drain, then repeat, again soaking for 2 hours. Drain, then cover with milk and soak overnight.

For the Tempura Batter, pour the soda water into a bowl. In a sifter, combine the flour, cornstarch, and salt, and sift it into the soda water. Whisk until evenly blended, with the consistency of thin pancake batter. Add a little more soda water if necessary to thin it. Cover and refrigerate for 45 minutes.

For the *Skordalia*, cook the potatoes in boiling salted water until very tender. Meanwhile, purée the garlic and vinegar in a food processor until very smooth.

Put the potatoes through a ricer into a bowl and stir in the garlic-vinegar mixture. Stir in the olive oil, 1 tablespoon kosher salt, and a generous grinding of pepper. The *Skordalia* should be the consistency of applesauce. Keep warm.

To assemble, in a pot half full of oil or a deep fryer, heat the oil to 350°F. Drain the cod and cut into about 8 rectangles. Season with kosher salt and pepper, and dip the cod pieces in the Tempura Batter. Fry until golden brown.

Add the onions and herbs to the beets. Dress with olive oil and season with salt and pepper. Make a pool of *Skordalia* on each plate and top with some of the fried cod. Place some Pickled Beets on the side and serve with lemon wedges.

☀ Make some *Tsatziki* (page 189). Put a dollop on top of the pickled beet salad.

DEEP-FRYING TIP

When you deep-fry, hold each piece of food, as you add it, with a pair of long tongs. Lower gently into the hot oil and hold just below the surface for 5 seconds before releasing. This will seize the exterior and stop it from sticking to the bottom of the pot or any other items already in the oil.

HANGER STEAK WITH BRAISED DANDELION, LEMON & OIL

BRIZOLA ME AGRIA RADIKIA KAI LADOLEMONO

SERVES 4

This steak greatly benefits from a long time in the marinade, so start it the night before if you can. Otherwise, let it marinate at least 4 hours.

¾ cup extra-virgin olive oil, plus more
   for brushing and finishing
3 cloves garlic, smashed
3 to 4 large sprigs thyme
1 fresh bay leaf
2 sprigs rosemary
2 shallots, sliced
Kosher salt and cracked black pepper

2 pounds hanger steak
1 small bunch dandelion greens, tough
   stems removed

¼ cup strained or Greek yogurt
2 tablespoons distilled white vinegar
1 tablespoon extra-virgin olive oil
2 cloves garlic, smashed and chopped
1 pepperoncini (pickled yellow pepper),
   chopped
1 teaspoon fresh lemon juice
¼ cup water
1 tablespoon Garlic Purée (page 264)
   or cold, unsalted butter
Sea salt

In a deep baking dish or roasting pan, combine the olive oil, garlic, thyme, bay leaf, rosemary, shallots, and a generous amount of kosher salt and pepper. Marinate the steak in this mixture overnight, covered with plastic wrap that is pressed down onto the surface of the meat.

Prepare an ice water bath. In a large pot of well-salted boiling water, cook the dandelion greens until tender, about 5 to 7 minutes. Drain and shock the greens in the ice water bath. Drain again, squeeze dry, and chop coarsely. Reserve.

In a small bowl, whisk the yogurt and vinegar together and season with kosher salt and pepper.

Preheat a charcoal or gas grill, or ridged cast-iron griddle pan, until very, very hot. Brush the steak with olive oil and season liberally with kosher salt and pepper. Grill until the meat is firm and char-marked, about 8 minutes, turning once. Set aside to rest for 10 minutes.

In a skillet, warm the olive oil over medium-high heat. Add the garlic and pepperoncini and sauté for 1 minute. Add the reserved dandelion greens, lemon juice, and ¼ cup of water. Season with kosher salt and pepper and add the Garlic Purée or butter.

With tongs, transfer the dandelion greens to a plate. Spoon a little yogurt mixture on the greens. Cut the steak into thick slices and place on top. Drizzle with olive oil and scatter with a little sea salt.

☀ If you have leftovers, make a quick hot sandwich: Sauté some sliced onion in olive oil with a teaspoon of gyro spice (fennel, mustard, and cumin seeds, and peppercorns, see page 150) until softened, deglaze the pan with sherry vinegar, and add the meat just to warm through. Pile into a pita and top with a spoonful or two of *Tsatziki*.

SAUSAGE, PEPPERS, ONION & TOMATO
SPETSOFAI

SERVES 4 TO 6 FAMILY-STYLE

This dish is a version of Italian sausage and peppers, with the added Greek dimension of cloves and mint. It's more of a side dish, good for a big table full of different dishes—perhaps a Super Bowl party. It can also easily be turned into a main course by serving over rice or rigatoni.

1 tablespoon blended oil (90 percent canola, 10 percent extra-virgin olive)

1½ pounds *loukanika* sausages, cut into 1-inch lengths (a chunky sweet or hot Italian sausage may be substituted)

1 Spanish or sweet onion, thickly sliced

1 red pepper, cored, seeded, and sliced

1 green pepper, cored, seeded, and sliced

1 yellow pepper, cored, seeded, and sliced

6 cloves garlic, smashed and chopped

3 pepperoncini (pickled yellow peppers), chopped

2 tablespoons tomato paste

½ cup white wine

1 (28-ounce) can Italian plum tomatoes, hand-crushed, with the juices

2 cups water

6 leaves fresh mint

6 whole cloves

1 teaspoon dry Greek oregano

Kosher salt and cracked black pepper

2 tablespoons Garlic Purée (page 264)

Extra-virgin olive oil

¼ cup crumbled feta cheese

Small handful torn fresh herbs, such as dill, mint, and/or parsley

In a very large, deep skillet, warm the blended oil over medium-high heat. Add the sausage, thoroughly brown, and reserve. To the same pan, add the onions and all the peppers; cook for 3 to 5 minutes. When the peppers are tender, throw in the chopped garlic and the pepperoncini and cook for 1 minute, then stir in the tomato paste and cook for 1 minute more.

Deglaze the pan with the white wine and let it evaporate completely. Add the reserved sausage, tomatoes, water, mint, cloves, oregano, 1 tablespoon of kosher salt, and a generous grinding of pepper. Bring the mixture to a boil. Reduce the heat, partially cover, and simmer until it thickens, about 25 minutes. Fold in Garlic Purée.

Transfer to a platter with all the pan juices. Drizzle with a little olive oil. Scatter with the feta and fresh herbs.

❈ If you don't like pepperoncini, leave them out, but be sure to add some acidity, such as a touch of red wine vinegar, because you need some brightness to play off all the fat that's coming out of the sausages, and to keep the palate coming back for more.

POTATO, EGG, TOMATO & PEPPERS

TIGANITES PATATES ME AVGA, TOMATES KAI PIPERIES

SERVES 4 TO 6

Every Greek mother has a go-to dish like this in her repertoire. When my mom was running around taking us four kids to soccer practices and ballet, this was a hearty meal she could throw together at the drop of a hat. Most Mediterranean cultures have an egg and potato dish. It is also one of the first things I ever cooked.

3 Idaho potatoes, peeled, cut into French-fry-sized batons

Canola, peanut, or sunflower oil, for deep-frying

Kosher salt and cracked black pepper

1 tablespoon olive oil

1 Spanish or sweet onion, finely chopped

1 red pepper, cored, seeded, and thickly sliced

1 green pepper, cored, seeded, and thickly sliced

1 yellow pepper, cored, seeded, and thickly sliced

2 large leaves sage, slivered

2 cloves garlic, smashed and chopped

2 plum or cherry tomatoes, cut into rough wedges

2 teaspoons white wine vinegar

12 large eggs, beaten well with a tablespoon of milk

Small handful torn fresh herbs, such as dill, parsley, mint, and/or chives

⅓ cup crumbled feta cheese

Crusty bread, for serving

Deep-fry the potatoes (see page 154). Drain on absorbent paper towels, and season with kosher salt and pepper.

In a large skillet, warm the olive oil over medium heat. Add the onion, all the peppers, and the sage and garlic. Cook until soft, about 3 to 6 minutes. Add the tomatoes and white wine vinegar, and continue to cook until the liquid evaporates. Add the fried potatoes, then pour in the beaten eggs. Let this cook undisturbed for 1 minute, then begin gently scrambling the mixture until it reaches your desired consistency. Just before serving, scatter with the fresh herbs and feta.

❁ If you like spicy flavors, add 2 to 3 chopped pepperoncini while you are sautéing the pepper mixture.

TOMATO & STRING BEAN SALAD
TOMATOSALATA ME FASOLAKIA

SERVES 4, OR MORE AS PART OF A LARGER SPREAD

This is my version of a Greek steak house salad—it's fantastic with a steak or any kind of protein. Add toasted bread and it's a Greek version of the Italian dish panzanella. I recommend going a step further by adding a grilled onion: the char flavor works perfectly with the ripe fruit and vegetables.

¼ pound green beans, ends trimmed

¼ pound yellow wax beans, ends trimmed

⅓ to ½ cup Red Wine and Feta Vinaigrette (page 271)

2 tablespoons crumbled feta cheese

4 vine-ripe tomatoes, preferably heirloom, cut into rough wedges

1 teaspoon dry Greek oregano

½ small red onion, thinly sliced and separated into rings

6 small, picked sprigs parsley, torn

6 small, picked sprigs dill, torn

16 leaves fresh mint, torn

Kosher salt and coarsely cracked black pepper

Prepare an ice water bath and bring a pot of salted water to a boil. Blanch the beans until tender but still snappy, about 3 minutes, then shock them in the ice water bath and swish around. Drain well and dry on a clean towel.

In a bowl, combine the beans, vinaigrette, feta, tomatoes, oregano, red onion, and torn herbs. Toss well with clean hands. Taste and adjust the seasoning with kosher salt and pepper.

❄ If you wish, add toasted chunks of day-old bread, brushed with extra-virgin olive oil and seasoned with sea salt and pepper.

❄ Or try adding half a grilled Spanish or sweet onion, separated into rings (page 270).

DRIED FRUIT SALAD WITH THYME-HONEY VINAIGRETTE
SALATA ME APOXIRAMENA FROUTA KAI LADOXYDO ME THYMARISIO MELI

SERVES 6

This is not a traditional Greek salad, but I love the interplay between the sweet fruits and the tart vinaigrette. Greece has a great tradition of fruit served with cheese, and this salad plays right into this palate-tantalizing combination. I've chosen dried fruits to show their versatility and to create a salad that's wonderful during the cooler months. Of note also is the variety of fruit being used. Although not all are necessary, each provides its own unique flavor and texture, which allows the salad to evolve with each bite.

¾ cup sliced almonds
¼ cup red wine vinegar
½ cup raspberry vinegar
3 cloves garlic, smashed
1 clove shallot, thickly sliced
1 tablespoon Dijon mustard
1 sprig picked thyme
1 teaspoon dry Greek oregano
1 teaspoon honey, preferably
  thyme honey
⅔ cup extra-virgin olive oil

⅓ cup canola oil
Kosher salt and cracked black pepper
¾ cup tart dried cherries
12 plump, dried apricots, slivered
6 dried pears, slivered lengthwise
6 dried figs, slivered
9 dates, slivered lengthwise
16 ounces baby arugula leaves
6 hearts frisée, coarsely chopped
5 ounces *manouri* cheese, coarsely grated

Preheat an oven to 350°F. Spread the almonds on a baking sheet and toast until golden, about 10 minutes.

In a blender or food processor, combine the vinegars, garlic, shallot, mustard, thyme, oregano, and honey. Process until smooth. With motor running, slowly pour in the extra-virgin olive oil, followed by the blended oil. Season with kosher salt and pepper.

In a large serving bowl, combine all the dried fruits, arugula, and the frisée. Toss until lightly coated with the vinaigrette. Scatter the toasted almonds and *manouri* on top and grind a generous amount of cracked pepper over all.

YOGURT WITH CANDIED QUINCE & CRUSHED JORDAN ALMONDS
YAOURTI ME ZAXAROMENA KYDONIA KAI COPANISTA KOUFETA

SERVES 4

If you make the candied quince for this dish, be sure to also make the skate recipe on page 44; as the quince is the most difficult and time-consuming element of both recipes, you will be able to create the other dish in no time at all. By pairing the sweet fruit with the tart flavor of yogurt, you create a simple, not-too-sweet dessert. Standard supermarket yogurt will not work here unless you drain it overnight (see page xiv; in fact, it will not work with any dish in this book that calls for Greek yogurt).

In Greece, Jordan almonds—whole almonds with a colored, hard sugar-candy coating—are traditionally wrapped in tulle and given as party favors to guests at weddings and christening celebrations. Here, they provide texture and beauty, but you can also choose crumbled halvah, or crystallized ginger. I prefer a combination of all three. So much more fun than the typical granola mix!

⅓ cup Jordan almonds
1¼ cups (10 ounces) goat's or sheep's
  milk yogurt, labne, kefir, or strained,
  full-fat yogurt

2 Candied Quinces (page 277),
  with syrup
4 leaves fresh mint, slivered

Crush the Jordan almonds with the side of a knife, then chop coarsely to a chunky granola-like consistency. (If this is difficult or messy, you can pulse quickly in a food processor.)

With an ice cream scoop or two large spoons, form quenelles (oval dollops) of the thick yogurt and put two on each plate. Sprinkle the Candied Quinces on top and drizzle with some of their spicy syrup. Scatter with the crushed Jordan almonds and a few slivers of mint.

the hunting trip

W ould you like to come?"

The silhouetted figure of my father loomed over my bed.

It was three o'clock in the morning. I was seven years old.

"Come where?" I mumbled, confused and disoriented.

"Hunting," he said. "With me."

I sat bolt upright. For as long as I could remember, I'd been begging my father to let me join him on one of his fabled hunting trips. Up until then the answer had always been "We'll see," and when I would wake up the morning of the trip, I'd find him already gone.

I jumped out of bed and hugged my father as hard as I could. I ran into my parents' bedroom, where my mother was still asleep, and I woke her to tell her the good news. Finally, I was going with my father, uncles, and male cousins on a family hunting trip. I knew what this meant. This was more than just fluorescent orange vests and beer in a cooler. This invitation meant that—in my father's eyes and in the eyes of my family—I was becoming a man.

When my father was a boy growing up in Crete, hunting wasn't about sport. It was the difference between meat on the table and going without. To come home without some kind of catch meant that he would go hungry, and so would his family. By joining this hunt, I was about to cross a threshold, and I embraced the opportunity—and the responsibility.

My mother had already laid out hunting clothes for me. As my father carefully loaded an arsenal into the back of our wood-paneled station wagon, I scrambled to get dressed. I could hardly contain my excitement.

We started the drive north, first on local roads, then onto the highway. The whole drive couldn't have taken more than a couple of hours, but to me even fifteen minutes seemed like an eternity. It was still pitch-dark outside, and I fell asleep in the back of the station wagon. When I awoke, Theio Jimmy and his son, my cousin Manoli, and Theio Antonios and his son, my cousin Teddy, and Theio Manousos were sitting in the vehicle too.

We arrived at our destination in the mountains of upstate New York and unloaded the guns. Every man took a weapon. My father told us all to line up in a row, four men and three boys, and we proceeded single file up a mountain. With this, as with most things in my life as it pertained to my father, there was an order to things—a rationale. We walked in a line so when someone was taking aim at an animal, a person would not inadvertently get caught in the line of fire. That line also determined the order in which we got a turn to shoot.

Buzzing with energy, I couldn't stop chattering as we started uphill. My father kept hushing me until I was quiet. Then, still in a row, we marched in silence. A rabbit hopped into view. Theio Jimmy, first in line, took aim and missed. The next person, Theio Antonios, took a shot and killed the rabbit. When we reached the rabbit, it was dead and I felt . . . odd. This meat was not the antiseptic product from the grocery store, shrink-wrapped in a Styrofoam tray. This was an animal that had been alive moments before, hunted by me, my father, my cousins, and my uncles, just as game had been hunted by my father's father and his father before him. And it was then that I realized, So, this is what I have to do to earn the privilege to come on these trips, to be *here* with my father.

We had a picnic breakfast in a clearing. All around us there were trees laden with bright red apples. As I bit into one, I thought, This is the best apple I've ever tasted. Whether that was a function of the freshness of the apple or the thrill of being allowed to join my father on a hunting trip, the taste was so pronounced that, to this day, I remember the sweet, crisp flesh of that apple in my mouth.

It was then that my father asked me if I was ready to shoot a gun. I had been waiting so long to have this chance that there was no hesitation when I shouted, "Yes!," jumped up, and hurried to his side. He helped me position the rifle and pointed to a nearby tree.

"See that bird on the branch over there? Try to shoot it," my father instructed.

I sighted along the barrel of the rifle and took aim, but I couldn't pull the trigger by myself so one of the adults assisted me. The gun fired, and it was as if I'd been punched in the shoulder. I stumbled backward and fell on my butt to a chorus of loving laughter. Even though my shoulder ached dearly from the kick-back, I hopped right back on my feet and begged my father to let me shoot again. I wanted the chance to prove that I belonged here; that I could pull that trigger and stay upright.

The blast had scared off any potential prey, so I took aim at a leaf. "See that leaf over there?" I announced. "I'm going to hit it."

I planted my feet on the ground, trying to take root like a tree. I pulled the trigger again. This time, while I stumbled back a couple of steps, I remained on my feet. Needless to say, I missed the leaf, but that neither deterred me nor diminished the pride that was so apparent on my father's face and that in turn made my chest swell.

When we got home, we skinned the rabbit and handed it to my mother to cook for dinner. The women took over and transformed our catch into *kouneli stifado* (a hearty rabbit stew) for the family. Nothing went to waste, not even the pelt, which my father, a furrier, would bring to work the next day.

We all sat around the table, enjoying the meal my mother and sisters had prepared for us, with meat we had just that day hunted to feed our family. The talk at our table that night was all about our journey.

When I first started out as a chef, every time I'd put a game dish on the menu I'd call my father and invite him in to the restaurant to sample it. Feeding people and making them feel welcome always brings me great pleasure, and seeing my father's joy in eating these particular dishes was especially gratifying. Whether you use meat from game you have hunted yourself or purchased from a butcher, I hope the recipes in this chapter will help to sustain and nourish those you invite to join you at your own table.

The satisfaction I get from hunting—and from bringing back something to eat—is huge. It's hard to explain, but the idea of sharing both the experience of hunting and the pleasures of cooking and eating the catch is a profound fulfillment for me. You become close to the people you hunt with, and it's not just the excitement of the hunt itself, but also reliving the stories that then become part of your personal lore.

Here in New York City, we are so removed from the origins of our food that to see the animal in its natural habitat is to learn a new respect for the food we eat and the people with whom we share our food. The food is more special because we know where it came from, and the respect that we show for it—by cooking it well, by enjoying it, and by gaining nutrition and life from the animal that gave its life— are part of the Greek culture that most of us don't get a chance to experience.

GRILLED RABBIT CONFIT
SIGOPSIMENO KOUNELI STIN SCHARA

SERVES 4 TO 6 FAMILY-STYLE, OR MORE AS PART OF A LARGER SPREAD

As I've mentioned, the muscle formation in the legs of most animals makes for tough, stringy meat. Confit involves cooking slowly, which allows these formations to break down and yield a luscious result. The added dimension of grilling provides a brilliant smoky char that takes this dish to new levels. Serve with Greek Salad, Spinach Rice, Artichokes and Potato, or Dried Fruit Salad.

1 whole rabbit, skinned and cut into
   8 pieces (the saddle in 2 pieces)
1 whole shallot
10 cloves garlic, peeled
3 fresh bay leaves or 6 dried leaves
8 cloves
15 to 20 whole black peppercorns
8 star anise pods
16 juniper berries
6 cardamom pods

10 sprigs thyme
4 sprigs rosemary
1 teaspoon mustard seeds
Kosher salt and cracked black pepper
Blended oil (90 percent canola,
   10 percent extra-virgin olive)
Roasted Lemon Purée (page 149,
   optional)
Lemon wedges, for squeezing

Preheat the oven to 300°F. Rinse the rabbit in cold water and dry thoroughly with paper towels.

In a heavy lidded pot or a large Dutch oven, combine the rabbit with the shallot, garlic cloves, bay leaves, cloves, peppercorns, star anise pods, juniper berries, cardamom pods, thyme, rosemary, mustard seeds, and 1 tablespoon of kosher salt. Add enough oil to cover by about half an inch, then lightly press a piece of parchment paper down on the surface of the oil. Cover the pan and cook until tender but not falling apart, about 3 hours. Check occasionally—the oil should never come to a full simmer; reduce the heat as necessary. (When done, you may cool to room temperature and refrigerate overnight, or up to 3 days. However, you must slowly heat the rabbit pieces in confit oil in a warm oven before grilling, otherwise the center will be cold.)

Preheat a charcoal or gas grill, or ridged cast-iron grill pan, until very hot. Lift the rabbit pieces out of the confit oil and season with kosher salt and pepper. Reserve the oil until serving time. Lightly sear the rabbit to imbue the smoky char flavor of the grill (remember, the rabbit is already cooked). Drizzle with a little of the confit oil and squeeze a wedge of lemon over, or, if you have Roasted Lemon Purée on hand, paint the rabbit with some of the lemon purée instead. You may also use the rabbit-infused confit oil to make a quick vinaigrette or to roast some mushrooms to serve alongside. The oil will add another dimension of flavor in both cases.

☀ Lightly cure the rabbit before making it into a confit: mix 3 tablespoons kosher salt with 1 tablespoon sugar. Rub the mixture all over the rabbit pieces and place on a rack in your refrigerator overnight, uncovered. Rinse well and pat dry thoroughly with paper towels before you begin the confit.

☀ Make the confit with a mixture of 50 percent extra-virgin olive oil and 50 percent canola or safflower oil instead of a 10 percent/90 percent blend.

☀ Rabbit confit makes the very best deep-fried rabbit you'll ever have: smear the pieces of rabbit with Dijon mustard, and bread as you would for deep-frying, using milk, flour, beaten egg, bread crumbs or panko; fry until golden brown.

RUSTIC BRAISED RABBIT WITH HILOPITES PASTA
HORIATIKO SIGOVRASMENO KOUNELI ME HILOPITES

SERVES 4 TO 6

Most of a rabbit's meat is on its legs, but in this dish all the meat will be falling off the bones, so you'll get more meat than usual in the sauce. Rabbits have tasty belly flaps, one on each side, below the rib cage. The flaps are very thin and small, but if you cut them off and save them until you have enough, you can bread them in the same way you would to make a Milanese, or any other way you would use a veal or pork scallopine. Imagine serving rabbit soffrito to your foodie friends . . . so cool, so haute, so easy!

In Greek, *hilo* means sun, and *pita* means bread. So, it is literally "sun-bread." If you prefer to make pasta in an electric stand mixer, by all means substitute that for the food processor used here. Because of the cake flour, this is a very delicate pasta.

1 dressed rabbit (with all its innards),
    cut into 8 to 10 pieces
Kosher salt and cracked black pepper
2 tablespoons blended oil (90 percent
    canola, 10 percent extra-virgin olive)
1 Spanish or sweet onion,
    finely chopped
2 carrots, finely chopped
2 stalks celery, finely chopped
8 cloves garlic, smashed and chopped
3 tablespoons tomato paste
1 cup white wine
4 quarts water

1 cup tomato purée (or good
    store-bought marinara sauce)
2 teaspoons dry Greek oregano
4 large sprigs thyme
1 large sprig rosemary
4 cinnamon sticks
2 tablespoons red wine vinegar
2 tablespoons Dijon mustard
Hilopites Pasta dough (page 76)
    or 2 pounds dried pappardelle
    pasta, cooked
Semolina and all-purpose flour,
    for dusting

Set the innards aside. Season the rabbit pieces liberally with kosher salt and pepper. In a large Dutch oven or heavy braising pan, warm the oil over medium-high heat. When the oil is very hot, sear the rabbit pieces until golden brown on all sides, shaking the pan and turning frequently. Add the onion, carrots, celery, and garlic and cook until soft, about 3 to 5 minutes. Add the tomato paste and stir for 1 minute. Deglaze the pan with the white wine and let it evaporate completely.

Add the rabbit's innards, water, tomato purée, 1 tablespoon salt, a generous grinding of pepper, and the oregano, thyme, rosemary, cinnamon sticks, vinegar, and mustard. Bring to a boil. Reduce the heat, partially cover the pan, and simmer gently for 1¾ to 2 hours (skim off any scum that rises), until the meat is falling off the bones and the sauce thickens.

Remove the rabbit pieces, pick the meat off the bones, and return it to the sauce. Fish out the whole herb sprigs and cinnamon sticks.

For the *Hilopites* Pasta dough, follow the first 2 steps for the pasta on page 76. Dust a parchment-lined, rimmed baking sheet very generously with flour and semolina. Cut 5 or 6 rectangles of parchment paper to fit the pan; you will be layering the finished noodles between the sheets as you work, scattering with more flour and semolina for each layer.

Starting with the largest setting, put the dough through a pasta machine and continue feeding, lowering the settings by two after each pass, until it's about the thickness of fettucine, no. 6 or no. 7. Scatter with flour only if the dough threatens to stick. Keep rolling until the dough is silky and flexible and, again, not at all tacky.

With a pizza cutter or a long knife, trim the edges of the dough straight and even. Cut lengthwise into 2 very long, 2-inch-wide strips. Cut these crosswise into rustic and slightly uneven domino-sized rectangles. As you work, place the shapes onto the flour-dusted parchment in single layers.

Cook and drain the pasta: for the fresh *hilopites*, boil 1 to 2 minutes, depending on how long it has dried. For dried pasta, cook according to the package instructions. Toss with the braised rabbit and sauce to make a rustic, hearty dish.

Fresh pasta is usually used right away, but you can open-freeze a single layer of the rectangles on parchment-lined baking sheets, then layer the frozen shapes between sheets of plastic wrap and place inside zipper-lock bags for up to 1 month. The frozen pasta will take slightly longer to cook.

PHEASANT WITH SPAGHETTI

PHASIANOS ME MAKARONIA

SERVES 4 TO 8 FAMILY-STYLE

In all my restaurants, I constantly observe the plates returning from the dining room. A clean plate is the only acceptable result. To me, the definition of food greatness is when a dish is so good that you want to continue eating it after you have become satiated. It's so European in mentality, but it means that you just can't stop because you don't know if you'll ever find that food bliss again. If plates come back unfinished, then we failed to reach that greatness.

This dish says "home" to me; it's home-style Greek cooking at its very best. Serve up a platter, and your friends won't be able to keep their hands off it. You can also make this dish with chicken or any other poultry or game bird.

1 pheasant, 2½ to 3¾ pounds, cut into breast-wing and leg-thigh pieces; backbone cut into 3 pieces
Kosher salt and cracked black pepper
3 tablespoons blended oil (90 percent canola, 10 percent extra-virgin olive)
4 cloves garlic, smashed
½ Spanish or sweet onion, roughly chopped
1 small carrot, roughly chopped
1 stalk celery, roughly chopped
3 tablespoons tomato paste
1 cup red wine
4 large sprigs thyme
2 large sprigs sage

1 large sprig rosemary
1 cinnamon stick
¼ cup red wine vinegar
2 teaspoons dry Greek oregano
1 tablespoon Dijon mustard
2½ cups water
1 pound dried spaghetti
12 dried dates, pitted and quartered lengthwise
⅓ cup yellow raisins
⅓ cup pine nuts
¼ cup torn fresh herbs, such as dill, mint, and/or parsley
Extra-virgin olive oil

Rinse the pheasant pieces in cold water and pat dry. Season all sides liberally with kosher salt and pepper. In a large, heavy pot or Dutch oven, warm the blended oil over medium-high heat. When the oil is very hot, add and sear the pheasant pieces, without crowding, until golden on all sides. Transfer to a platter and discard most of the oil. Add all the vegetables and sweat for 3 to 5 minutes, without browning. Add the tomato paste and stir for 1 minute. Deglaze the pan with the red wine and let it reduce completely.

Return the seared pheasant pieces to the pot and add the thyme, sage, rosemary, cinnamon, vinegar, oregano, mustard, water, 1 tablespoon salt, and a generous grinding of pepper. Bring to a boil, then reduce the heat, partially cover, and simmer until the meat is nearly falling off the bones, about 50 minutes, occasionally skimming off any scum. (Cooking time will depend on the size of the pheasant; males are much larger than females.)

Transfer the pheasant pieces to a platter. Remove and discard thyme, sage, and rosemary sprigs, and cinnamon stick. Add ½ to 1 cup of water if there is less than 2 inches braising liquid remaining. Bring the liquid to a boil, crack the spaghetti in half, and add to the pot along with the dates, raisins, and pine nuts. If desired, pick the pheasant meat off the bones, all the time watching and aggressively stirring the spaghetti in the pot—especially toward the end of the cooking time—to keep it moistened with the reduced braising liquid and stop it from sticking. Return the pheasant meat to the spaghetti and season with salt and pepper to taste. The spaghetti should take about 10 minutes to cook until tender. Transfer to a warm platter and scatter with the fresh herbs; drizzle with the olive oil. (Serve immediately, or the starch from the spaghetti will thicken the liquid too much.)

❉ For an extra dimension of flavor and texture, cure the pheasant pieces overnight, then confit them (both techniques are described for the rabbit on page 116), before roasting as directed here.

ROASTED PHEASANT WITH CANDIED ORANGE PEEL & LEEK CONFIT

PSITO PHASIANOS ME ZAHAROMENO PORTOKALI KAI SIGOVRASMENA PRASSA

◈———◈

SERVES 2

This recipe is a bit involved, but it will showcase your talents in the kitchen. I suggest leaving this dish for a Sunday afternoon cooking extravaganza. For me, cooking is like therapy—a calming, soothing, relaxing place that somehow always makes me feel better. And then we get to eat!

Note: If you buy a whole pheasant, remove the legs and confit them as for the Grilled Rabbit on page 116. Serve with this dish, in which case the recipe will serve 4.

2 pheasant breasts, if available, or
   1 whole pheasant
2 pieces (1 whole leek) Leek Confit (page
   268), with 3 tablespoons of the oil
Kosher salt and cracked black pepper
2 tablespoons sherry vinegar

2 tablespoons water
1 tablespoon cold, unsalted butter
1 teaspoon finely chopped dill
6 to 10 thin strips Candied Orange Peel
   (page 279), with a little of the syrup,
   to taste

Rinse the pheasant breasts in cold water and pat thoroughly dry with paper towels. (If you think ahead, allow the breasts to dry on a rack in the refrigerator for at least a few hours, and up to a few days. It will intensify the game flavor and also dry out the skin, resulting in a crisper skin.)

continued

Have all of the ingredients prepared and on hand, and preheat the oven to 375°F.

Place two skillets on the stove, one of them ovenproof. In the ovenproof skillet, warm about 2 tablespoons of the Leek Confit oil over medium-high heat. Season the pheasant breasts liberally on both sides with kosher salt and pepper. When the oil is hot, sear the breasts skin-side down for 2 minutes, then turn and sear the flesh side for 1 minute. Turn the breasts back to skin-side up and transfer the pan to the oven for 3 minutes (you'll be using these 3 minutes to heat the pan for the garnish). After 3 minutes, remove the pan from the oven and let the breasts rest.

In the other skillet, warm the remaining tablespoon of the Leek Confit oil over high heat. When the oil is hot, add the Leek Confit pieces with any oil still clinging to them. Sauté for 1 minute, then deglaze the pan with the vinegar and water. Simmer for 1 minute, then remove from the heat and swirl in the butter, dill, Candied Orange Peel, and 1 teaspoon syrup from the orange peel. Keep swirling until the sauce is creamy. Spoon the leek-orange garnish onto the plates and top with the pheasant breasts, thickly sliced. Spoon the remaining pan juices over the top.

GRILLED QUAILS WITH
SWEET-&-SOUR CHARRED ONION & RED WINE GLAZE
ORTYKIA STIN SCHARA, GLYKOXINA KREMMYDIA GLASSARISMENA
ME KOKKINO KRASI

❖───❖

SERVES 4 AS A PLATED ENTRÉE, OR MORE FAMILY-STYLE
(IF THE QUAILS ARE SPLIT), AS PART OF A LARGER SPREAD

In this glaze, charring the onion reinforces the open-flame flavor of the grill. The result reminds me of a refined Mediterranean barbecue sauce. It works perfectly with any kind of grilled meat, poultry, or game. Keep in mind that the glaze will thicken as it cools, so remove it from the heat before it seems ready. It will cool to the perfect consistency.

FOR THE GRILLED QUAILS
4 quails, dressed or partially boned
Kosher salt and cracked black pepper
4 large sprigs rosemary
8 large sprigs thyme
16 large leaves fresh mint
1 cup red wine
¼ cup balsamic vinegar

1 cup extra-virgin olive oil
1 shallot, roughly chopped
2 cloves garlic, smashed and chopped
2 fresh bay leaves or 4 dried leaves
Pinch dry Greek oregano
2 sprigs rosemary
2 tablespoons honey, preferably
    thyme honey

FOR THE ONION & RED WINE GLAZE

1 Spanish or sweet onion, thickly
  sliced and separated into rings
2 cups red wine
1 cup red wine vinegar
¼ cup raspberry vinegar
1½ cups water
½ cup granulated sugar
3 tablespoons honey, preferably
  thyme honey
1 fresh bay leaves or 2 dried leaves
1 sprig rosemary
Extra-virgin olive oil

Rinse the quails well in cold water, and dry thoroughly with paper towels. Season inside and out with kosher salt and pepper. Stuff each quail's cavity with 1 sprig of rosemary, 2 sprigs of thyme, and 4 mint leaves.

Make the marinade: in a container, combine the wine, vinegar, olive oil, shallot, garlic, bay leaves, oregano, rosemary, and thyme honey. Place the quails in the marinade, turning to cover, and press a large sheet of plastic wrap over the quails to exclude any air. Marinate for at least 2 hours, but not more than 6, turning over halfway through. Return the quails to full room temperature if you have held them in the refrigerator.

Meanwhile, make the glaze: in a blistering hot skillet filmed with a little oil, char the onion rings, tossing until blackened in several places, and transfer to a medium-sized pot. Add all the remaining glaze ingredients, bring to a boil, and reduce the heat to a simmer. Reduce the liquid until it thickens enough to coat the back of a spoon. Remove the glaze from the heat and strain through a sieve, pushing all the liquid out of the onions. Reserve the onions.

Preheat a charcoal or gas grill, or ridged cast-iron grill pan, until hot. Remove the quails from the marinade, season with kosher salt and pepper, and grill, moving the quails around a little if flames spring up (but don't be afraid of a little flame). Turn the quails over after 2 to 3 minutes, and cook for another 1 to 2 minutes until firm and char-marked.

Transfer the quails to the pan of glaze and turn to coat them all over. Transfer to a platter with the onions and all the pan juices. Drizzle with a little olive oil.

BRAISED QUAIL WITH FENNEL & APRICOTS

SIGOVRASMENA ORTYKIA ME MARATHO KAI VERIKOKA

SERVES 4

This is a refined dish, not as rustic as many of the tomato-based braises elsewhere in this chapter. The anise flavor of the fennel pairs brilliantly with the apricots to create an elegant sauce all in one pan. This dish illustrates how a little refinement can produce exquisite results and endless possibilities. Have fun and be prepared to be blown away by something you produced with your own hands.

4 dressed quails
Kosher salt and cracked black pepper
2 tablespoons blended oil (90 percent canola, 10 percent extra-virgin olive)
½ Spanish or sweet onion, roughly chopped
½ bulb fennel, roughly chopped
1 stalk celery, roughly chopped
2 sprigs rosemary
½ cup white wine

½ cup *metaxa* (rose-scented Greek brandy)
1½ tablespoons white vinegar or champagne vinegar
2 cups water
Scant tablespoon Dijon mustard
12 plump, dried apricots
1½ teaspoons honey
1 tablespoon Garlic Purée (page 264) and/or cold, unsalted butter

Rinse the quails in cold water and pat completely dry, inside and out. Season all sides and the cavities with kosher salt and pepper. In a wide, heavy pot or Dutch oven, warm the blended oil over medium-high heat. When the oil is very hot, add the quails and sear on all sides until golden brown.

Add the vegetables and rosemary to the pot and reduce the heat slightly. Wilt the vegetables until tender, about 4 to 6 minutes. Deglaze the pot with the white wine, *metaxa*, and vinegar and let it reduce completely. Add the water and mustard. Bring to a boil, reduce the heat, and partially cover the pot. Simmer for 30 minutes, occasionally skimming off any scum. Add the apricots and honey, and simmer until the quails are very tender, about 20 to 35 minutes. (Check to be sure the water has not cooked away and add a bit more if necessary.)

Transfer the quails to a warm platter. Add half the braising liquid to half the vegetables and a couple of the apricots and purée, using an immersion or standard blender. Pass the puréed mixture through a fine sieve or the finest disk of a food mill, and return the mixture to the original braising liquid. Swirl in the Garlic Purée and/or cold butter until fully incorporated. Season to taste and pour the mixture over the quails.

VENISON STEW

ELAFI STIFADO

◆——◆

SERVES 4 TO 6 AS A PLATED ENTRÉE, OR MORE FAMILY-STYLE,
AS PART OF A LARGER SPREAD, WITH POTATOES, RICE, OR ORZO

This stew, as with all braises, benefits texturally from the muscular, marbled meat. The long braises allow the natural collagens to break down, resulting in a fork-tender consistency. Luxury cuts like the saddle or the rack should be reserved for roasting or grilling. This dish is part of the "poverty cooking" tradition of Greece, where every cut of the animal is used and the cooking technique is tailored to suit.

2 tablespoons blended oil (90 percent canola, 10 percent extra-virgin olive)

1¼ pounds venison leg meat, cut into 1-inch cubes

Kosher salt and cracked black pepper

20 small, whole cipolline onions, pearl onions, or baby shallots, peeled

3 tablespoons tomato paste

1 cup red wine

¼ cup red wine vinegar

2 fresh bay leaves or 4 dried leaves

6 juniper berries

4 cloves

2 cinnamon sticks

4 quarts water

1 tablespoon Dijon mustard

2 tablespoons honey, preferably thyme honey

2 teaspoons dry Greek oregano

2 sprigs thyme

1 large sprig rosemary

8 fresh figs, quartered

2 small parsnips, peeled and cut into large chunks

1 tablespoon Garlic Purée (page 264) or cold, unsalted butter

In a large, heavy pot or Dutch oven, warm the oil over medium-high heat. Season the venison liberally with kosher salt and pepper, and sear on all sides for 3 to 5 minutes. Add the onions and sauté for 1 minute. Add the tomato paste and stir for 1 minute, then deglaze the pot with the red wine and vinegar and allow the liquid to evaporate completely. Add the bay leaves, juniper berries, cloves, cinnamon, water, mustard, honey, oregano, thyme, and rosemary. Bring the mixture to a boil, then reduce the heat and partially cover. Simmer briskly for about 30 minutes, until around one third of the liquid evaporates. Add 8 of the fig pieces and the parsnips, and simmer for another 30 minutes.

Check the meat. If it is tender, add the remaining figs to warm (continue cooking for 20 to 30 minutes more, if not). Season with salt and pepper, and serve.

VENISON SAUSAGE
LOUKANIKO APO ELAFI

MAKES 9 2-OUNCE SAUSAGES, PERFECT FOR MEZE

This is a play on a Cypriot sausage called *tseftelia*. Rather than using sausage casing, these fresh sausages are held together with caul fat, the lining of a pig stomach. I love caul fat—it's basically a weblike sheet of translucent fat that melts away as it cooks. Once you start using it, I guarantee it will change the way you cook. After all, what isn't better wrapped in dissolved fat? Caul fat is typically purchased frozen, so you will have to plan ahead. It's best to soak the caul fat overnight in salted water and squeeze dry before using. However, you may substitute a sausage casing if caul fat is unobtainable.

Note: If you don't have a spice mill, substitute 1¼ teaspoon ground fennel and ¾ teaspoon ground cumin for my spice mixture.

2 (¼-inch-thick) slices Spanish
  or sweet onion
Extra-virgin olive oil
Kosher salt and cracked black pepper
1 teaspoon coriander seeds
1 teaspoon cumin seeds
2 juniper berries
1 teaspoon fennel seeds
12 ounces ground venison, from the leg
6 ounces fatty, coarse-ground pork
  or fatback
2 teaspoons Garlic Purée (page 264)

2 teaspoons Dijon mustard
1 teaspoon honey
Large pinch dry Greek oregano
1 tablespoon finely chopped parsley
½ teaspoon orange zest
About 3 ounces pork caul fat or a
  sausage casing
Lemon wedges and extra-virgin olive oil
  or *Tsatziki* (page 189)
¼ cup loosely packed, picked herbs,
  such as dill, mint, and/or parsley

Brush the onion slices with a little olive oil and season with kosher salt and pepper. On a hot grill pan or in a cast-iron skillet, grill the onion until tender. Separate into rings and finely chop.

Toast the seeds and juniper berries in a preheated 325°F oven for 10 minutes. Transfer to a spice mill and grind to a powder (you will not use all of it).

In a large bowl, combine the grilled onion, 2 teaspoons of the spice mixture, and the venison, pork, Garlic Purée, mustard, honey, oregano, parsley, and orange zest. Season liberally with salt and pepper. With clean hands, combine the mixture evenly, and form 9 football-shaped sausages.

Wrap each sausage in a single layer of caul fat, trimming off any extra bits and pieces. If you like, refrigerate the sausages on a rack, uncovered, for 2 hours; this will help dry the surface and give you an even better sear on the grill.

continued

Vension Sausage continued from page 130

Preheat a charcoal or gas grill, or ridged cast-iron grill pan, until very hot. Brush the sausages lightly with a little olive oil and season with kosher salt and pepper. Grill until firm and char-marked all over. Transfer to a platter and drizzle with some lemon juice and extra-virgin olive oil, or top with a spoonful of *Tsatziki*. Scatter with picked fresh herbs.

❋ If you have some of the Candied Orange Peel (page 279), cut it into tiny dice and add to the venison mixture.

RACK OF VENISON WITH LEEK CONFIT & CANDIED CHERRIES
ELAFI ME SIGOVRASMENA PRASSA KAI ZAHAROMENA KERASIA

SERVES 4 TO 6 AS A PLATED ENTRÉE OR FAMILY-STYLE

Make sure the butcher cuts through or removes the chine bone, from the base of the rack, or you will have a very hard time carving the meat into individual chops for serving this hearty yet refined winter dish.

2 tablespoons blended oil (90 percent canola, 10 percent extra-virgin olive)
1¼-pound rack of venison, chined and cut in half crosswise
Kosher salt and cracked black pepper
20 Candied Cherries (page 276), with a little of the syrup
4 pieces Leek Confit (2 whole leeks, page 264), with some of their oil

6 to 8 ounces dried venison sausage or loukanika, thickly sliced on a diagonal
1 sprig sage
1 sprig thyme
1½ tablespoons cold, unsalted butter
⅓ cup sherry vinegar
⅓ cup water

Preheat the oven to 375°F. In an ovenproof skillet, warm the blended oil over medium-high heat. When the oil is very hot, season the 2 pieces of venison liberally with kosher salt and pepper and sear them in the pan. Turn occasionally, leaning the pieces up against the edge of the pan to make sure all sides—including the meaty, rounded ends—get seared. Discard the excess oil and return the venison to the pan bone-side down. Transfer the pan to the oven to finish cooking for 6 to 8 minutes, depending on size. Remove and allow to rest for 10 minutes.

In a small pan, warm the Candied Cherries in their syrup to room temperature, and reserve.

In a large skillet, warm a tablespoon of the Leek Confit oil over medium-high heat. Add the sausage slices and the Leek Confit and sauté for 1 minute. Add sage and thyme, and warm through for another minute. Deglaze the pan with the vinegar and water. Reduce liquid by half. Remove from heat, remove sage and thyme, and swirl in the cold butter until melted.

Mound the leek and sausage mixture on individual plates or a platter. Carve the racks into chops and place over the mixture, with the bones uppermost, and drizzle with the pan juices. Spoon a few cherries on the side and finish with a drizzle of cherry syrup and Leek Confit oil.

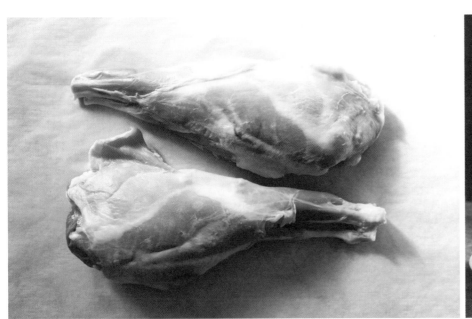

a lamb and a goat

W hen people talk about "coming of age" they're often thinking of their first sexual experiences. But my "coming of age" was closely tied to a lamb and a goat—technically, a kid.

It was the week before Easter and I was eleven years old. Easter is the most important holiday in the Greek Orthodox Church, with the Saturday night service preceding Easter Sunday being the holiest ceremony of all. We had been observing the forty days of Lent by not eating any animal products or anything that had had blood in it—no meat, no dairy, no eggs. We could eat shrimp and other shellfish but not "fin" fish. Mostly, we kids subsisted on a diet of peanut butter and honey sandwiches, vegetables, and a few Greek staples like *taramosalata*.

One afternoon, my father disappeared in our trusty Ford LTD station wagon. When he returned, he summoned me.

"Let's go to the barn and get the wheelbarrow," he instructed.

I followed along while he wheeled our blue, beat-up wheelbarrow from the garage-sized shed (which we called "the barn") back to our car. The rear window was already lowered, and now he reached inside to unlatch the tailgate. Inside were a couple of burlap sacks. Wriggling around on top of the sacks were two animals, lying on their sides.

"What are these?" I asked him, still not sure what to make of the situation.

"These are baby animals," he replied, without a hint of sarcasm.

There were a lamb and a goat, hogtied. First, we lifted the kid and put it in the wheelbarrow. It was thrashing around as much as it could, voicing its displeasure with all sorts of bleats and shrieks, the likes of which I'd never heard before. We wheeled the goat into the backyard, deposited it on the grass, and went back to get the lamb.

When both animals were in the backyard, my father said, "Go get a knife."

Thinking nothing of it, I raced inside to get a knife and presented it to my father. In one swift motion, my father cut the ties that bound the goat's legs. Up it sprang, and off it ran like a shot. He did the same with the lamb and, again, I was surprised by the speed at which the animal jumped up and scampered away.

Somehow, I hadn't yet made the connection between the animals in my yard and the meat that I had eaten all my life. All I knew was that Daddy had brought the farm home.

We called the rest of the family outside. The two animals raced around the yard with we kids chasing after them. My mother, concerned that we would catch some kind of disease, shouted to us repeatedly not to touch them. When she wasn't shouting at us, she was shouting at my father, expressing her displeasure with the situation. My father, meanwhile, could not have been more pleased.

We called up the cousins and invited them over to see the animals. Fifteen of our cousins lived nearby and were present at every family function we hosted. I was the oldest of the pack and the leader. The fifteen of us ran around the yard, trying to catch the lamb and the goat. Every time, we came up empty-handed. We threw balls to the animals, trying to teach them to play fetch, but they just ignored us and bounded away.

The aunts and uncles, along with my grandmother, watched the scene and laughed at the chaos. All the while, my mother continued to shout at us, "Don't touch the animals! Don't touch them!" as the lamb and the goat baahed and bleated and tried to keep as far away from us as possible.

It was starting to get late, so we all went inside for dinner—we weren't allowed to eat outside because my mother was afraid the animals would bite one of us. When we were all stuffed to the gills, the cousins went home and I went out to check on the animals. It was dark and I couldn't find them. I ran inside to get my father and he came with a flashlight. We searched all around the yard. My mother was shouting at us for letting the animals escape. Finally, we found them, huddled on their knees down in the dirt, hidden away between a couple of trees and the stacks of firewood that lined our back fence. I guess they were cold and had sought shelter.

Every day I raced home from school to play with and feed our animals, whom

I now considered my friends. I was bursting at the seams, dying to tell my school friends that we had two baby animals in our backyard, but I knew I'd get in trouble with my mother if I did. So instead of sharing this secret, I amused myself by trying (unsuccessfully) to lasso the animals, chasing after them, and generally driving them crazy—and all the while my mother continued to shout, "Don't touch them! Be careful! Don't touch them!" And that's pretty much how the week went.

Saturday night midnight mass was upon us, the pinnacle of our religious year. Following the service, which included a candlelit procession outside of the church and down the street, we returned to my grandmother's house for a big holiday dinner. By the time we left and I crawled into bed, it was four in the morning—same as every year.

Normally, on Easter Sunday my father would get up at 7:00 A.M. so he could prepare the barbecue. By 11:00, relatives would start showing up and begin snacking on cheese, olives, sausages, *spanakopita*, *tiropitas*—the usual *mezes* we would have around before the main meal was served.

But this year at 7:00, my father woke me up to help him. Though this was not routine, I still sensed nothing unusual about the day ahead. We went out into the yard and looked at the baby animals, something I had done multiple times every day since we'd got them. My father looked at me and announced, "Okay, now it's time to catch one."

I looked at my father quizzically. I thought he was joking, putting me on, testing me in some way. But when I saw the serious look on his face, I realized he wasn't joking. So off I went, chasing after the lamb and the kid, trying to catch one in my arms. It was almost comical how I ran, diving after them, often coming close to catching one but never actually succeeding. My pants were covered in grass stains and I shouted to my father:

"Mom's going to yell at me!"

"Just catch one," my father repeated, calmly.

Finally I caught the lamb by a leg and knocked him down. He was kicking and trying to run away, but I sat down on top of him.

As I sat on top of the lamb, watching it struggle to free itself, as if in slow motion my father came up behind me, reached down over my right shoulder with

a hunting knife, grabbed the lamb's head and ears, and, in one swift motion, slit the lamb's throat.

Blood shot out of the lamb like water from a high-pressure hose. The lamb started shaking and convulsing. I could feel an intense heat radiating out of its body, and I felt as though I was burning up. It all happened so quickly and yet, the way it seemed to me, I felt like it would never end.

I jumped off the lamb. I looked down at myself and saw that I was covered in blood. Now I was crying hysterically.

My father asked me, "Are you crying?"

This had always been a rhetorical question: in my family, men and boys didn't cry. So "Are you crying?" had always been more of a warning: I should pull myself together because crying would be unacceptable. Instinctively, I tried to stop the tears from flowing. I turned away and swiped at my eyes and running nose, attempting to get a grip.

But on this day, my father was really asking me this question. I tried to answer and tell him I wasn't crying. I didn't want my tears to disappoint him. But he beckoned me over and pulled me up onto his lap, something he rarely did. Gently he asked, "Why are you crying?"

I sobbed that he had just killed my friend, and that I had helped him do it. My father explained that he wanted to illustrate something very important to me: that every year we put a lamb on the spit and every year we ate lamb at Easter. And here was the lesson. He asked me, *"Where did you think that lamb came from?"* My response was one of childlike innocence. "I don't know," I told him, sniffling.

I was still on my father's lap. It was so unusual for him to hold me this way that I sensed I was about to be told something I would remember forever. Quietly and firmly, my father explained: "Michael, when Mommy cooks something for us to eat for dinner and it's something you think you might not like because it's a part of the animal you don't like the sound of, think before you say you're not going to eat it. Because when you reject that liver, tongue, or cheeks, you are essentially saying that this animal gave its life for nothing—this animal that someone else raised, cared for, and fed died for nothing because you don't want to eat it. It is okay to be sad that the lamb is dead. Hold on to that sadness, because the taking of a life is never something to joke about. When you think about that lamb and what it gave up for us so that we could eat, you understand that we killed a living thing, and we must always respect and honor that animal by using everything it has to offer."

I never forgot my father's words. When I first started cooking in restaurant kitchens, I wanted to use every part of the animals I was butchering. I wanted to honor those animals that had given their lives so I could feed the people who came to eat the food I created. I wanted to show them that I could create something beautiful and delicious from even the worst cuts of meat.

In this chapter, there are recipes that many people may want to skip over because they use unconventional parts. It is my sincerest hope that, rather than flipping ahead to the next chapter, you instead will consider making one of these dishes and honoring the animal that gave its life to sustain us.

Anthony Bourdain once told me that a true test of great chefs is not how well they can cook a prime or luxury cut of meat, but rather how they are able to use their talent to cook obscure or less desirable ones. This, of course, was after I had cooked a twelve-course offal dinner for him and David Kiley, who was writing a story for *BusinessWeek* on organ meat. The following recipes use both luxury and obscure cuts of lamb and goat to show how, in the right hands, all food is beautiful. Maybe you too will take Bourdain's challenge and give it a try.

ROASTED LEG OF LAMB

PSITO BOUTAKI ARNIOU

SERVES 6, OR MORE FAMILY-STYLE

Butterflying the lamb gives you options that you don't have with a bone. A good butcher will be happy to do this for you. (See my instructions on page 146.) Here, I've made a very flavorful stuffing from sun-dried tomatoes, which looks great when you carve the roast. Normally, I don't see the point of mincing herbs, but rosemary, with its woody sprigs, is hard to eat. If you're using it only as a flavoring agent, you can just pull the sprigs out at the end, but if you want to eat it—and lamb loves rosemary—it has to be *very* finely chopped.

FOR THE STUFFING

1½ cups large, plump sun-dried
   tomatoes, roughly chopped
¼ cup oil-cured black olives, pitted
1 teaspoon minced rosemary
Leaves only from 3 small sprigs thyme
1 teaspoon dry Greek oregano
1 tablespoon Dijon mustard
15 cloves Garlic Confit (page 264) or
   ⅓ cup Garlic Purée (page 264),
   if you have it
3 tablespoons extra-virgin olive oil
1½ tablespoons red wine vinegar
About 1 teaspoon cracked black pepper

FOR THE LAMB

3 to 3½ pound boneless leg of lamb,
   butterflied to flatten, some of the fat
   trimmed off
Kosher salt and cracked black pepper
Extra-virgin olive oil
1½ cup water
1 tablespoon Dijon mustard
1 tablespoon Garlic Purée or 2 to 3
   cloves Garlic Confit, if you have it
3 large sprigs rosemary
3 tablespoons blended oil (90 percent
   canola, 10 percent extra-virgin olive)

In a food processor, combine all of the ingredients for the stuffing and purée to a smooth, thick paste, about 45 to 60 seconds. Reserve about 2 tablespoons of the stuffing.

Lay the lamb out on a work surface with the fattier side down. Season generously with kosher salt and pepper and spread an even layer of stuffing over it, pressing the stuffing down into the crevices. Drizzle with a little olive oil and roll the lamb up in a spiral, seasoning the fatty side with salt and pepper as you roll. Tie in 3 or 4 places crosswise and 1 or 2 places lengthwise (twist the string around itself 3 times instead of just once before you pull it tight, so it won't loosen as soon as you let go). Ideally, allow the meat to sit on a rack, uncovered, in the refrigerator overnight, to dry the surface well and develop all the Greek flavors.

Bring the lamb to room temperature while you preheat the oven to 375°F. In a small roasting pan, whisk the reserved stuffing with the water, mustard, and Garlic Purée. Throw in the rosemary sprigs. Place a rack in the pan; the rack should not touch the liquid.

continued

Roasted Leg of Lamb continued from page 142

Again, season the lamb on all sides very generously with kosher salt and pepper. In a large, heavy skillet, warm the oil over medium-high heat. When the oil is very hot, sear the lamb well on all sides, using tongs and leaning the meat up against the sides of the pan to sear the thinner sides and cut ends. Transfer the lamb to the rack *seam-side up* and roast for about 1 hour, basting every 15 minutes with the pan liquid. (When the meat is medium-rare—140°F—a skewer inserted at the thickest point should feel warm when pressed against your lower lip.)

Rest the meat for about 15 minutes. Slice ¼-inch-thick pieces, drizzle with the pan sauce, and finish with a little extra-virgin olive oil.

❀ Optional: Peel and cut a few potatoes into rough wedges, toss with a little olive oil, season with salt and pepper, and throw in the roasting pan.

❀ To butterfly a piece of boneless lamb from the leg, lay the piece out flat, fatty-side down. Make 8 to 10 shallow cuts in the thicker parts, then open them out like a book and press flat. Your goal is a relatively flat surface, but don't worry if it's a little uneven—it will be concealed inside, with the stuffing.

FAMILY PACKS

Sometimes, a boneless leg of lamb is much larger than you want to serve. If so, make the most of it! Cut off a piece, freeze it, and use later for *souvlaki*, or in lieu of the venison in the stew on page 129. Alternatively, you can put it through a grinder and have meat for a ragout for Open Goat Moussaka, *Papoutsakia*, *Seftalia*, or the Lamb Burger. Buying family packs for the home cook is always a great way to save money. Be sure you double-wrap all items to be frozen and label them with weights and dates.

SUN-DRIED-TOMATO-CRUSTED LOIN OF LAMB
WITH WILTED ARUGULA & TSATZIKI
ARNI ME KROUSTA APO LIASTES TOMATES, HORTA KAI TZATZIKI

SERVES 6 AS A PLATED ENTRÉE

This dish screams "Greek" to me: lamb, yogurt, and greens. What else do you really need? Try to find the large, bright red sun-dried tomatoes that are soft and pliable, like a good dried peach, not the dark purple, papery variety. Mince the rosemary here, because it's so tough that even in the food processor, it will not reach the very small size necessary.

FOR THE CRUST
¾ cup large, plump sun-dried tomatoes, roughly chopped
2 tablespoons oil-cured black olives, pitted
½ teaspoon minced rosemary
1 small sprig thyme, leaves only
½ teaspoon dry Greek oregano
1½ teaspoons Dijon mustard
7 cloves Garlic Confit (page 264) or 2 tablespoons Garlic Purée (page 264), if you have it

1½ tablespoons extra-virgin olive oil
2 teaspoons red wine vinegar
About ½ teaspoon cracked black pepper

FOR THE LAMB
3 lamb loins, at room temperature
Kosher salt and cracked black pepper
2 tablespoons extra-virgin olive oil, plus more for drizzling
2 shallots, finely chopped
6 cups (about 6 ounces) baby arugula leaves
⅓ to ½ cup *Tsatziki* (page 189)

For the crust, in a food processor, combine all the ingredients and purée to a very smooth, thick paste, about 45 to 60 seconds. Reserve.

For the lamb, preheat the oven to 400°F. Season the lamb loins liberally on all sides with kosher salt and pepper. Warm an ovenproof pan over medium-high heat with the olive oil and sear the loins well on all sides. Discard the oil and transfer the pan to the oven; roast 5 to 6 minutes per side. (A skewer inserted at the thickest point of the meat should feel warm when pressed against your lower lip.) Remove the loins from the oven and smear the sun-dried tomato crust over the top. Allow to rest for about 10 minutes before serving.

Meanwhile, warm a heavy skillet over medium-high heat and add the remaining olive oil. Add the shallots and sauté for about 1½ minutes. Add the arugula and wilt briefly, about 30 seconds. Divide the arugula among 6 plates and top with a spoonful of *Tsatziki*.

Carefully slice the lamb into ½-inch pieces and place on top of the arugula and the *Tsatziki* sauce. Finish with a drizzle of extra-virgin olive oil.

GRILLED LAMB HEART WITH CRISPY & SHAVED FENNEL SALAD

KARDIA ARNIOU STIN SCHARA KAI MARATHOSALATA

SERVES 4 TO 6 AS AN APPETIZER, OR MORE FAMILY-STYLE,
AS PART OF A LARGER SPREAD

Don't be afraid of this dish! The lamb gave its life to make a meal for someone, and the least we can do in return is use every part of it. Lamb hearts are very lean and beefy-tasting—they look like filet mignon. Ideally, ask your butcher to trim and butterfly them for you; an Italian butcher would know how to do this, and he'll probably be thrilled if you ask. Keep the vegetables for the salad very cold. Serve this to a bunch of foodie friends, and they'll think you're a rock star!

4 large lamb hearts
1 large bulb fennel (very cold),
  shaved crosswise on a mandoline
  or sliced paper-thin
½ small red onion (very cold), shaved
  on a mandoline or sliced paper-thin
2 tablespoons finely snipped chives
8 leaves fresh mint, slivered

2 tablespoons roughly chopped dill
2 tablespoons plus ¼ cup fresh
  lemon juice
¼ cup extra-virgin olive oil, plus more
  for brushing
Kosher salt and cracked black pepper
¼ cup Greek yogurt, drained

If your butcher has not already done so, first butterfly and trim the lamb hearts: trim off the very top of each heart at the wider end, crosswise, to expose the ventricles. Trim off any white fat, and go inside each of the ventricles to trim any veins, leaving just the deep red muscle. Turn the cut sides down and trim downward to remove any fat from the outside (don't be obsessive about this). Cut through the ventricles close to the dividing piece, and open out like a book to butterfly. From each heart, you should have 1 small piece (from the smaller ventricle) and 2 bigger pieces (from the larger ventricle).

In a large bowl, combine the fennel, red onion, chives, mint, and dill. Season generously with kosher salt and pepper, toss well with clean hands, and reserve.

Whisk together the yogurt and 2 tablespoons lemon juice; season to taste.

Preheat a charcoal or gas grill, or ridged cast-iron grill pan, until hot. Paint both sides of the pieces of lamb heart with olive oil and season with salt and pepper. Grill the lamb hearts for about 1 minute on each side, until only just firm and char-marked. Let rest for 2 to 3 minutes.

Slice the hearts about ¼ inch thick on the diagonal; combine with the fennel salad, dress with the ¼ cup lemon juice and the ¼ cup olive oil. Toss well, season to taste. Put a spoonful of the yogurt mixture on each plate. Top with the salad.

BRAISED LAMB TONGUE WITH WHITE BEANS & MUSHROOMS
SIGOVRASMENI GLOSSA ARNIOU ME LEFKA KOUKIA KAI MANITARIA

SERVES 4 TO 6 AS A PLATED ENTRÉE WITH RICE, POTATOES, OR PASTA,
OR MORE FAMILY-STYLE, AS PART OF A LARGER SPREAD

If you are a good customer, the butcher may *give* you cuts like these because there is so little demand. When preparing this dish, try to envision what it was like to live in a time when people were impoverished and never allowed any part of an animal to go to waste. This food is a celebration of that animal, and we are lucky to have it. Peeling the lamb's tongues is advisable but not absolutely necessary.

10 lambs' tongues

Kosher salt and cracked black pepper

3 tablespoons blended oil (90 percent canola, 10 percent extra-virgin olive)

4 cloves garlic, smashed and chopped

½ small Spanish or sweet onion, finely chopped

1 small carrot, finely chopped

1 stalk celery, finely chopped

3 tablespoons tomato paste

1 cup red wine

5 large sprigs thyme

1 large sprig rosemary

2 fresh bay leaves or 4 dried leaves

3 quarts water

½ pound white beans, soaked overnight

4 ounces button mushrooms, cleaned and quartered

Extra-virgin olive oil

Small handful torn fresh herbs, such as dill, parsley, and/or chives

Wash the lambs' tongues in cold water, pat dry with paper towels, and season liberally with kosher salt and pepper. In a large, heavy pot or Dutch oven, warm the oil over medium-high heat. When the oil is hot, add the tongues and brown very well all over. Transfer the tongues to a plate and pour off most of the cooking oil. Add the garlic, onion, carrot, and celery and wilt for 3 to 5 minutes. Add the tomato paste and stir for 1 minute. Deglaze the pan with the red wine and allow it to reduce away completely.

Return the tongues to the pot and add the thyme, rosemary, bay leaves, water, 1 tablespoon kosher salt, and a generous grinding of pepper. Bring to a boil, then reduce the heat, partially cover, and simmer gently for 30 minutes. Drain the beans and add them to the pot. Continue simmering for 30 minutes more, then add the mushrooms.

Continue simmering for about 30 minutes more or until the beans and tongues are tender, for a total of about 1½ hours. Remove from the heat.

Transfer the tongues to a cutting board. With a small, sharp knife, trim any fat and gristle from the base. Optional: Place smooth-side up and slit the thin outer skin from the tip to the base. Use the knife to loosen the skin at the slit. Then, with your fingers, work the skin free and peel it off. Return the peeled tongues to the braising liquid to warm through. Drizzle with a little olive oil and scatter with the fresh herbs.

GRILLED LAMB CHOPS
PAIDAKIA STIN SCHARA

◆————————————————————————◆

MAKES 12 TO 18 CHOPS

I like to serve these chops as an appetizer, straight off the grill, while everyone is hanging out and chatting. And make sure you keep them coming! Or, serve as an entrée, with Greek Salad (page 213) or Spinach Rice (page 167) on the side.

Souvlaki marinade (page 74)
12 to 18 lamb rib chops,
   French-trimmed, patted dry with
   paper towels
Kosher salt and cracked black pepper

Roasted Lemon Purée
   (recipe follows, optional)
2 lemons
Extra-virgin olive oil
1 tablespoon dry Greek oregano

Marinate the chops in the *Souvlaki* Marinade, refrigerated, for 24 hours.

Preheat a charcoal or gas grill, or ridged cast-iron grill pan, until hot. Lift the chops from the marinade, letting all of it drain away. Season liberally with kosher salt and pepper. Grill the chops until firm and char-marked, about 1½ minutes on each side, depending on their thickness and how you like the meat done. Rest the meat for a minute or two. Paint the chops with Roasted Lemon Purée (optional) and arrange on serving platter. Squeeze fresh lemons over the top, drizzle with extra-virgin olive oil, and finish with a sprinkle of oregano.

This creamy, bright yellow sauce is all lemon and no eggs. Roasting the lemons caramelizes their natural juices and imparts both sweet and sour flavors. The purée works well with any number of dishes, but particularly with lamb chops. On the plate, it mixes with the lamb's natural juices to create a "plate sauce" that blends all of the flavors. The purée will keep in the refrigerator for up to 2 weeks.

4 scrubbed lemons, preferably Meyer or Sorrento (always scrub supermarket lemons, to remove the wax)

About ⅓ cup kosher salt

2 tablespoons fresh lemon juice or orange juice

1 tablespoon Dijon mustard

Garlic Purée (page 264, optional) or 2 crushed and pressed garlic cloves

1 cup extra-virgin olive oil

Pinch superfine sugar, or as needed

Cracked black pepper

Preheat the oven to 325°F. Place each lemon on a large square of aluminum foil. Roll the lemon in the foil lengthwise, then fold under the sides to meet in the center. Make 4 mounds of salt on a baking sheet, and place a wrapped lemon on top of each mound with the folded sides downward (this keeps the lemon flesh from burning).

Roast until the lemon packages feel very soft and squishy, about 1½ to 2 hours. Unwrap and let cool slightly, then quarter the lemons lengthwise. Scoop all the roasted flesh into a sieve and work it through to remove the seeds, saving the juices. Lay the strips of peel on a surface, pith-side up, and halve again lengthwise so they will lie flat. Scrape and shave off as much white pith as possible, keeping the knife parallel to the surface (place on a kitchen towel to stop the peels from sliding around as you trim them). Coarsely chop the resulting zest.

In a food processor, combine the chopped zest, strained flesh, and any juices with the fresh lemon juice, mustard, and Garlic Purée. Process to a fairly smooth purée, scraping down the sides. Add the olive oil through the feed tube and keep processing until the purée is completely smooth. Taste for sweetness and seasoning, and add a pinch of sugar, and some salt and pepper.

☀ Fold the purée into a homemade mayonnaise or aioli.

☀ Make a quick pan sauce after sautéing any kind of protein. Mix some Roasted Lemon Purée with a little chicken stock, then pour into the very hot pan after your chop or chicken breast is finished cooking. Boil to reduce slightly, then finish with a tablespoon of Garlic Purée or cold butter.

KEFI LAMB GYRO

GYROS ARNIOU

SERVES 6

Very few people make their own gyro—it's like making your own prosciutto or sausage. Homemade gyro makes a statement about how much you care about your food, and we are very proud of the gyro we make at Kefi. The gyro itself is actually a terrine that you might like to serve cold if you are making a charcuterie plate.

1 recipe Lamb Gyro (recipe follows)

FOR THE SPICED OIL
2 teaspoons fennel seeds
2 teaspoons mustard seeds
2 teaspoons cumin seeds
10 whole black peppercorns
⅓ cup extra-virgin olive oil

¼ recipe Greek Salad (page 213),
   vinaigrette on the side

⅔ cup *Tsatziki* (page 189)
6 rounds pita bread
Extra-virgin olive oil
Kosher salt and black pepper

First make the Lamb Gyro as directed on the page opposite.

Then make the spiced oil: In a toaster oven or 350°F oven, toast the seeds and the peppercorns in a single layer just until they release their aroma, about 1 to 3 minutes. Cool and grind in a spice grinder. Combine with the oil.

In a bowl, combine all ingredients for Greek Salad and reserve. (Do not dress!)

With a hot, sharp knife, slice the gyro about ⅜ inch thick. In a very large skillet, warm the spiced oil over medium-high heat. When the oil is very hot, add the gyro slices and sauté for about 2 minutes, shaking the pan around to thoroughly coat the slices with the spiced oil.

Paint the pita with extra-virgin olive oil, season with kosher salt and pepper, and grill until firm and char-marked on all sides. Toss the Greek Salad with the vinaigrette. Smear some *Tsatziki* in the center of each pita round. Divide the gyro meat among the pitas, on top of the *Tsatziki*. Add some Greek Salad. Pull the sides of the pita up to meet in the center, like a taco. Serve like a taco, or wrap and secure with a wide strip of parchment. Messy and great!

Be sure the meat is finely ground, otherwise you will not get the proper dense result. If coarsely ground meat is all that's available in the cold case, ask your butcher to put the meat through the grinder again.

2 ¼-inch-thick slices Spanish or sweet onion

Extra-virgin olive oil

Kosher salt and coarsely cracked black pepper

1 pound well-marbled, finely ground lamb (from the shoulder)

8 ounces finely ground pork

1 teaspoon Dijon mustard

1 tablespoon Garlic Purée (page 264)

1 teaspoon ground coriander

1 teaspoon espelette pepper or best-quality chile powder

2 tablespoons minced fresh herbs, such as dill, parsley, and/or chives

1 whole scallion, minced

2 large eggs, beaten

Brush the onion slices with a little olive oil and season with kosher salt and pepper. On a hot griddle pan or in a cast-iron skillet, grill the onion until tender. Separate into rings and chop very fine.

Lightly brush a 7½ x 11-inch baking dish with olive oil and preheat the oven to 375°F.

In a large mixing bowl, combine the grilled onion, lamb, pork, mustard, Garlic Purée, coriander, espelette, fresh herbs, scallion, and eggs. Season liberally with kosher salt and pepper and thoroughly combine the mixture with clean hands. Transfer to the baking dish and spread out evenly to the edges, smoothing the top flat. Place the dish inside a larger roasting pan and add boiling water to about halfway up the sides of the baking dish.

Bake for 45 minutes, or until the gyro shrinks away from the sides and is quite hot in the middle when pierced with a metal skewer (around 150°F). Remove the pan from the water bath and cool to room temperature. Cover and refrigerate for at least 3 hours or, ideally, 24 hours, to develop the flavors.

Place a large, flat platter upside down over the baking dish. Turn both over, and carefully remove the gyro.

❁ Scatter a little fennel pollen on the dressed salad just before serving.

❁ Serve with homemade French Fries on the side (page 154).

LAMB BURGER

BIFTEKI ARNIOU

This dish came about when we were looking for a Greek "hamburger" with the flavors of Cypriot cuisine. The recipe evolved from the more traditional Little Sausages (*Seftalia*, page 186). I highly recommend using a ring mold for the hamburgers, so that you can maintain consistency in their size, which aids in the cooking process. If you don't have a ring mold and have an extra plastic pint or quart container, like those delis use, you can make one with a pair of kitchen shears. Simply poke a hole about 2 inches from the top and cut around the container to form a ring. Just remember to work with the wider side of the makeshift ring mold down on a clean work surface, to allow for easy removal of the patty.

2 (¼-inch-thick) slices Spanish
   or sweet onion
Blended oil (90 percent canola,
   10 percent extra-virgin olive),
   as needed
Kosher salt and cracked black pepper
7 ounces ground lamb
3 ounces ground pork
1 tablespoon Dijon mustard
½ teaspoon ground coriander
1 tablespoon finely chopped parsley
1 tablespoon finely chopped dill

1 scallion, green part only, finely chopped
1 tablespoon Garlic Purée (page 264,
   optional)
½ teaspoon ground cumin
½ teaspoon ground fennel
About 2 ounces pork caul fat
2 kaiser rolls or sesame buns, or the roll
   or bread of your choice, brushed with
   olive oil and toasted
Htipiti (page 195) or lemon wedges and
   extra-virgin olive oil
French Fries (recipe follows, optional)

Brush the onion slices with a little oil and season with kosher salt and pepper. On a hot grill pan or in a cast-iron skillet, grill until tender. Separate the onion into rings and chop fine.

In a bowl, combine the chopped grilled onion, lamb, pork, mustard, coriander, parsley, dill, scallion, and Garlic Purée. Season liberally with kosher salt and pepper. With clean hands, combine the mixture evenly and divide in half.

Place a 4- to 5-inch ring mold on a clean work surface (if one side is wider, place the wider side down). Lay a piece of caul fat over the top with a few inches overhanging all around. Place half the lamb mixture in the center and press down to form a thick, flattened disk. Wrap the overhanging caul fat up and over the top, overlapping a bit but trimming off extra bits and pieces. Smooth the caul fat so that it is flat to the surface. Repeat to make the second burger, and place them on a piece of parchment. Cover with another piece of parchment and refrigerate for a couple of hours if not using immediately.

continued

Lamb Burger continued from page 152

Preheat a charcoal or gas grill, ridged cast-iron grill pan, or cast-iron skillet, until hot. Brush the burgers lightly with olive oil and season with kosher salt and pepper. Place the side with the caul fat down first, grill, and turn over until firm and char-marked on both sides, to your desired doneness. Transfer to the bun of your choice and top with a spoonful of *Htipiti* (or drizzle with some lemon juice and extra-virgin olive oil). Serve with French Fries (optional).

✺ When you grill the onion for the burger mixture in the first step, grill two extra slices of onion. Leave whole and use to top the finished burgers.

✺ Instead of using the ground versions of coriander, cumin, and fennel, you can toast and grind your own. The flavor will be far more complex. In a small, dry skillet, toast a pinch each of coriander, cumin, and fennel seeds. Cool and grind to a powder in a spice grinder.

FRENCH FRIES

SERVES 6–8

When my mom was in a rush—juggling kids, shopping, cleaning the house—her standby quick meal was scrambled eggs and French Fries. And she never used fast-food fries.

3 Idaho potatoes, peeled, cut into
  French-fry-sized batons
Canola, peanut, or safflower oil,
  for deep-frying

Kosher salt, sea salt, and cracked
  black pepper

Place the potato batons in a large bowl of cold water, in the sink. Rinse very thoroughly under slow-running cold water, until all the starch is removed, about 20 minutes or until the water runs clear. Dry the potatoes thoroughly between kitchen towels. Prefry in 250°F oil until tender but with no color. Drain well and hold in the refrigerator, uncovered, for up to 4 hours.

Just before serving, deep-fry the potatoes again, this time at a higher temperature of 375°F, until golden brown. Drain on absorbent paper and season with sea salt and pepper.

✺ For Pickled French Fries: Make the brine in the recipe for *Souvlaki* (page 74). After the first, low-temperature frying of the potatoes, immerse the potatoes in the brine and refrigerate overnight. Dry thoroughly and fry at the higher temperature.

POACHED GOAT AVGOLEMONO

KATSIKI AVGOLEMONO

SERVES 4 TO 6 FAMILY-STYLE, OR MORE AS PART OF A LARGER SPREAD

After you make this recipe, there will be leftover braising liquid, essentially a light goat stock—a wonderful by-product. I suggest you cool and freeze it. It will greatly enrich almost any other braise in this book. I like to serve this over orzo.

2 tablespoons blended oil (90 percent canola, 10 percent extra-virgin olive)

5 cloves garlic, roughly chopped

½ Spanish or sweet onion, finely chopped

½ bulb fennel, finely chopped

2 stalks celery, finely chopped

1 cup white wine

1 goat leg, on the bone, cut crosswise into 4 pieces (plus, if you like, the neck)

4 quarts water

4 fresh bay leaves or 8 dried leaves

1 large sprig sage

1 small bunch dill

1 teaspoon cumin seeds

1 teaspoon fennel seeds

2 star anise pods

5 cardamom pods

Kosher salt and cracked black pepper

3 large eggs, at room temperature, separated

4 tablespoons lemon juice

⅓ cup small, picked sprigs dill

Kosher salt and cracked black pepper

Warm a large, heavy pot or Dutch oven over medium heat and add the blended oil. Add all the vegetables and sweat until tender, without coloring at all. Deglaze the pan with the white wine and let it reduce completely away. Add the goat and the water, then add the herbs and spices. (If you have a bag or sachet for bouquet garni, wrap up the herbs and spices so they'll be easy to remove later.) Season with 2 tablespoons of kosher salt and a generous grinding of pepper. Bring to a boil, reduce the heat, and partially cover the pot. Skim off the scum once or twice at the beginning. Keep at a simmer until the meat is almost falling off the bones, about 2 to 2½ hours.

Transfer the goat pieces and any vegetables that remain (most will have melted away) to a platter. Pour a few tablespoons of liquid over the goat and keep warm. Strain the braising liquid to get half a cup. (Reserve the leftover liquid for another braising project.)

Make the *Avgolemono:* Get everything together so you can work quickly. Add the egg yolks to the half cup of braising liquid and quickly whisk to incorporate. Place the egg whites in a food processor and turn it on. When the whites begin to froth, after about 20 seconds, add the lemon juice, keeping the motor running all the time. When the whites are very frothy and thick, another 25 to 35 seconds, add the dill and process for 10 to 15 seconds more, while you season liberally with kosher salt and pepper. Pour in the egg yolk mixture and immediately turn the machine off. Spoon the *Avgolemono* over the goat, drizzle with extra-virgin olive oil, and serve at once, or the foam will quickly start to deflate.

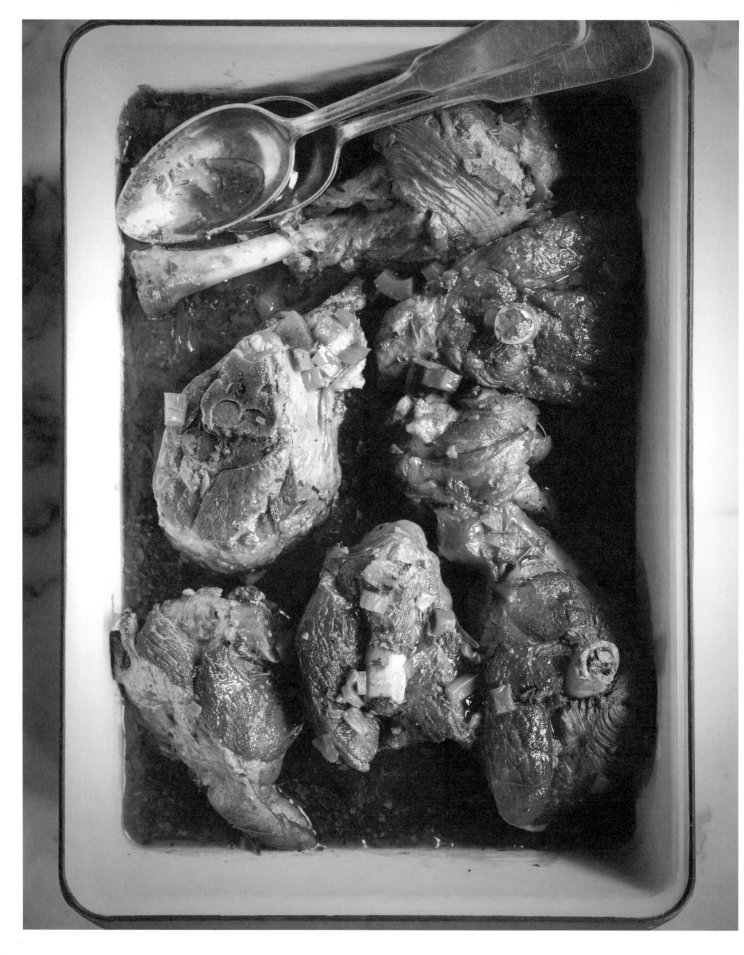

BRAISED GOAT

SIGOVRASMENO KATSIKI

SERVES 4 TO 6 FAMILY-STYLE, OR MORE OVER POTATOES, RICE, OR ORZO

I think that goat is going to become wildly popular over the next few years. It is very lean meat with a subtle game flavor and a lot of versatility. However, it tends to take longer to cook than lamb and is less forgiving of technical errors. Be patient and precise; it will be worth the wait and effort. If you prefer, you can substitute veal, on the bone, for the goat.

1 goat leg, on the bone, cut crosswise into 4 pieces (plus, if you like, the neck)

Kosher salt and cracked black pepper

3 tablespoons blended oil (90 percent canola, 10 percent extra-virgin olive)

5 cloves garlic, roughly chopped

½ Spanish or sweet onion, roughly chopped

1 carrot, roughly chopped

2 stalks celery, roughly chopped

3 tablespoons tomato paste

1 cup red wine

2 tablespoons red wine vinegar

2 teaspoons dry Greek oregano

2 tablespoons Dijon mustard

4 quarts water

5 large sprigs thyme

2 sprigs rosemary

1 tablespoon Garlic Purée (page 264)

1 tablespoon chopped dill

1 tablespoon chopped fresh mint leaves

Extra-virgin olive oil

Season the goat pieces liberally with kosher salt and pepper. Warm a large, heavy pot or Dutch oven over medium-high heat and add the blended oil. When the oil is very hot, add the goat pieces and sear until deep golden brown on all sides. Transfer the meat to a platter and pour off most of the oil.

Add the vegetables to the pot and stir until soft, about 3 to 5 minutes. Add the tomato paste and stir for 1 minute. Deglaze the pot with the red wine and vinegar, allowing the liquid to cook away almost completely. Add the oregano, mustard, water, thyme, and rosemary. Return the goat pieces to the pan and season with 1½ tablespoons kosher salt and a generous grinding of pepper. Bring to a boil, reduce the heat, and partially cover the pan.

Simmer until the meat is tender and almost falling off the bone, up to 2½ hours. At the beginning, occasionally skim off any scum that arises. When done, transfer the goat and any vegetables that haven't melted away to a platter and keep warm. Over high heat, reduce the pan juices until thickened and swirl in the Garlic Purée and fresh herbs. Remove the remains of the thyme and rosemary. Drizzle over the goat. Finish with a drizzle extra-virgin olive oil.

☀ If you have any leftover braised goat, make my Open Goat Moussaka (next page).

OPEN GOAT MOUSSAKA

ANIKTOS MOUSSAKAS KATSIKIOU

The shredded, braised goat meat called for in this dish should be prepared exactly as in Braised Goat (previous page). If you have a free Saturday afternoon, this is an impressive dish that combines the wonderful, earthy flavors of moussaka with a refined presentation. Or, make the dish whenever you have some leftover braised goat (or braised lamb). The fresh pasta used in this recipe is about halfway between the thickness of the rustic *Hilopites* and the *Manti*.

2 Idaho potatoes, peeled and sliced paper-thin on a mandoline into rounds

2 Japanese eggplants, sliced paper-thin on a mandoline

Kosher salt and cracked black pepper

Large pinch ground cinnamon

2 tablespoons blended oil (90 percent canola, 10 percent extra-virgin olive)

About 2 cups Béchamel Sauce Without Eggs (page 276)

12 to 16 ounces shredded braised goat, with about 1 cup of the braising liquid

1½ tablespoons fresh lemon juice

1½ tablespoons finely chopped dill

1½ tablespoons finely chopped parsley

¼ cup Garlic Purée (page 264)

About ¼ *Hilopites* Pasta recipe (page 76), rolled out to no. 6 thickness

1 head frisée, torn into sprigs

Extra-virgin olive oil

Sea salt

Prepare an ice water bath. In salted boiling water, blanch the sliced potato disks for about 1 minute. Drain the slices and immediately shock in the ice water bath. Lay out in a single layer on a lightly oiled piece of parchment. Season the eggplant slices with kosher salt and pepper, and dust with a little cinnamon. In a large, medium-hot skillet, sauté the eggplant in the blended oil until pliable and slightly golden. Drain on absorbent paper.

Put a saucepan of well-salted water on to boil, for the pasta disks. Warm four plates in a low oven, warm the béchamel, and get all the necessary ingredients together.

In a saucepan, combine the shredded goat and braising liquid, lemon juice, dill, parsley, and Garlic Purée. Over medium-high heat, stir the mixture until hot.

With a 3-inch cutter, cut out 12 disks from the *Hilopites* Pasta sheet. Cook the pasta disks until pliable. Reserve on a lightly oiled sheet of parchment.

Place a spoonful of the warm béchamel on each plate and spread into a 3-inch circle. Top with 1 disk of pasta, 2 slices of eggplant, 2 to 3 slices of potato, and a spoonful of the goat meat (use a slotted spoon, to drain the liquid), keeping everything in a circle. Top with another spoonful of béchamel, another pasta disk, eggplant slices, potato slices, and a spoonful of goat, as before. Make a third layer, then finish with a final spoonful of béchamel. Repeat for the other three plates. Drizzle the remaining goat pan juices around the moussaka. Toss the frisée with lemon, oil, salt, and pepper, and place around the edges of each plate. Drizzle everything with a little olive oil and season with a little more sea salt and cracked black pepper.

psilakis birthday dinners

Don't get me wrong, I loved birthday gifts just as much as the next kid. But if you asked any of my siblings, I think they'd all agree that, for us, birthdays weren't about the gifts from our parents. Birthdays were *really* about the family dinners that marked the special day of our birth. The best gift was the honor of getting to choose the meal the whole family would have for dinner on that one day each year. Because dinner was the only time each day that was guaranteed to bring us all together, these birthday dinners held a special meaning, particularly to us kids. Choosing that one special meal, whatever *we* wanted, was sacrosanct.

In our family, food was far more than calories and nutrients. Food was the reason my parents left behind their homes, the country and friends they loved, and the language they knew for a new and unknown country where getting enough to eat would not represent the difference between life and death. The promise of a better life in America meant to my parents, literally, not starving. It's difficult to relate to those circumstances today given the bounty most of us know in America. This meant to my parents that every meal they put on the table had a spiritual dimension. We Psilakis children knew almost from birth that in our home food represented love.

For our birthday dinner, it became comical how each of the four of us would choose the same dish, year after year, to the point where each of those dishes became associated with the child who chose it. For me, until I became a teenager and my tastes shifted somewhat (and rebellion set in), that dish was always *giouvarlakia*, meatball soup.

My mother would take ground beef, mix it with uncooked rice, and form it into golf-ball-sized meatballs. She'd boil the meatballs in a pot of water seasoned with bay leaf and onions, until the rice was cooked. As the rice and meat cooked, they suffused the water with starch from the former and the juices from the latter. The meatballs bounced around in the boiling water, agitating like billiard balls knocking against one another. After about an hour and a half, so much flavor had been released from the meatballs that those simple ingredients transformed mere water into my favorite soup.

But it was the *avgolemono* sauce that transformed the soup into my favorite meal. My mother would take egg whites, to which she added lemon juice and dill, and whip them into stiff peaks. She'd temper the yolks with some of the soup from the pot and fold them into the peaked egg whites. The whites and yolks together made *avgolemono*, which she poured into the boiling soup. The addition of the *avgolemono* to the boiling soup created so much foam and froth that it was like adding bubble bath to a Jacuzzi.

When that pot of soup, made just for me with so much joy and love, was presented to the table, I felt like the guest of honor at a royal banquet. I felt celebrated and cherished, as my mother intended each of us to feel on our special day.

Of course, the birthday cake didn't hurt either. It's not really a Greek tradition to have dessert after meals. We viewed it as an American custom. When I was a kid, on a normal evening after the women had finished clearing the table and cleaning up after dinner, my mother and sisters would join us and we finished the meal with fruit. It was only on weekends when the cousins would come over—or at parties or on special occasions—that we would have pastries. But on our birthdays, we had a real American birthday cake with candles.

The meals we ate for our birthdays marked our special occasions—the *food* marked the occasion, not the other way around. That food, whether it was *giouvarlakia* for me or *gemista* (stuffed vegetables) for Maria, meant so much more

to my parents. It is difficult, even for me, to comprehend that a single bite of *giouvarlakia* could represent so much: culture, my parents' history and hardship, a new country, a new life, and now a family. But to my parents, all of these things were ingredients in every bite. The special food, made with love, was a vehicle to express the joy of that occasion—celebrating the birth of a child—and that was what made us feel special.

Now, any time I eat *giouvarlakia*, it transports me to my parents' table and my childhood birthdays. And when I cook *giouvesti* (lamb with orzo), my brother Peter's chosen birthday dish, at Kefi, I always think of him. In my home today, at my own table, we continue to celebrate this tradition. The same way my mother made our favorites with so much love, I too include that as an ingredient for my son.

This chapter is made up of the recipes for each of our favorite dishes from my family's childhood birthday dinners. Just as *garides me kritiko pilafi* (shrimp with Cretan pilaf) will always evoke thoughts of my sister Anna for me, I hope that you too can take these recipes and create memories of your own.

LAMB SHANKS WITH ORZO
PODARAKIA ARNIOU ME KRITHARAKI

SERVES 6 FAMILY-STYLE WITH POTATOES OR ORZO,
OR MORE AS PART OF A LARGER SPREAD

If you have some stock, this braise will have a richer, more intense flavor, but I make it here the way my mother would approach it. Note that whenever you braise something on the bone, the resulting liquid benefits from the marrow and you ultimately end up with a stock-flavored sauce. Plus, this recipe contains lots of herbs and flavorings, so the braise will still have great body and depth of flavor, even if you use only water.

6 lamb shanks, about 1 pound each
Kosher salt and cracked black pepper
2 tablespoons blended oil (90 percent canola, 10 percent extra-virgin olive)
1½ to 2 quarts water or meat stock, as needed
1 Spanish or sweet onion, roughly chopped
2 carrots, roughly chopped
2 stalks celery, roughly chopped

3 tablespoons tomato paste
¼ cup red wine
2 fresh bay leaves or 4 dried leaves
5 large sprigs fresh thyme
2 large sprigs fresh rosemary
1 tablespoon Garlic Purée (page 264) or cold, unsalted butter
Small handful torn fresh herbs, such as dill, mint, and/or parsley
Extra-virgin olive oil

Season the lamb shanks liberally with kosher salt and pepper. In a very large skillet, warm the blended oil over medium-high heat. Sear the lamb shanks on all sides until golden brown. Do this in batches if necessary to avoid overcrowding the pan. Transfer the shanks to a large Dutch oven. Pour off most of the oil from the skillet.

Preheat the oven to 325°F. Heat some water (or stock) for the braise. In the same skillet, add all the vegetables and soften for 3 to 5 minutes. Add the tomato paste and stir for 1 minute. Deglaze the pan with the red wine and let it reduce away.

Scatter the vegetable mixture over the lamb in the Dutch oven. Add enough of the hot water or stock to just cover the lamb, and add all the herbs, 1 tablespoon salt, and a generous grinding of pepper. Cover the pan and braise until the meat is falling off the bones, about 1½ to 2½ hours, depending on the size of the shanks.

Transfer the lamb and any remaining vegetables to a platter. Cover and keep warm in the turned-off oven. On the top of the stove, reduce the braising liquid over high heat until it starts to thicken (if you like it thicker, reduce further). Taste for seasoning and add the Garlic Purée or butter. Spoon the juices over the lamb, scatter with the fresh herbs, and finish with a drizzle of extra-virgin olive oil.

❋ If you have any leftover lamb, you can make a fantastic lamb ragout to toss with the *Hilopites* Pasta from page 76. Pull the meat off the bone and shred, then warm it in a skillet with some of the leftover braising liquid. Reduce the liquid to concentrate the flavors and create a textural sauce to coat the pasta. If you have any Garlic Purée, throw a spoonful into the pan, along with a few tiny picked sprigs of thyme and a pinch of minced rosemary. Cook the *Hilopites* Pasta in the usual way, drain well, and toss with the lamb mixture.

❋ Instead of serving orzo on the side, throw some cooked orzo into the liquid toward the end of the reducing time. The starch from the orzo will thicken the juices.

SPINACH RICE
SPANAKORIZO

SERVES 4 TO 6 FAMILY-STYLE AS A SIDE DISH, OR MORE AS PART OF A LARGER SPREAD

My mom made *spanakorizo*, or spinach rice, all the time, always with water. But if you have chicken stock, the flavor will be richer. If you use vegetable stock, you'll still have a vegan dish. This is another example of the type of food we would eat during Lent.

1 cup uncooked long-grain rice, well rinsed
1 tablespoon extra-virgin olive oil
2 shallots, finely chopped
6 whole scallions, thickly sliced

5 cups baby spinach leaves
Kosher salt and cracked black pepper
1 tablespoon fresh lemon juice
3 tablespoons cold, unsalted butter

In a large pot, cook the rice according to the package instructions (or the way you like to cook rice).

While the rice is cooking: in a large skillet, warm the olive oil over medium-high heat. Wilt the shallots and scallions for 2 to 3 minutes without browning. Add the spinach, turning it over with tongs to help it wilt evenly. Stir in 1 tablespoon of kosher salt, a generous grinding of pepper, and the lemon juice.

When the rice is done, add it to the spinach mixture. Stir in the butter, and season with salt and pepper.

❋ *Spanakorizo* is typically a side dish, but you can easily add shrimp, scallops, or mussels to make it into a main course. A scatter of crumbled feta or *manouri* cheese would add another layer of flavor.

PAN-ROASTED CHICKEN WITH LEMON POTATOES

KOTOPOULO ME PATATES LEMONATES

This dish can replace your usual roast chicken. Pan-roasting the pieces allows you to achieve much crisper skin than a straight oven roast. It will also drastically cut down on the cooking time. Partially boning the chicken helps to accomplish both of these goals. It is something you can ask your butcher to do, if he or she likes you. Don't skip the brining process—when we take away the bones, we need to replace their missing flavor with the brine. And for the best flavor and the crispiest skin, I suggest you marinate the chicken too, preferably overnight, but certainly for at least 4 hours. If you take these steps, it will be well worth the effort. This recipe uses water, but good chicken stock yields a tastier final product.

1 (3½-pound) chicken, preferably free
 range or pasture-raised
Brine and marinade for *Souvlaki*
 (page 74)
1 pound fingerling potatoes, scrubbed
Kosher salt and cracked black pepper
1 to 2 teaspoons blended oil (90 percent
 canola, 10 percent extra-virgin olive)
Extra-virgin olive oil

3 red bell peppers, cored, seeded, and
 thickly sliced
1 teaspoon dry Greek oregano
½ lemon, sliced
2 tablespoons fresh lemon juice
2 tablespoons water
1 tablespoon Garlic Purée (page 264)
 or cold, unsalted butter (optional)
Small handful torn fresh herbs, such as
 dill, mint, and/or parsley

First, bone the chicken: trim off the first two joints of the wings. With kitchen shears, cut down on either side of chicken's backbone and remove it. Open out the chicken with the breast-side down and make a shallow cut on either side of the keel bone (central cartilage). Trim the rest of it away with a sharp knife. Cut the chicken in half through the remaining breastbone. Remove the wishbone. Cut through the leg-thigh joints without slicing through the skin. Pop out the thigh bones, then cut along the top and scrape down and remove them, leaving the drumstick bones intact. Leave the breast and thigh connected by the skin. Save all the bones in the freezer, for stock.

Brine the chicken overnight (see page 74).

Marinate the chicken for at least 4 hours, or overnight. Cover it with plastic wrap and press the plastic down onto the surface, to exclude air.

Bring the chicken to room temperature. Meanwhile, put the potatoes into a small pot of liberally salted cold water and bring to a boil. Simmer until crisp-tender, about 3 to 4 minutes. Drain well and slice ½ inch thick. Reserve.

Preheat the oven to 375°F. Lift the chicken pieces from the marinade, allowing the liquid to drain away. Season the skin with a little kosher salt and pepper. In a 12-inch ovenproof skillet, heat a thin film of blended oil over high heat. When the pan is very hot, add the chicken halves skin-side down and don't move them at all until you get a nice golden sear, about 3 to 4 minutes. Turn over and cook for 2 minutes more. Spoon off some of the fat and turn the chicken pieces skin-side down once again. Transfer the pan to the oven and cook for 15 minutes.

Meanwhile, in a second pan, heat a thin film of extra-virgin olive oil. Add the peppers and sauté until softened. Add the potatoes, lemon slices, and oregano and continue to sauté until golden brown.

Transfer the chicken to absorbent paper, on a platter, skin-side up. Keep warm, uncovered, in the turned-off oven. Discard most of the fat from the skillet and place over medium-high heat. Deglaze the pan with the lemon juice and water. Stir in the Garlic Purée or butter and lemon slices and remove from the heat. Season with salt and pepper. Transfer the vegetables and pan juices to a large platter and place the chicken on top. Drizzle with a little olive oil and scatter with the fresh herbs.

✸ Instead of serving with peppers and potatoes, shred the cooked chicken and toss with some cooked orzo, pitted black olives, strips of roasted pepper, sun-dried tomatoes, feta cheese, and fresh herbs, and perhaps some caperberries or pepperoncini. Now you've got a fantastic Greek chicken salad.

✸ If you use store-bought imported red peppers, don't add them until the potatoes are golden and you've deglazed the pan.

MAKING YOUR OWN COOKBOOK

I always ask young cooks in my kitchens to keep a notebook at their stations to make notes and keep track of adjustments to the recipes that they are cooking. When you cook, keep notes on scrap paper. Then, when you've got the recipe down exactly the way you like it, transcribe it and your notes into a nice leather-bound journal; it will be your own personal cookbook. The recipes you include might be my recipes, or dishes from someone else's book, or something you saw on TV. Make sure to keep notes on how you changed each recipe. Gradually, you will become known for your special dishes, and friends and family will say, "Hey, can you bring that great whatever-you-made-the-last-time-I-was-at-your-house?" I don't think there is any better compliment for a cook. Cooking is therapy and food is a gift. Sharing it among people who appreciate its value is the ultimate high for someone who loves to cook.

BEEF & RICE MEATBALLS IN EGG-LEMON SOUP

YOUVARLAKIA

SERVES 4 TO 6, OR MORE FAMILY-STYLE, AS PART OF A LARGER SPREAD

This is the dish I requested on virtually every birthday. It couldn't be more kid-perfect—meatball soup!

1 pound ground beef

½ cup uncooked long-grain rice

2 tablespoons finely chopped dill

2 tablespoons finely chopped parsley

2 tablespoons finely chopped fresh mint leaves

1 shallot, finely chopped

8 cloves Garlic Confit (page 264) or 3 tablespoons Garlic Purée (page 264, optional)

½ large egg, beaten

Kosher salt and cracked black pepper

4 slices Wonder bread, crusts removed

½ cup milk

4 fresh bay leaves or 8 dried leaves

3 quarts water

FOR THE AVGOLEMONO

3 large eggs, at room temperature, separated

4 tablespoons fresh lemon juice

⅓ cup small, picked sprigs dill

In a large bowl, combine the beef, rice, dill, parsley, mint, shallot, Garlic Confit, beaten egg, and liberal amounts of kosher salt and pepper. In a small bowl, soak the bread in the milk until most of the milk is absorbed, squeeze out the milk, and add to the mixture in the large bowl.

With clean hands, combine the meatball mixture thoroughly, evenly distributing the rice and bread. Using a large ice cream scoop, form firmly packed, golf-ball-sized meatballs of about 2 ounces each (about 18).

Bring water to a boil in a very large pot. Salt liberally, and add the bay leaves. Drop all the meatballs into the water. Partially cover the pot, reduce the heat, and simmer gently until firm and cooked through, about 45 to 60 minutes. (Taste to be sure the rice is cooked through to the center.) Discard the bay leaves.

Make the *Avgolemono:* Get everything together so you can work quickly. With a ladle, scoop out ½ cup of the braising liquid and strain into a small bowl. Add egg yolks and whisk together. Place the egg whites in a food processor and turn it on. When the whites begin to froth, after about 30 seconds, add the lemon juice, keeping the motor running all the time. When the whites are very frothy and thick, another 45 to 60 seconds, add the dill, and process for 10 to 15 seconds more while you season liberally with salt and pepper. Pour in the egg yolk mixture and immediately turn the machine off. Spoon the *Avgolemono* over the soup and serve at once, as it will quickly start to deflate.

STUFFED PEPPERS WITH BEEF & RICE
YEMISTES PIPERIES ME MOSCHARAKI KAI RIZI

SERVES 6, OR MORE FAMILY-STYLE, AS PART OF A LARGER SPREAD

The stuffing in this recipe may be used to stuff all kinds of vegetables, such as tomatoes, zucchini, and eggplants. Whenever the vegetable has pulp, scoop it out, chop it up, and add it to the celery, onion, and fennel before you begin to soften them.

2 tablespoons blended oil (90 percent canola, 10 percent extra-virgin olive)
1 stalk celery, finely chopped
½ small Spanish or sweet onion, finely chopped
¼ bulb fennel, cored and finely chopped
12 ounces ground beef
½ cup white wine
Kosher salt and cracked black pepper

½ cup uncooked long-grain rice
3 cups water or light stock, any variety
⅔ cup roughly chopped fresh herbs, such as dill, mint, and/or parsley
2 tablespoons fresh lemon juice
3 tablespoons Garlic Purée (page 264)
6 red or green bell peppers, or a combination
Extra-virgin olive oil

In a heavy pot over medium-high heat, warm the blended oil. Add the celery, onion, and fennel and soften for 3 to 5 minutes without browning. Add the beef and brown well. Deglaze the pot with the white wine, and cook until it's all evaporated. Season liberally with kosher salt and pepper, and add the rice. Stir for 2 minutes, then add the water, stir well, and bring to a boil. Remove the mixture from the heat and stir in half of the fresh herbs, the lemon juice, and the Garlic Purée. Let stand *briefly* while you prepare the peppers.

Preheat the oven to 400°F. Cut off the top 1 inch of the peppers and remove the seeds and large white ribs through the top. Reserve the tops. Place the peppers in a Dutch oven or small roasting pan. It should be just large enough to hold all the vegetables securely upright, so that the stuffing—which is initially quite wet but firms up as the rice cooks—absorbs the excess moisture.

Spoon the stuffing into the peppers to within half an inch of the top rim. Distribute the pan juices evenly between the peppers, and drizzle each one generously with olive oil. Season with kosher salt and pepper, and replace the tops of the peppers. Cover the pan with a lid or aluminum foil.

Steam-roast in the oven until the peppers are tender, about 45 minutes. Scatter with the remaining chopped herbs and drizzle with a little more olive oil.

❋ For a more traditional version of this dish, add 2 tablespoons of tomato paste to the stuffing mixture.

STUFFED BABY EGGPLANTS

PAPOUTSAKIA

❖——❖

SERVES 12 AS AN APPETIZER OR PART OF A LARGER SPREAD, OR 6 AS A MAIN COURSE

Papoutsakia translates from Greek as "cute little shoes." Try to find very small, young eggplants—they have not yet matured and so have fewer seeds, which tend to be bitter.

6 very small globe or Japanese eggplants, halved lengthwise

Extra-virgin olive oil

Kosher salt and cracked black pepper

Pinch ground cinnamon, plus 2½ teaspoons, for the filling

1 tablespoon blended oil (90 percent canola, 10 percent extra-virgin olive)

½ Spanish or sweet onion, finely chopped

12 ounces ground beef

1 fresh bay leaf or 2 dried leaves

2 tablespoons tomato paste

⅓ cup red wine

1 quart water

1 teaspoon small, picked thyme

1 cup Greek Béchamel Sauce (page 274, with one egg whisked in)

⅓ cup finely grated *graviera* cheese

Small handful torn fresh herbs, such as dill, mint, parsley, and/or chives

Preheat the oven to 400°F. Make deep, crisscross slashes in the cut sides of the eggplant halves. Brush the eggplant with olive oil and season with kosher salt, pepper, and a little cinnamon. Wrap each half in a square of foil and roast until quite tender, about 35 to 40 minutes. Scoop out the eggplant flesh without piercing the shell. Chop the eggplant flesh.

Warm a large, heavy pot over medium-high heat, add the blended oil, and sweat the onion (2 to 3 minutes). Add ground beef and brown thoroughly. Add the chopped eggplant, bay leaf, 2½ teaspoons cinnamon, and tomato paste; stir for 1 minute. Deglaze the pot with the red wine and let it all evaporate. Add the water, thyme, 1 tablespoon salt, and a generous grinding of pepper. Bring to a boil. Reduce the heat, partially cover the pot, and simmer until the sauce is quite dry, about 60 to 65 minutes, checking and stirring frequently.

Preheat the oven to 350°F. Put the eggplant halves in a small roasting pan and stuff with the meat mixture. Spoon a layer of béchamel sauce over the stuffing and scatter with the *graviera*. Roast for about 15 minutes, until golden brown. Drizzle the top with some of the rendered fat from the roasting pan and scatter with fresh herbs.

GRILLED PORGIES

SINAGRIDA STIN SCHARA

SERVES 4 TO 8, DEPENDING ON THE SIZE OF THE FISH

This is an amazing process! By leaving the scales on the fish you protect it from the fierce heat of the grill, and the layer of fat underneath the skin bastes the flesh, keeping it moist and tender—almost like whole fish baked in salt. The skin puffs up as the fish chars on the hot grill, and when it's done you can easily lift it away. Don't make this recipe unless you have a real grill; charcoal is best, but gas will work too. This dish does not lend itself to a grill pan.

4 whole porgies or any kind of sea
   bream, gutted but not scaled
Extra-virgin olive oil
Kosher salt and cracked black pepper

Ladolemono (page 270)
Small handful torn fresh herbs, such as
   dill, mint, parsley, and/or chives

Preheat a charcoal or gas grill until very, very hot. Brush the fish on all sides with a little olive oil and season liberally with kosher salt and pepper.

Grill the fish until firm and very char-marked. The skin will blister and raise slightly, and may crack a little.

Lift away the skin, then flip over and remove the skin from the other side. Lift off the fillet, then remove and discard the skeleton. Drizzle the meat generously with *Ladolemono* and scatter with the fresh herbs. Serve the heads and tails to anyone who asks for them.

SHRIMP WITH ORZO & TOMATO

GARIDES, KRITHARAKI, TOMATA

This is a one-pot meal that should take, at the most, 15 minutes to throw together. The results, however, would suggest otherwise. This dish is also a great example of the interesting combination of fish and cheese. Historically, the Greeks have had a long love affair with cheese, and it is used in many dishes where it would be absolute heresy in other cuisines. I'm sure after trying this recipe, however, you'll side with us. Of course, I am a little biased.

16 U-15 shrimp, peeled
Kosher salt and cracked black pepper
1½ cups orzo
2 tablespoons extra-virgin olive oil
2 cloves garlic, smashed and finely chopped
3 shallots, finely chopped
9 whole scallions, thickly sliced
½ cup water
3 plum tomatoes, roughly chopped

1½ cups smooth tomato sauce or purée (or a good, store-bought marinara)
¼ cup Garlic Purée (page 264)
¾ cup crumbled feta cheese, divided in half
6 cups baby spinach leaves (about 8 ounces)
Small handful torn fresh herbs, such as dill, mint, and/or parsley
Extra-virgin olive oil

Preheat the oven to 275°F. Season the shrimp with kosher salt and pepper.

Cook the orzo according to instructions and toss with 1 tablespoon of the oil. Reserve, keeping warm.

In a large, heavy soup pot, Dutch oven, or wok, warm the remaining tablespoon of olive oil over high heat. When the pot is very hot, add the garlic and shallots, and sauté for 1 minute. Add the scallions and shrimp, and sear for 30 seconds. Add the water, tomatoes, tomato sauce, and Garlic Purée. Cook for 2 minutes and remove the shrimp to the reserved orzo. Continue to reduce the liquid until the mixture has thickened (2 to 3 minutes), and season with salt and pepper.

Place a serving bowl in the preheated oven for 2 minutes to warm.

To the pot, add the orzo and shrimp, half of the feta, and the spinach, and toss to combine. As soon as the spinach has wilted (about 1 minute), transfer to the preheated bowl.

To finish, scatter the remaining feta, the fresh herbs, and a drizzle of olive oil over the top.

Left to right: Costas Psilakis, far left, and Cretan Dance Group; Michael Psilakis dancing on a bottle, 1987; Chef Psilakis in his father's dancing costume

kefi—a time to dance

There is a single word in Greek, *kefi*, that explains a philosophy of life. *Kefi* is the culmination of a celebration when music, dance, food, liquor, and the company you share intersect. The effect is so ethereal and the feeling so euphoric that you realize this is what life is about. It isn't material possessions—the size of your house or the kind of car you drive—that are important. It's the joy you derive from celebrating life with the people you love.

When I was five years old, my parents sent me to Greek school at our local Greek Orthodox church on Long Island. We learned not only how to read and write Greek, but also about Greek culture and the country our parents had left behind. The religious component of the program wasn't dominant (because the church also had Sunday school, which of course I had to attend) but the culture is tied into the religion and vice versa, so religion was a unifying aspect of all of the other elements of our program.

I found my time at the church for Greek school to be very peaceful. It wasn't because of any deep-seated religious beliefs, but rather because of the friendships that I made there. I found a support system I desperately needed among the other children of Greek immigrants. They understood me in a way that only children growing up in the same cultural bubble could comprehend.

As part of the curriculum, we learned traditional Greek folk dancing. Initially, the forty-five minutes of dance instruction every Saturday was relatively casual. Mrs. Benes was a good recreational folk dancer, but she was not a professional. It was when Mrs. Sopasis, a retired professional dancer, came to Greek school to teach us that I really became interested in Greek, especially Cretan, dancing.

As Mrs. Sopasis and her daughter, Debbie (later my dance partner), whipped us into shape, requests for our dance troupe started to come in. We were regularly asked to perform at church bazaars and festivals. As I became more passionate about my dancing, I also became more determined to be the best in our troupe.

Before every performance, my father would come backstage to help us dress. Then, before I ever took my first step onto the stage, he would be back in his seat in the audience to watch me dance. My father was also a dancer. He had danced as a boy in Crete and continued to dance in a Cretan troupe long after his arrival in America. As part of traditional Greek dance, we wore the traditional Greek costume: bloomer-style long wool pants, a wraparound sash about twenty feet long, and a long-sleeved, baggy white shirt. I had my own costume for these performances, but it was my father's costume for which I had been begging him half of my life. Greek dance was so important to my father that he commissioned a portrait of himself in his full dance costume. It still hangs in my mother's dining room.

On one occasion, when I was twelve years old, our dance troupe was invited to a church bazaar that would be four days long. We prepared feverishly. All went according to plan on the first three days of the festival. My father, as usual, was there watching his son with pride.

On the fourth day, we dancers had a special agenda. Unbeknownst to her, we planned to bring Mrs. Sopasis onto the stage to dance with us, present her with flowers, and acknowledge all of her hard work and dedication. I was very excited, as were the other dancers. Our energy was palpable, and the air felt like it was resonating with our adrenaline-pumped anticipation.

It was a shock to all of us then when the priest suddenly and casually canceled our performance. It wasn't his fault, really. He didn't know that we had a special program planned. There was no way for him to know how much work, love, and devotion we had tied up in this, the last performance of the festival.

The blow, however, was tremendous. I ran off and in my fury and frustration I punched a cinder-block wall. I then proceeded to chug wine, one bottle after another. As I stumbled around, my cousin took me to the bathroom, propped me against a wall, and started beating on me, just to keep me conscious.

I remember my friends around me. Some of them, including my best friend, Alex, were crying as I was strapped to a stretcher and taken away in an ambulance. In addition to breaking my hand, I had to have my stomach pumped. My father, president of the church and upstanding member of the Greek community, had to watch his son very publicly rushed off to the hospital, siren wailing.

It can be difficult to look back on your life and see a mistake you've made that was not only painful to yourself but to others too. It's amazing, though, that despite my behavior, my father seemed to understand my actions. He too knew the passion of dance, the intersection of wine and spirits, the sacrifice and commitment to become an accomplished dancer. To him, my behavior was a gross embarrassment, but still he understood it—he understood me.

I was about thirteen years old when Mrs. Sopasis asked me to join the Minos dance troupe in Astoria, Queens. The dancers at Minos were on an entirely different level than my peers at Greek school. My passion for Greek dance had grown, and even at Minos I was determined to be the best. Every day after school I would run home and my mother would rush me over to the church or to Queens so I could practice, for hours, the dances that Mrs. Sopasis was teaching us.

When I wasn't practicing under Mrs. Sopasis's direction, I was practicing on my own. I became obsessed with learning how to do *figoures*—tricks like jumps, twists, and turns. But the one *figoure* that consumed me was one that only a rare few could execute. I wanted to learn how to do the *figoure* in which, while dancing, the dancer jumps onto a bottle and balances himself on its mouth.

I worked alone in my basement for hours, standing on a rickety card table so I could hang from the rafters in order to lower myself onto a bottle. I fell again and again, sometimes to the floor, other times falling on the card table and toppling the table and glass bottle along with me. I worked tirelessly, first trying to balance myself on the bottle and, once I had mastered that, trying to jump off the bottle and into the air, slap my hands to my feet, and then land back on the mouth of the bottle again. I worked on this for weeks and weeks.

A famous *lyratzi* (lyrist) was coming over from Crete to play to a full house of thousands. I, the lead dancer of this Cretan dance troupe, felt the weight of my father's life and history upon my shoulders. I led the troupe onto the stage and we began to dance to the *lyratzi*'s accompaniment. In the middle of the performance, all the other dancers stepped back and I took center stage.

Debbie placed an empty glass bottle on the floor in front of me. I jumped up onto the bottle and balanced myself. And then I started to jump and dance. I was doing the *figoure*—I was doing *my figoure*. Debbie placed a full bottle of *metaxa*, Greek brandy, and an empty shot glass on the floor next to me while I continued to balance all of my weight on this single, empty glass bottle. I did a jump in the air, landed on the mouth of the bottle, balanced on my right leg, and bent and tucked my left leg behind my right knee. Then I bent down, picked up the bottle of *metaxa*, poured a drink into the shot glass, placed the glass on top of my head, stood up, and again started to dance.

I was so engrossed in my dancing, I was so consumed by the music (which sounds like a mix of Arabic, Indian, and Turkish folk music) of this famous *lyratzi*, that up until that point I had not realized that my father was standing there, front and center, directly before me as I bent down to pick up the glass. At my past performances, my father had always been there. He always came backstage and he always watched from the audience, but he never stood up front. He was not one to draw attention to himself.

I looked at him and saw that his cheeks were streaked with tears. I had never seen my father cry before, and I never saw him shed a tear after. Our eyes locked, and I could read the depth of pride and emotion in his expression. I knew my passion for Greek dance made my parents proud, but I could not have anticipated the profound effect it would have on my father and, as a result, on me. I realized at that moment that to my father, this dancing was the most important thing I ever did in my life. Then I was again consumed by *kefi* and the spirit and soul of the dance.

My grandparents, parents, their brothers and sisters, and all of my relatives—they worked so hard. And when it came time to celebrate, they celebrated with all of their hearts, bodies, minds, and souls. Wine, beer, and spirits—*ouzo* and *metaxa*—these, just like the food overflowing from the tables, were integral to our celebrations and to our culture.

With the recipes that follow, I hope you'll take the opportunity to celebrate your lives with some of the drinks and spirit suggestions I have included and be sure to whip up some *mezes* to complement the drinks too!

FRIED PORK & BEEF MEATBALLS
SOUTZOUKAKIA

These meatballs are a crowd-pleaser and were awarded Best Meatball of 2007 by both the *New York Times* and *New York* magazine. They are time-consuming by nature, but they are loved by grown-ups and children alike and are equally terrific for family gatherings and big parties.

FOR THE CHUNKY TOMATO SAUCE
1 (15-ounce) can whole plum tomatoes, with all the juice
1 tablespoon extra-virgin olive oil
½ large Spanish or sweet onion, thinly sliced lengthwise
6 cloves garlic, smashed
½ cup red wine
1 fresh bay leaf or 2 dried leaves
Large handful basil leaves
1½ cups water

FOR THE MEATBALLS
15 slices Wonder bread (crusts trimmed off)
1½ cups milk
1 pound ground beef
½ pound ground pork
½ large Spanish or sweet onion, finely chopped
½ cup finely chopped parsley
2 tablespoons dry Greek oregano

½ cup grated *graviera* cheese
1 large egg, lightly beaten
Kosher salt and cracked black pepper
All-purpose flour
Blended oil (90 percent canola, 10 percent extra-virgin olive), for shallow-frying
¼ cup olive oil
2 whole scallions, sliced
2 plum tomatoes, seeded and roughly chopped
12 cracked, brined green olives, pitted and torn
12 Kalamata olives, pitted and torn
12 cloves Garlic Confit (page 264, optional)
15 small, picked sprigs parsley
15 small, picked sprigs dill
15 leaves basil, torn
Extra-virgin olive oil

For the Tomato Sauce, in a food processor, purée about one third of the tomatoes.

Warm the olive oil in a large, heavy saucepan over medium heat. Add the onion and sauté until almost tender. Add the garlic and cook for 1 minute more, then deglaze the pan with the red wine and add the bay leaf, basil, and water, and the puréed and whole tomatoes and all their juices. Simmer for 5 minutes, all the time breaking up the tomatoes with a wooden spoon. Have the Tomato Sauce standing by on the stove in a very large pot.

For the meatballs, in a large bowl, soak the Wonder bread with milk. Squeeze most of the milk out of the bread, and transfer to another large bowl. Tear the bread into small pieces. Add the beef, pork, onion, parsley, oregano, *graviera*, and egg; season liberally with kosher salt and pepper. With clean hands, mix thoroughly until evenly blended. Use an ice cream scoop to form firmly packed, golf-ball-sized meatballs.

Spread a generous bed of flour on a large platter. Warm about ¼ inch of blended oil in your largest skillet over medium-high heat. Dredge the meatballs in the flour, coating them evenly. Fry in batches until golden brown on all sides. As they brown, transfer the meatballs to the pot of tomato sauce, keeping the sauce at a very low simmer. Cook gently until all the meatballs are tender and very juicy, about 1 hour.

In a skillet, warm the olive oil over medium heat. Add the scallions and sauté for 2 minutes, then add the tomatoes, olives, and Garlic Confit. Sauté for 1 minute, then add the mixture to the pot of meatballs and stir *very* gently, to combine. Simmer for 1 or 2 more minutes and transfer onto a platter. Scatter with the herbs and drizzle with a little extra-virgin olive oil.

❋ If making the night before, follow the recipe through the cooking of the meatballs, then cool and reserve in refrigerator. Before serving, warm through in a 325°F oven, stirring only very gently so you don't break up the meatballs. At this point, continue with the last step to complete.

LITTLE SAUSAGES

SEFTALIA

MAKES 6 SAUSAGES

These superfresh mini homemade sausages from Cyprus are terrific on a table of *meze*. Caul fat is traditionally used to make this sausage, but you may substitute regular sausage casing if caul fat is not available.

If your caul fat is frozen, when thawing be careful that it doesn't pull apart into small pieces. You can freeze, or even refreeze, any leftover caul fat, which is helpful because you will probably not be able to buy a small quantity. If you plan to refreeze, try not to bring it past 45°F. The best way to defrost caul fat is to place it in salted water in the refrigerator.

2 (¼-inch-thick) slices Spanish or sweet onion

Extra-virgin olive oil

Kosher salt and cracked black pepper

8 ounces ground beef

4 ounces ground pork

1 tablespoon Dijon mustard

1 teaspoon ground coriander (optional)

1 tablespoon finely chopped parsley

1 tablespoon finely chopped dill

1 scallion, green part only, finely chopped

1 teaspoon dry Greek oregano

1 tablespoon Garlic Purée (page 264, optional)

About 2 ounces pork caul fat

Lemon wedges and extra-virgin olive oil or *Tsatziki* (page 189), for serving

1 tablespoon chopped fresh herbs, such as dill, mint, parsley, and/or chives

Brush the onion slices with a little oil and season with kosher salt and pepper. On a hot grill pan or in a cast-iron skillet, grill the onion until tender and slightly char-marked. Separate into rings and finely chop.

In a bowl, combine the onion, beef, pork, mustard, coriander, parsley, dill, scallion, oregano, and Garlic Purée. Season liberally with kosher salt and pepper. With clean hands, combine the mixture evenly, and form six football-shaped sausages.

Wrap each sausage in a single layer of caul fat, trimming off any extra bits and pieces. If you like, refrigerate, uncovered, for a couple of hours; this will help dry the surface and give you an even better sear on the grill.

Preheat a charcoal or gas grill, or ridged cast-iron grill pan, until hot. Brush the sausages lightly with a little olive oil and season with salt and pepper. Grill until firm and char-marked. Transfer the meat to a platter and drizzle with some lemon juice and extra-virgin olive oil, or top with a spoonful of *Tsatziki*. Scatter with chopped fresh herbs.

☀ Skewer the sausages lengthwise after grilling, for a fantastic, hand-passed *meze*. Top with a dollop of *Tsatziki* and grated lemon zest.

EGGPLANT SPREAD

MELITZANOSALATA

Melitzanosalata is a very versatile spread that keeps well and is relatively easy to make. I love to prepare a variety of spreads, grill some pita, and make a beautiful *meze* table for a cocktail party or a pre-dinner snack with wine.

1 large eggplant
2 tablespoons extra-virgin olive oil
6 shallots, roughly chopped
2 cloves garlic, smashed and roughly chopped
½ small fire-roasted red bell pepper, home-roasted (page 270) or store-bought, cut into strips
½ roasted yellow pepper (or increase above to 1 whole red pepper), chopped

1 tablespoon fresh lemon juice
12 cloves Garlic Confit (page 264) or 3 to 4 tablespoons Garlic Purée (page 264), if you have it
¼ cup red wine vinegar
¼ cup extra-virgin olive oil
Small handful roughly chopped fresh herbs, such as dill, mint, basil, and/or chives

Preheat the oven to 350°F. Hold the eggplant with long tongs or a fork and char it over an open flame, turning it until blackened and flaky all over. Wrap the eggplant in foil and roast it in the oven until very soft, about 45 minutes. Cool slightly, then peel off the skin and discard it. Line a colander with a double thickness of cheesecloth and place it over a bowl. Drain the eggplant pulp overnight (don't skip this step or the texture will be too loose).

In a skillet, warm the olive oil over medium-high heat. Add the shallots and cook until tender, about 3 minutes. Add the garlic and roasted peppers, and cook for 1 minute more. Deglaze the pan with the lemon juice and remove from the heat.

In a food processor, combine half the drained eggplant and the Garlic Confit. Purée until very smooth, and add the red wine vinegar. With the motor running, drizzle in the extra-virgin olive oil. Coarsely chop the remaining drained eggplant, and in a large bowl, combine with the pepper mixture. Add the puréed eggplant and fold together. Season generously with salt and pepper and fold in the fresh herbs.

※ For a Cretan version of Eggplant Spread, toast 1 teaspoon each cumin seeds, fennel seeds, and mustard seeds in a dry pan. Cool, grind in a spice mill, and add to Eggplant Spread.

※ To make eggplant and chickpea *keftedes:* In a food processor, combine 1 cup Eggplant Spread with 1 cup drained Chickpea Confit (page 266). Add an egg yolk and pulse until chunky. Use an ice cream scoop to form the mixture into balls, dredge in flour, and deep-fry until golden brown, for an arancini-like fritter. For a vegetarian *souvlaki* (kind of like falafel), put one fritter into a pita and top with Greek Salad (page 213). Spoon in a little *Tsatziki*, and perhaps some tahini.

☸ Smear a little Eggplant Spread on a plate, and top with a *keftede* and a spoonful of *Tsatziki*.

☸ Add a little cooked bulgur to the Eggplant Spread. Make a larger ball and flatten into a disk. Chill for 4 hours, then pan-fry for a superior vegetarian burger.

◈ The Wedge: Smear a little Eggplant Spread on a triangle of pita and top with a little shaved *graviera* cheese, a few rings of fried shallots (page 77), and a sprig or leaf of any fresh herb.

TSATZIKI

MAKES 1 QUART

This is the one sauce you *must* make. It's a classic and very easy to prepare, but be sure you use only a superior quality Greek yogurt or labne spread. I cannot emphasize this strongly enough—it makes all the difference.

1 English cucumber, peeled
10 cloves garlic, smashed and finely chopped
1 cup distilled white vinegar
4 shallots, thickly sliced
1 cup small, picked sprigs dill

2½ cups strained or Greek yogurt or labne spread
2 tablespoons extra-virgin olive oil
2 tablespoons fresh lemon juice
Kosher salt and cracked black pepper

Quarter the cucumber lengthwise and trim off the triangular wedge of seeds. Cut the cucumber into a very small, even dice. Transfer it to a mixing bowl.

In a food processor, combine the garlic, vinegar, shallots, and dill. Pulse until finely chopped but not puréed. Add the mixture to the cucumbers; add the yogurt. Fold together with a rubber spatula, adding the olive oil and lemon juice. Season liberally with kosher salt and pepper, starting off with 1 tablespoon salt. Taste for seasoning. You can store *Tsatziki* in a covered, clean jar in the refrigerator for up to 1 week.

◈The Wedge: Smear some *Tsatziki* onto a pita triangle. Top with a tiny pinch of dry Greek oregano, a few pieces of diced tomato or a halved grape or cherry tomato, and a few salami matchsticks.

FAVA SPREAD

In Greek cuisine, the term *fava* always refers to dried yellow split peas, not the fresh green favas used in Italian cooking. Note that this mixture always thickens as it sits. If it is too thick, return it to the food processor and stream in extra-virgin olive oil with the motor running until you reach the desired consistency. With the addition of heavy cream (water, if you're vegan), this makes an absolutely divine split pea soup.

FOR THE PEA MIXTURE
2 tablespoons blended oil (90 percent canola, 10 percent extra-virgin olive)
10 shallots, finely chopped
6 to 7 cloves garlic, smashed and finely chopped
1 pound yellow split peas, well rinsed
1½ quarts water
2 fresh bay leaves or 4 dried leaves

Kosher salt and cracked black pepper

8 cloves garlic, smashed
2 shallots, roughly chopped
1 tablespoon fresh lemon juice
2 pepperoncini (pickled yellow peppers), roughly chopped
½ cup extra-virgin olive oil
Small handful small, picked sprigs dill

In a large pot, warm the blended oil over medium-high heat. Add the shallots and garlic, reduce the heat a little, and sweat until softened but not browned, about 3 to 4 minutes. Add the split peas and stir for 2 minutes. Add the water, bay leaves, 1 tablespoon kosher salt, and a generous grinding of pepper. Cover and simmer gently until very soft but not mushy or falling apart, about 45 to 50 minutes. Transfer to a sieve over a bowl and drain well. (Reserve all the liquid for another use.) Let stand for at least 15 minutes, to ensure all the liquid drains away. Remove the bay leaves.

In a food processor, combine the garlic, shallots, lemon juice, and pepperoncini. Add about one third of the split pea mixture and pulse until smooth. With the motor running, drizzle in the olive oil to form an emulsion. Add the dill, 1 tablespoon salt, and more cracked pepper. Pulse again to blend, then turn out into a large bowl and combine with the remaining split pea mixture. Blend with a large spatula until evenly mixed. You can store the spread in a covered, clean jar in the refrigerator for up to 1 week.

❧ The Wedge: Smear some fava spread onto a pita triangle. Top with a pinch of grated *manouri*, a few slivers of sun-dried tomato or dried apricots, and a sprig of dill.

TARAMOSALATA

Tarama (carp roe) is available at Middle Eastern specialty shops and, of course, on the Internet. It is deep red and looks like shad roe. Transferring the mixture to a stand mixer may seem a bit of a hassle, but it's the only way you will get a beautiful, fluffy consistency. If you finish the *Taramosalata* in the food processor, it will still be delicious, but the consistency will be more dense.

3 shallots, roughly chopped
2 cloves garlic, smashed
1 tablespoon Dijon mustard
¾ cup tarama (Krinos brand is a
    good one)
2 tablespoons fresh lemon juice

12 slices Wonder bread, crusts removed
1¼ cups milk
1¾ cups extra-virgin olive oil
1¼ cups canola oil
Freshly ground black pepper

In a food processor, combine the shallots, garlic, mustard, half of the tarama, and lemon juice. Pulse to create a smooth paste.

In a large bowl, soak the bread in milk, turning over. Squeeze the bread to remove most of the milk, transfer to a food processor, and pulse to combine evenly.

Transfer the mixture to a stand mixer fitted with a whisk attachment. With the motor running, slowly drizzle in the extra-virgin olive oil and canola oil until the mixture is completely emulsified; it will have a mousselike, mayonnaisey consistency. Add a generous grinding of pepper and fold in the remaining tarama. If the mixture is too thick, add a little milk. You can store in a covered, clean jar in the refrigerator for up to 1 week.

❖The Wedge: Smear a little *Taramosalata* onto a triangle of pita. Top with a bit of trout or salmon roe, some fresh lemon zest (or Dried Lemon Zest, page 270), and a sprinkle of fresh chives.

Overleaf, clockwise from top left: Kalamata olives; Tsatziki, *page 189;* pita; *Eggplant Spread, page 188; Fava Spread, opposite; Roasted Pepper & Feta Spread, page 195;* Taramosalata, *above*

CHICKPEA SPREAD

REVYTHOSALATA

⬦————————————————————————————————————⬦

MAKES I QUART

This is a Greek version of hummus that captures the soul of the Mediterranean. For this recipe, be sure to use premium-quality imported sun-dried tomatoes; they should be plump and soft with a red hue.

½ Spanish or sweet onion, thickly sliced

Extra-virgin olive oil

Kosher salt and cracked black pepper

40 large, plump sun-dried tomatoes (about 2 cups)

6 cloves garlic, smashed

2 large shallots, thickly sliced

8 leaves basil

1 teaspoon ground cumin

1 cup extra-virgin olive oil

3 tablespoons fresh lemon juice

3 cups Chickpea Confit (page 266), drained

Brush the onion slices with a little olive oil and season with kosher salt and pepper. On a hot griddle pan or in a cast-iron skillet, grill until tender and slightly char-marked.

In a food processor, combine the grilled onion, sun-dried tomatoes, garlic, shallots, basil, and cumin. Pulse into a chunky purée. With the motor running, slowly drizzle in the olive oil, then the lemon juice. The mixture should be quite smooth.

Transfer to a large bowl and add the Chickpea Confit. Fold together to blend. Return to the food processor in batches, and purée until the mixture is smooth and thick. Season to taste with pepper and salt (if the sun-dried tomatoes are very salty, you may not need much). The texture is a matter of taste; if it is very thick, add a little more olive oil to yield a creamier result. Well covered, the spread will last for at least a week in the refrigerator.

※ For two different textures, purée half the spread until very smooth and pale, and leave the other half chunky.

※ If you refrigerate the spread overnight, you can return it to a nice creamy texture by rewhipping in the food processor (pulse on and off for 1 minute).

⬦The Wedge: Cut a small triangle of pita and smear with Chickpea Spread. Top with a pinch of crumbled feta and some sliced scallions, picked sprigs of parsley or dill, and a few slivers of olive.

ROASTED PEPPER & FETA SPREAD

HTIPITI

MAKES 1 QUART

This traditional spread resembles a Greek *romesco*. It goes well with just about anything and is wonderful on its own as a dipping agent for crudités or potato chips. I like to use it anywhere you would use an aioli.

½ Spanish or sweet onion,
   thickly sliced
Extra-virgin olive oil
Kosher salt and cracked black pepper
1 cup crumbled feta cheese
2 fire-roasted red bell peppers, home-
   roasted (page 270) or store-bought,
   cut into strips
1 to 2 pepperoncini (pickled yellow
   peppers) to taste, sliced

½ teaspoon dry Greek oregano
2 pinches ground coriander
2 pinches ground cumin
4 small, picked sprigs parsley
4 small, picked sprigs dill
1 tablespoon snipped chives or scallion
   greens, sliced
½ teaspoon Dried Lemon Zest
   (optional, page 270) or ¼ teaspoon
   grated lemon zest

Brush the onion slices with a little olive oil and season with kosher salt and pepper. On a hot grill pan or in a cast-iron skillet, grill the onion until tender and slightly char-marked. Separate into rings.

In a food processor, combine all the remaining ingredients and process until very smooth. Taste for seasoning, but be careful not to add too much salt, as the feta is very salty.

❖The Wedge: Smear a pita wedge with *Htipiti*, top with a slice or two of pepperon-cini, and add a sprig of dill.

WARM FETA WITH TOMATO, OLIVE & PEPPER SALAD
ZESTI FETA

SERVES 10 TO 12 AS A *MEZE*

This supereasy and fast dish is a play on *saganaki*, a typical tavern dish where you melt cheese by grilling, broiling, or pan-frying. You could grill a large plank of feta and top it with this salad, but since this is a *meze*, I don't want anyone to have to use a fork.

1 small Spanish or sweet onion, thickly sliced

Kosher salt and cracked black pepper

9 caperberries, halved lengthwise

2 tablespoons capers

9 cherry or grape tomatoes, halved

9 cracked green olives, pitted and torn

9 Kalamata olives, pitted and torn

1 small red onion, roughly chopped

2 fire-roasted red bell peppers, home-roasted (page 270) or store-bought, roughly chopped

9 Greek sardines or white anchovies (optional), diced

9 small, picked sprigs dill

9 small, picked sprigs parsley

9 leaves fresh basil

⅓ to ½ cup Red Wine–Black Pepper Vinaigrette (page 273) or 3 tablespoons extra-virgin olive oil plus 1½ tablespoons fresh lemon juice

1 teaspoon dry Greek oregano

12 ounces feta cheese, crumbled

3 warmed or toasted pita breads, cut into wedges

Brush the onion slices with a little olive oil and season with kosher salt and pepper. On a hot grill pan or in a cast-iron skillet, grill the onion until tender and slightly char-marked. Separate into rings.

In a large bowl, combine the grilled onion, caperberries, capers, tomatoes, olives, red onion, roasted peppers, sardines or anchovies (optional), dill, parsley, and basil. Drizzle with the vinaigrette, season with kosher salt and pepper, sprinkle with oregano, and toss the salad until evenly coated.

Scatter the feta evenly over the base of an ovenproof baking dish or gratin. Warm the feta until slightly softened, 30 seconds in a microwave, or under a broiler for 3 minutes. Top with the salad and serve with the pita wedges. Scoop feta and salad onto a wedge with a knife and eat out of hand.

※ Grill a couple of sirloin steaks and when warming them up after the resting period (page 67), scatter with some crumbled feta. Then make the salad as above and pile it on top of the steak.

※ Grill a pounded, seasoned chicken breast and top it with feta, broil to soften—but not melt—the feta, and top with this salad.

FIGS STUFFED WITH FETA WRAPPED WITH PASTOURMA
SIKA YEMISTA ME FETA TYLIGMENA SE PASTOURMA

MAKES 20 TO 30 MOUTHFULS

I love this incredibly easy *meze* because you get a variety of great flavors in one mouthful: barnyard/earthy (depending on the cheese), salty, sweet. Wrap the figs the night before if you like. Store in a covered container and bring back to room temperature before serving raw or searing as below. If you can find very moist, dark purple dried figs, they can be substituted for fresh figs. *Pastourma* is a heavily spiced version of *bresaola*, with a thick spice layer visible on the outside.

10 ripe black Mission figs
3 to 4 ounces feta cheese, in a block
Leaves only from 2 small, picked
   sprigs thyme

Cracked black pepper
10 thin slices of *pastourma*
   or *bresaola*

Halve the figs through the stem (or if you find very large figs, quarter them). Scoop up about 1 teaspoon of the feta and place in the center of the cut side; the feta should be just big enough to cover the pink part of the fig. Push a few small leaves of thyme into the cheese and grind a little pepper over the top.

Halve the *pastourma* or *bresaola* slices crosswise. Place a stuffed fig on one short end and wrap up snugly. Prepare the remaining figs in the same way.

Serve the figs as is, or grill or sauté them briefly to crisp the meat and release the woodsy flavor of the thyme. To grill: lightly brush the outside of each wrapped fig with a little olive oil and place on a hot charcoal or gas grill for 30 to 45 seconds, turning with tongs, just to char the meat slightly. To sauté: in a hot pan with a tablespoon of olive oil, sear the figs just until the meat is slightly golden and crisped in a few places.

❋ For an earthy, woodsy flavor, substitute blue cheese for the feta.

❋ Try a soft goat cheese, or any soft and stinky cheese you like.

❋ Substitute very soft, plump dried apricots for the figs.

FRIED CALAMARI & WHITEBAIT
WITH CRISPY CHICKPEAS & LEMON

TIGANITO KALAMARI KAI MARIDA, ME TRAGANISTA REVYTHIA KAI LEMONI

SERVES 6 TO 8 AS A *MEZE*

This is the Greek take on *fritto misto*, and you can add all kinds of things—vegetables, meat, poultry—here as long as they are cut in pieces small enough to cook at about the same time. I prefer you use really, really fresh calamari (squid) here. However, if you use frozen calamari, make sure you take the calamari out of the frozen juices as soon as it is thawed and use it the same day.

Everyone is familiar with fried calamari, that Italian staple most often served with a heavy tomato sauce. In the Greek kitchen, we prefer to complement fried fish with a tart, acidic sauce to keep the palate alive and kicking.

1 pound calamari (squid) cleaned, heads separated from the bodies
12 small oil-packed Greek sardines or white anchovies, fresh whitebait, or fresh smelt
About 2 cups milk
Canola, safflower, or blended oil, for deep-frying
All-purpose flour
Kosher salt and cracked black pepper

1 cup drained Chickpea Confit (page 266) or canned chickpeas, well rinsed and drained
2 shallots, cut into ¼-inch rings
1 lemon, sliced paper-thin
⅓ cup small, picked sprigs parsley
⅓ cup small, picked sprigs dill
10 leaves fresh basil or mint
Tsatziki (page 189), for serving (or just serve with lemon wedges)

Cut the bodies of the calamari into ½-inch rings; leave the heads whole. Soak the calamari and the small fish of your choice in just enough milk to cover for 20 minutes.

In a large, heavy pot no more than half filled with oil, or a deep fryer, heat the oil to 350°F. Meanwhile, spread about 2 cups of flour in a large, shallow bowl. Drain the calamari and the fish and season them liberally with kosher salt and pepper. Season the Chickpea Confit, shallots, and lemon slices as well.

Throw the calamari, little fish, Chickpea Confit, shallots, and lemon slices into the bowl of flour, and toss well with your hands until evenly coated. Transfer everything to a colander or sieve and shake to get rid of the excess flour. Fry in the hot oil until golden brown, 2 to 3 minutes. Just before everything is done, throw the fresh herbs into the fryer for about 10 seconds. Lift all ingredients out of the oil and drain briefly on absorbent paper. Season with salt and pepper. Immediately turn out onto a large, warm platter. Serve with *Tsatziki* for dipping and wedges of lemon.

❋ Add a couple of sliced pepperoncini to the frying list.

SWEETBREADS WITH CAPERBERRIES, ARTICHOKES & WHITE WINE

GLYKADAKIA ME KAPARI, AGINARES KAI LEFKO KRASI

SERVES 4 TO 8 AS A *MEZE* OR STAND-UP FOOD

Make sure everything is ready and near the stove before you begin sautéing the sweetbreads, so you can prepare and serve this dish quickly. If you don't have any Garlic Purée on hand, finish up with 2 or 3 tablespoons of cold, unsalted butter.

12 ounces calf sweetbreads
Kosher salt and cracked black pepper
All-purpose flour
2 tablespoons blended oil (90 percent canola, 10 percent extra-virgin olive)
1 tablespoon extra-virgin olive oil
12 sage leaves, torn
2 large shallots, finely chopped
1 tablespoon fresh lemon juice
¼ cup white wine
¼ cup water
6 tablespoons Garlic Purée (page 264)
12 caperberries, halved
4 cups loosely packed baby spinach leaves
Extra-virgin olive oil
Sea salt

Plunge the sweetbreads into rapidly boiling salted water. Cook for 4 minutes, then remove and cool. Using your fingers, pull off the white membranes—the sweetbreads will fall apart into large, lumpy nuggets. (You can do this the night before: place on a paper towel on a plate, then cover with a damp towel and refrigerate. The next day, return to room temperature for 10 minutes before proceeding.)

Season the sweetbreads with kosher salt and pepper. Warm a very large skillet over medium-high heat and add the blended oil. While the oil is heating, dredge the sweetbreads thoroughly in the flour and shake off the excess. When the oil is hot, add the sweetbreads to the pan and sauté until golden brown on all sides, turning as necessary (use the side of the pan as a support, to help you brown the thinner sides), about 5 minutes. Drain on absorbent paper.

Working quickly, pour off the oil from the pan and wipe it out with a paper towel. Still over medium-high heat, add the olive oil. When the oil is hot, add and sauté the sage and shallots for 30 seconds. Deglaze the pan with the lemon juice, wine, and water; stir in the Garlic Purée and caperberries. Add the spinach leaves and wilt for a few seconds. Return the sweetbreads to the pan and toss gently. Drizzle with a little extra-virgin olive oil and scatter with a few grains of sea salt; serve immediately.

❋ Add 10 pieces of Artichoke Confit (page 267) to the pan with the baby spinach.

❋ At serving time, garnish with 1 large fried shallot (page 77).

big-party cooking

My family was legendary for throwing big parties. There was always an occasion to celebrate, whether it was a birthday, the Fourth of July, New Year's Eve, or my father's name day. And naturally, we wanted our friends and family there to turn the celebration into a real party.

On the occasion of my sixteenth birthday, my mother decided to throw one of these grand bashes in my honor. Ordinarily, my mother and maternal grandmother would start preparations for a big party a day or two in advance, and for some parties they would begin as much as a week beforehand. But this time, my mother was trying to pull off a surprise party and I—being in the throes of my malcontented, angry teen phase—did not make it easy for her. So, my mother came up with a strategy of her own. She called upon my best friend, Alex, to get me out of the house for a sleepover to give her at least thirty-six hours to get ready.

My mother and I had just had (another) big fight, so when Alex called, I busted his chops too. He was so persistent that I snarled at him and told him to back off. Out of options, he came clean and revealed that my mother was trying to throw me a big surprise party. My instant reaction was "Tell her I don't want a party. Tell her not to do it. Tell her I won't come."

My mother had another ploy, which she got my aunt to execute: after I returned from Alex's on the morning of the party, my aunt came to take me off her hands. My mother had made up some absurd story about my aunt needing my help at work that day, and that I had to dress a certain way in order to go with her. Before my aunt picked me up, my father started in on me about the way I was dressed.

I had bandanna strips wrapped around my forearm like bracelets. It drove my father crazy. He had been after me for months to remove them and, on this day, he was relentless. In a fury, I stood up, grabbed a knife, and—with the blade pointing away from my forearm and up toward my face—swiftly cut the tattered fabric off my arm. As I cut the last bracelet free, the blade came up with the force of my fury and I sliced myself on the brow, only millimeters from my right eye. I grabbed my eye as the blood poured down. Slowly, I removed my hand so my father could see. A plastic surgeon and sixteen stitches later, I was on my way to my aunt's office to "help" her.

The party I came home to continues to live on in infamy more than twenty years later. We ate and drank, laughed and chatted for hours. The party to which I had been so rabidly opposed transformed my spirits as I visited with friends and cousins, aunts and uncles—each and every one of them there to celebrate with me and my family.

On this occasion my father at last presented me with his traditional dance costume, something I had so desperately coveted for years. His presentation of that costume to me meant far more than the costume itself. It was his acknowledgment that I had earned it, along with his respect, and I was walking forward into manhood. I had his beloved costume and, in time, I would present it to my own son.

As the night wore on and the party ramped up, the kids went downstairs to the basement and the adults continued their festivities upstairs. I ran up and down between the two parties, from the teenagers making out in the basement to the adults getting drunker by the hour upstairs.

It was when my father came downstairs to resupply the moonshine for the contingent upstairs, with nary a comment to Alex (who was so engrossed in his activities with a girl on the couch that he was the only one who hadn't disentangled and straightened himself up upon my father's arrival), that my father attained legendary status among my friends. He simply looked at Alex and the girl (who were oblivious), went over to the bar, picked up two bottles of moonshine, and walked back upstairs. At this point, I realized the adults must be having one hell of a party too. So I ran up to see what was happening.

My godfather grabbed me and nodded to Skalidis, the famous *lyratzi* who had been hired to play at the party. Skalidis played a *pendozali*, a very fast Cretan dance. My *theio* linked up with me, shoulder to shoulder, and other men joined the line. The women seated all around us cheered wildly. As the pace picked up, my uncle directed us to do what he did—and he proceeded to take his clothes off, piece by piece.

The women were shouting, laughing, and throwing the plastic flowers that were in the vases adorning the room. We danced at a feverish pitch. As I looked around the room, for a moment I stepped outside myself. I could see the sheer joy, delight, and reckless abandon on the faces of everyone around me. These were the people I shared my life with and the people who loved me. These are the moments in life that are frozen in my mind forever—and they are priceless. This is *kefi*.

And just like that, I was inside myself and back at the party again, my shirt in my hand, twirling it over my head and following the instructions of my increasingly naked uncle.

When I look back on my life to the snapshots that populate my memory, many of my fondest memories are of events that happened at the parties we hosted at our house when I was growing up. Entertaining, however, and especially throwing big parties, can seem like a daunting proposition. But a good party doesn't have to be a huge party. Gather together any number of people you want—thirty, twenty, or fifteen of your close friends and family. With a couple of days' advance planning, a little organization, and the help of your friends, you can create memories of your own to last a lifetime. I guarantee that once you throw your first party, you'll be planning your second before the last bites of *pastitsio* have been eaten and before the last of the paper plates, plastic cups, and empty bottles have been taken to the trash.

The recipes that follow in this chapter are all-time party favorites. These recipes are no more difficult to make for four people than for thirty—a five-pound roast is no more challenging than a twenty-pound roast and *spanakopita* for four is no more difficult to make than for twenty. Save the fine china and crystal for another day, grab your friends as they walk in the door, and enlist them to help you. I promise, your friends will thank you and the effort you make will be rewarded tenfold with the memories you create.

Big-party cooking is not about one person doing all the work. A single person can't make all the food in a day—it's impossible. My mother used to cook for 250 people out of a home kitchen four or five times a year, but she cooked for a week beforehand. My aunts and grandmothers would arrive in the morning and help her put together everything she had prepared in advance. Just to have someone to wash all the pots and pans will make your life so much easier, because you'll be using them over and over again. Hire someone, or rope in a friend or relative, if you can. Thinking about how and when you will do the cooking will help you create a menu that is realistic for yourself and your home. Quite a few vegetable dishes can be made in the morning and safely kept at room temperature. If you have a grill and someone to take charge of grilling, that also saves time and real estate on the stove and in the oven.

The dishes in this chapter are designed to be part of a big buffet, so I don't give the portion sizes in the usual way. If you serve mussels as an appetizer, followed by a main course, you need ten or twelve per person, but when they are part of a huge spread that includes a table of *meze*, a lamb roasting on the spit, *spetsofai*, a huge dish of *spanakopita*, and artichoke fricassee, three or four mussels per person might be more realistic. Slice the lamb right off the spit so it's still hot and juicy, and two or three hours into the party, when people have been eating for a while, bring out the casserole-style dishes and salads—Potatoes, Olives & Capers with Anchovy Vinaigrette, and Greek Salad—and let everyone continue to graze. Look at the big picture when you gauge how much food to make. But always remember one thing: be sure there is too much food, rather than too little. Not enough food at a Greek party? Embarrassing. At my family parties, even after everyone is full, there should be more food to feed them all over again!

WHOLE SPIT-ROASTED LAMB

OLOKLIRO ARNI STIN SOUVLA

THE EQUIPMENT

Motorized roasting spit

20 feet of 14-gauge aluminum wire

2 pairs of pliers that can cut wire

2 U-Bolt clamps

6 (25-pound) bags of charcoal

30 pounds wood chips (preferably hickory), soaked in water overnight

New paintbrush

FOR THE LAMB

1 lamb, skinned, gutted, hung for two days in a cool, dry place

Kosher salt and cracked black pepper

2 quarts fresh lemon juice

1 quart extra-virgin olive oil

¼ cup dry Greek oregano

Decapitate the lamb, if necessary (reserve the head for oven roasting or braising). Working on a large, flat surface and starting from the back of the lamb, take the spit and push it through until the lamb is secured by the rear fork on the spit. The fork should go into the upper quarter of the two hind legs. Then, take the second fork and slide that into the front shoulder and secure. Use a hammer if necessary. Now, turn the lamb on its back and, using the wire, fasten the neck of the lamb to the spit by wrapping it around both. Make sure to fasten it firmly, using the pliers to twist the wire.

Take the front legs and pull them above where the lamb's head would be, as if the "elbows" were next to the "ears." Fasten the front legs to the spit using wire in a similar fashion to securing the neck. Extend the hind legs and tie them to the spit in the same fashion as the front legs. Turn the lamb onto its side. Unbolt the two U-Bolt clamps. Take the first clamp and pierce it through the back of the lamb under the rib cage. Go through the backbone into the cavity of the animal. Place the bar that holds the clamp together and bolt the two bolts as tightly as possible to the clamps against the spit. Move 6 inches to the rear and fasten the other clamp to the spit.

Now, light the fire using the charcoal and adding the wood chips for flavor. Wet the lamb down with water inside and out. Generously season with kosher salt and pepper; *do not be shy*. In a mixing bowl, combine the lemon juice, olive oil, oregano, salt and pepper to taste, and whisk. Transfer to a bucket. This will be your basting liquid. Spread the charcoal and wood chips to the sides, front, and rear of where the lamb will hang so there is no direct heat. (Indirect heat is key.) The heat should be approximately 300 to 325°F. If you can hold your hand next to the lamb as it spins for 10 seconds, it is the right temperature. If you cannot last 10 seconds, it's too hot. Put the lamb on the rack and fasten to the motor. Put the motor on the slowest setting. For the next 6 to 7 hours, baste frequently, using the paintbrush, and maintain the temperature. The lamb is ready when you can take a rib and pull it off with your hands without any resistance. Any animal roasted on a spit is best eaten right off the spit. I personally don't recommend transferring this to a table. Go right at it with a fork!

ARTICHOKE FRICASSEE
AGINARES FRIKASE

SERVES 10 AS A SIDE DISH, AS PART OF A LARGER SPREAD

This is a delicious match for roasted lamb or grilled lamb chops, especially with a little rice pilaf to soak up all the juices. The gaminess of the lamb is a perfect partner for the bold, rich flavor of the artichokes. It's a soulful combination.

8 medium artichokes, long stems
    left on, if present
2 lemons
2 tablespoons extra-virgin olive oil
2 large Spanish or sweet onions,
    thickly sliced
2 bulbs fennel, thickly sliced crosswise
2 cups white wine

2 quarts water
2 fresh bay leaves or 4 dried leaves
Kosher salt and cracked black pepper
2 tablespoons Garlic Purée (page 264)
Generous handful small, picked sprigs dill
4 ounces (1 stick) cold, unsalted butter,
    cut into pieces

Pull off the tough artichoke leaves until you reach the pale yellow leaves. Cut off the pointed tops about half an inch above the base. Trim the dark bits from the stem and base with a vegetable peeler. As you work, throw the trimmed artichokes into a bowl of cold water acidulated with the juice of 1 lemon.

In a large, heavy pot or Dutch oven, warm the olive oil over medium heat. Add the onion and fennel, and sauté until slightly wilted, about 5 to 7 minutes. Deglaze the pan with the white wine and simmer briskly until completely evaporated. Add the drained artichokes, water, bay leaves, 1 tablespoon kosher salt, and a generous grinding of pepper. Bring to a boil. Reduce the heat, partially cover the pan, and simmer until the artichokes are soft and offer almost no resistance to the point of a knife, about 35 minutes.

Drain the artichokes and vegetables, reserving all the braising liquid (discard the bay leaves). Let cool for 10 minutes. Pour 2 cups of the braising liquid into a blender and add three quarters of the fennel and onion pieces (reserve the remaining vegetables and the artichokes). Purée until completely smooth. (Reserve the remaining braising liquid for another use.) Return the puréed liquid to the pan; simmer very actively over high heat to reduce and thicken the juices, 10 to 15 minutes.

Stir in the Garlic Purée, the juice of the remaining lemon, and the dill. Return the artichokes and remaining vegetables to the pan. Reduce to a simmer and swirl in the butter until melted. Remove from the heat.

PASTITSIO

This is a classic Greek dish, which I often refer to as a Greek version of lasagna. You will need a deep, lasagna-style pan, and it may be hard to find the *pastitsio* noodles called for here. Try a Greek or Middle Eastern market or, of course, the Internet. The crucial thing is that the noodles be both hollow and straight, so you may substitute bucatini, percia-telli, ditali, or long, straight ziti laid end-to-end. This casserole, as with lasagna, must rest before serving to set, or it will be difficult to serve.

3 tablespoons blended oil (90 percent canola, 10 percent extra-virgin olive)

1 large Spanish or sweet onion, finely chopped

3 fresh bay leaves or 6 dried leaves

2 cinnamon sticks

2 pounds ground beef

1¼ teaspoons ground cinnamon

Pinch ground nutmeg (optional)

Pinch ground cloves (optional)

¼ cup tomato paste

2¼ quarts water

1 (28-ounce) can plum tomatoes, crushed slightly, with all the juices

1 tablespoon red wine vinegar

1 teaspoon sugar

Kosher salt and cracked black pepper

1 (500-gram) package Misko Macaroni *Pastitsio* no. 2 (see above)

1¾ quarts Greek Béchamel Sauce (page 274, *with* eggs)

1 cup coarsely grated *graviera* cheese

Make the *kima* sauce: in a large, heavy pot over medium-high heat, add the oil and wilt the onion with the bay leaves and cinnamon sticks for 3 to 5 minutes. Add the ground beef and brown thoroughly. Add all the spices and the tomato paste and stir for 1 to 2 minutes. Add the water, tomatoes, vinegar, sugar, about 2 tablespoons of kosher salt, and a generous grinding of pepper. Bring to a boil.

Reduce the heat, partially cover, and simmer for 65 to 75 minutes. Skim off the fat once or twice. Reduce until the sauce is almost completely dry. Proceed with the recipe, or cool and refrigerate.

Preheat the oven to 350°F. In a large pot of generously salted boiling water, cook the macaroni until almost tender, a minute or so before the *al dente* stage. Drain well. Spread 1 cup of the Greek Béchamel Sauce on the bottom of a deep roasting pan or lasagna pan, and sprinkle with ⅓ cup *graviera*. Lay half of the noodles out on top of the béchamel. You should have 2 to 3 layers of noodles. Spread another cup of the béchamel over the noodles, without disturbing the direction of the noodles, to bind them. Scatter with ⅓ cup of the *graviera*. Spoon all of the *kima* sauce over the top and smooth flat. Spread 1 more cup of the béchamel over the *kima* sauce, scatter with ⅓ cup *graviera*.

Layer remaining pasta noodles over the béchamel. Spoon on the remaining béchamel and scatter with the remaining ⅓ cup of *graviera*. Bake uncovered until crusty, golden, and set, about 1 hour. If you don't have a convection oven, you may want to increase the heat to 400°F at the end, to brown the top. Cool for at least 40 minutes, to allow the custard to set so that the squares will remain intact when you cut them. Or, cool to room temperature, then refrigerate overnight.

GREEK SALAD

HORIATIKI SALATA

SERVES 10 TO 15 AS PART OF A LARGE BUFFET

Some people think a Greek salad is a few olives, some cucumbers, tomatoes, and a block of feta on top of some lettuce. This refined version of the quintessential Greek side dish can be assembled up to an hour ahead of time, and kept in the refrigerator. As always, don't dress the salad until just before serving. This salad turns a grilled chicken breast, lamb chop, or any protein into a fresh and bright meal.

1 large Spanish or sweet onion, thickly sliced

Extra-virgin olive oil

Kosher salt and cracked black pepper

1 large head iceberg lettuce, sliced paper-thin

1½ pounds whole trimmed bulbs of fennel, sliced crosswise paper-thin

4 small fire-roasted red bell peppers, home-roasted (page 270) or store-bought, cut into strips

24 cherry or grape tomatoes, halved

¾ pound English cucumber, peeled, halved, seeds scooped out, and thickly sliced

8 whole scallions, thinly sliced

1 red onion, sliced paper-thin

½ cup small, picked sprigs dill, roughly chopped

½ cup small, picked sprigs parsley, roughly chopped

1 tablespoon dry Greek oregano

About 50 mixed green and black olives, brined and/or oil-cured, pitted and halved

16 whole caperberries

¾ cup Red Wine & Feta Vinaigrette (page 271)

⅔ cup crumbled feta cheese

4 pepperoncini (pickled yellow peppers), sliced

Brush the onion slices with a little olive oil and season with kosher salt and pepper. On a griddle pan or in a cast-iron skillet, grill the onion until tender. Separate into rings.

In a large bowl, combine all the remaining ingredients except the Red Wine and Feta Vinaigrette, feta, and pepperoncini. Toss.

Drizzle with the vinaigrette and toss the mixture aggressively with clean hands. Scatter with the feta and pepperoncini.

SPANAKOPITA

I call this dish *spanakopita*, but it's really more a hybrid of Greek-scented creamed spinach and *spanakopita*. This version captures the flavors of my mom's *spanakopita*, but it's presented in my own special way.

16 sheets phyllo dough (about
  6 ounces), thawed
⅔ cup clarified butter
2 tablespoons extra-virgin olive oil
8 large shallots, finely chopped
8 whole scallions, thickly sliced
16 ounces baby spinach leaves,
  roughly chopped

Kosher salt and cracked black pepper
2 cups Béchamel Sauce Without Eggs
  (page 276)
⅓ cup roughly chopped dill
½ cup plus ¼ cup coarsely grated
  graviera cheese
½ cup plus ½ cup crumbled feta cheese

Preheat the oven to 375°F. On a large baking sheet, paint 1 sheet of phyllo with clarified butter and layer on 3 more sheets, painting each one and keeping the edges lined up. On a dry surface, make another, separate stack of 4 butter-painted sheets. Fit the second stack into a 9 x 12-inch (or similar-sized) baking dish, with the edges hanging over the dish all around. Layer on 6 more painted sheets of phyllo, fitting them into the base of the dish and rotating each sheet 1 inch to the right, again letting all the edges overhang. Prick the bottom in a few places and place on a baking sheet to catch any dripping butter.

Bake the flat stack for 9 to 10 minutes and the baking-dish pastry for about 15 minutes, until both are golden brown. (Depending on the humidity, both may be kept, uncovered at room temperature, for a couple of hours or even overnight.)

In a large, heavy pot, warm the olive oil over medium heat. Add the shallots and cook until softened, about 3 to 4 minutes. Add the scallions and spinach, and cover the pan for a minute, to begin wilting the spinach. Toss for 1 to 3 more minutes, to wilt without melting completely. Season liberally with kosher salt and pepper. Thoroughly stir in the Greek Béchamel Sauce, dill, ½ cup *graviera*, and ½ cup feta.

Spoon the very thick, hot mixture into the prepared pan of overhanging phyllo and smooth it level. Scatter the remaining feta and *graviera* cheeses and crumble the extra, flat stack of phyllo in rough shards over the top. If you are not serving it immediately, you may keep the dish warm in the oven for up to 10 minutes before serving.

❀ If you're a fan of mac and cheese, combine the creamed spinach mixture (above) with 8 cups cooked elbow macaroni, ¾ cup crumbled feta, and ¼ cup grated *graviera* cheese. Turn into a 9 x 12-inch or similar-sized gratin dish and top with some toasted bread crumbs (homemade or, in a pinch, store-bought) and another 1¼ cups grated *graviera*. Bake at 350°F until warmed through, and then broil for a minute to brown the top.

☀ For individual servings of creamed spinach in a phyllo shell: cut the creamed spinach mixture in half. Make two 4-sheet, *flat* stacks of butter-painted phyllo. Cut one of the stacks into four smaller squares (to do this, you'll have to trim the larger rectangle into a square first). Fit one of the smaller 4-sheet squares down into each of four 4- to 5-ounce ramekins, with the edges overhanging. Prebake the ramekin containers and the flat pile of phyllo (opposite) until golden and crisp. Just before serving, fill the phyllo ramekins with hot creamed spinach and top with crumbled shards of the extra stack of phyllo. This is fantastic garnish for the Steak with Bone Marrow *Htipiti* (page 66).

TWICE-COOKED GIGANTE BEANS
GIGANTES PLAKI

MAKES 2½ QUARTS

Gigante beans are a perennial favorite side dish at Greek parties. The dish requires the beans to be cooked twice, so save some time by chopping the vegetables in a food processor. To prevent the onion from becoming a purée, add it after the carrot and celery are partially chopped.

3 tablespoons olive oil
1 large Spanish or sweet onion, finely chopped
2 large carrots, finely chopped
2 stalks celery, finely chopped
3 fresh bay leaves or 6 dried leaves
¼ cup tomato paste

2 pounds dried gigante beans (large limas/habas grande), soaked in water overnight
Water as needed
Kosher salt and cracked black pepper
½ cup Garlic Purée (page 264)
2 cups crumbled feta cheese
9 whole scallions, thickly sliced
1 cup coarsely grated *graviera* cheese

In a large pot, warm the olive oil over medium-high heat. Add the onion, carrots, celery, and bay leaves and cook to soften without browning, about 3 to 5 minutes. Add the tomato paste and stir for 1 minute. Add the drained beans and enough fresh water to cover everything by about 1 inch. Bring to a boil and add 1 tablespoon of kosher salt and a generous grinding of pepper. Reduce the heat, partially cover, and simmer until the beans are soft, about 45 minutes to 1½ hours. Check occasionally, and add a little water if the level drops below the surface of the beans.

continued

Drain the beans, transferring all the liquid back into the pot and the bean mixture to a large bowl; reserve.

Place the liquid over medium-high heat and reduce until very thick. (This will take some time.) To the beans, add the Garlic Purée, feta, scallions, and just enough of the reduced liquid to lightly coat the beans. Fold together and taste for seasoning.

Preheat the oven to 400°F. Transfer the beans to one large dish or several small gratin dishes. Top with the *graviera* and bake just until warmed through and the cheese is melted, about 25 to 30 minutes.

POTATOES, OLIVES & CAPERS WITH ANCHOVY VINAIGRETTE
PATATES, ELIES, KAPARI ME LADOXYDO ANJOUYAS

SERVES ABOUT 15, AS A SIDE DISH, AS PART OF A LARGER SPREAD

Don't crowd the pan, or the potatoes will steam instead of browning. To avoid this, use a 12-inch sauté pan, wok, Dutch oven, or heavy soup pot, and cook in batches. To achieve a golden brown surface, the trick is to add a little butter to the olive oil: as the butter solids caramelize, the vegetables begin to brown. If you cook in batches, however, wipe the pan clean after each one. Serve hot or warm.

2 pounds fingerling potatoes, scrubbed
Kosher salt and cracked black pepper
3 to 4 tablespoons extra-virgin olive oil
1¼ cup small, picked sprigs parsley
½ cup small, picked sprigs dill
18 whole caperberries
½ cup capers

18 mixed green and black olives, pitted and split
12 whole scallions, thickly sliced
About half the recipe of White Anchovy Vinaigrette (page 273, optional) or any of my other vinaigrettes

Put the potatoes in a large pot of generously salted cold water and place over high heat. Bring to a boil, then reduce the heat and simmer gently until just crisp-tender, about 7 to 9 minutes. Drain the potatoes and spread out on a plate. Refrigerate for at least 30 minutes and up to overnight. Cut into rustic, bite-size chunks and season with kosher salt and pepper.

In a very large skillet, sauté pan, or pot, warm the oil over medium-high heat. When the oil is very hot, add the potatoes (no crowding!). Roast the potatoes, shaking the pan, for several minutes, until most pieces turn a golden color. Add the herbs, caperberries, capers, olives, and scallions and shake the pan for 1 minute more, just to wilt the herbs and scallions. Add the White Anchovy Vinaigrette and warm through; transfer to serving platter and serve immediately.

❋ Add some crumbled feta to the last batch of potatoes just before they're done, then fold all together.

❋ If you have leftover fish from, for example, the Striped Bass *Plaki*, fold chunks of fish into this dish and serve at room temperature.

OCTOPUS WITH CHICKPEA SALAD

OKTAPODI ME REVYTHOSALATA

Octopus is perhaps one of the most recognized of Greek dishes, but many people are afraid of it because they think it's difficult to cook. The technique in this recipe solves that problem—it comes out beautifully tender. Once you have this technique down, you can add diced octopus to a cold seafood salad, or a bowl of pasta with tomato sauce, or risotto.

1 (4- to 6-pound) octopus, cleaned, whole legs only

Kosher salt and cracked black pepper

Blended oil (50 percent canola, 50 percent extra-virgin olive), as needed

6 whole cloves garlic, peeled

2 fresh bay leaves or 4 dried leaves

¼ teaspoon red chile flakes

1¾ cups Chickpea Confit (page 266)

2 cups cooked black-eyed peas

½ small red onion, roughly chopped

8 scallions, green part only, thinly sliced

10 large, plump sun-dried tomatoes, cut into thick strips

1 tablespoon finely chopped parsley

1 tablespoon finely chopped dill

⅓ to ½ cup Red Wine–Black Pepper Vinaigrette (page 273) or 3 tablespoons extra-virgin olive oil plus 1½ tablespoons fresh lemon juice

Ladolemono (see page 270)

Small handful torn fresh herbs, such as dill, mint, and/or parsley

Sear the legs in batches of two, to avoid overcrowding the pan. Season the legs liberally with kosher salt and pepper. Place a large skillet over the highest heat and let it get smoking hot. Film the pan with a little blended oil and add two of the legs, tentacle-side down. Sear, turning, to a reddish brown, 1 to 2 minutes. Transfer to a Dutch oven or roasting pan and sear the remaining legs, returning the pan to superhot each time.

Preheat the oven to 375°F. Add the garlic, bay leaves, and chile flakes and cover with the lid or aluminum foil. Braise for 1 to 1½ hours, depending on the size of the octopus, until fork-tender. (Do this the night before, if you like.)

Preheat a charcoal or gas grill, or ridged cast-iron grill pan, until hot. In a large bowl, combine the Chickpea Confit, black-eyed peas, red onion, scallions, sun-dried tomatoes, parsley, and dill. Season with kosher salt and pepper and drizzle with the Red Wine–Black Pepper Vinaigrette. Toss the salad mixture thoroughly and transfer to a large platter.

Grill or pan-grill the octopus legs again briefly to char and warm. Transfer the legs onto the salad. Drizzle the legs generously with *Ladolemono* and scatter with the fresh herbs.

✺ Substitute one 15-ounce can of black-eyed peas for the cooked black-eyed peas; be sure to rinse and drain well.

STRIPED BASS PLAKI

LAVRAKI PLAKI

This dish is much better when made with a whole fish, but you could also use halibut tail or a big piece of cod. There are lots and lots of vegetables in here that meld with the garlic-herb-citrus flavors and the delicious pan juices that develop as the fish steam-cooks. Serve over rice or orzo to serve an even bigger crowd.

2 to 3 pounds whole sea bass, black bass, blue fish, or weakfish, gutted and scaled, gills removed

Extra-virgin olive oil

Kosher salt and cracked black pepper

About 1 teaspoon dry Greek oregano

1 lemon, thinly sliced

6 large sprigs thyme

6 large sprigs rosemary

4 fresh bay leaves or 8 dried leaves

16 whole cloves garlic, peeled

½ small red onion, very thinly sliced

3 plum tomatoes, cut into rough wedges

2 Idaho potatoes, quartered lengthwise and cut crosswise into big chunks

1 large zucchini, thickly sliced on a diagonal

1 Spanish or sweet onion, cut into thick julienne

About 16 Kalamata olives, pitted

Small handful torn fresh herbs, such as dill, mint, and/or parsley

⅓ cup capers

1½ cups white wine

2 tablespoons Garlic Purée (page 264) or cold, unsalted butter

2 lemons, cut into wedges, for serving

Preheat the oven to 450°F. Rinse the fish well under cool running water. Pat dry thoroughly. Film a large roasting pan with the olive oil and place the fish in the center. Season liberally with kosher salt, pepper, and a big pinch of oregano inside and outside. Stuff the cavity with about half the lemon slices, 4 sprigs each of the thyme and rosemary, the bay leaves, and a few garlic cloves.

Cover the fish with overlapping slices of the red onion, then top with the remaining lemon slices. Scatter the tomatoes, potatoes, zucchini, Spanish onion, olives, and the remaining thyme, rosemary, and garlic around the fish. Scatter the fresh herbs and capers over all. Season the fish liberally with salt, pepper, and oregano, and pour in the wine. Cover the pan with foil, sealing well.

Steam-bake until the fish is flaky and cooked, and all the vegetables are tender, about 45 minutes. (If you push a metal skewer into the center of the fish for a moment, then hold the tip against your lip, it should feel somewhere between warm and hot.)

Discard the herb sprigs if you like, and carefully transfer the fish and all the vegetables to a big platter. Whisk the Garlic Purée or butter into the pan juices until melted, and drizzle over and around the dish. Squeeze the lemon wedges over the top.

MUSSELS WITH GIGANTE BEANS & FETA
MYDIA ME GIGANTES KAI FETA

Make the gigante beans the night before, if you like. At that point, the mussels will be a breeze. If you don't have any Garlic Purée, purée a few of the cooked beans and braising vegetables with just a little of the cooking liquid. Use it to thicken the bean mixture.

FOR THE BEAN MIXTURE
1 tablespoon extra-virgin olive oil
½ Spanish or sweet onion, finely chopped
1 stalk celery, finely chopped
1½ fresh bay leaves or 3 dried leaves
1 pound dried gigante beans (large limas/habas grande), soaked in water overnight
Kosher salt and cracked black pepper
½ cup Garlic Purée (page 264)
1½ cups crumbled feta cheese

3 tablespoons extra-virgin olive oil

6 cloves garlic, smashed and finely chopped
5 large shallots, finely chopped
12 whole scallions, thickly sliced
6 plum tomatoes, roughly chopped with seeds
50 mussels
⅓ cup fresh lemon juice
2 cups white wine
1½ teaspoons dry Greek oregano
1 cup crumbled feta cheese
Large handful torn fresh herbs, such as parsley, dill, mint, and/or chives
Crusty bread, for serving

For cooking the beans, in a large pot, warm the olive oil over medium-high heat. Add the onion, celery, and bay leaves and cook to soften without browning, about 3 to 5 minutes. Add the drained beans and enough water to cover everything by about 1 inch. Bring to a boil and season liberally with kosher salt and pepper. Reduce the heat, partially cover, and simmer until the beans are very soft, about 45 minutes to 1½ hours. Check occasionally, and add a little water if the level drops below the surface of the beans.

Strain the beans. In a large bowl, fold together the beans, Garlic Purée, and feta. Refrigerate overnight, if you like.

In a very large stockpot, warm the oil over high heat. Add the garlic and shallots and wilt for 2 minutes. Add the scallions and tomatoes and let cook for 1 to 2 minutes.

Add the mussels and, after 30 seconds, the lemon juice, wine, and oregano. Cover the pan and cook, shaking it around occasionally while you hold the top on, until the mussels open, about 4 to 6 minutes. Add the beans and ¾ cup of the feta; toss to slightly melt the feta into the liquid.

Transfer the mussels to a large platter and throw the herbs into the liquid to warm. Drizzle all the pan juices and herbs over the mussels and scatter with the remaining feta. Serve with crusty bread.

anthos—the new world

The stories you read earlier in this book are the foundation of who I am today. The lessons learned in my childhood and the values instilled in me by my parents and our larger Greek community are the ingredients that inform my cooking and have shaped me into who I am as a chef. Food is our most elemental and basic need. Like the air we breathe, we need it to survive. And yet for me, and so many others, food is also a vehicle for communication.

When I decided to close my restaurant on Long Island and take my chances opening a restaurant in New York City, I had one very specific goal in mind: to shatter the confines, boundaries, and expectations that had been imposed on Greek cuisine. I aimed to elevate the way in which Greek cuisine—the cuisine of my heritage—is perceived by critics and diners alike. Through my cooking, I hoped to reach people not only on a sensual level but on a cerebral level as well, opening doors and showcasing the love and pride I have for the country and the people that made Greece what it is today. To do that, I needed a larger stage than Long Island, and to my mind there is no larger stage in the culinary world than New York City.

It is through food and cooking that I am able to share with diners my passion for my culture and elevate food beyond the five senses. I cook with the aim that, with every bite, you will not only smell and taste the food but also explore with your mind the identity of the dish I have created. Through that process, you are gaining a deeper understanding of the beauty that underlies the culinary traditions of Greece, and you will have a greater ability to interpret what I'm doing in the kitchen.

Greece is the birthplace of democracy and Western civilization as we know it today. It is also the birthplace of cuisine. Because of the trials and tribulations that Greece endured—war, famine, and centuries-long occupations—Greeks as a people are deeply rooted to their culture and cuisine. With the country under foreign occupation, Greek food evolved, and the influences of Mediterranean, Italian, and, of course, Turkish flavors are undeniable. What we see from a cultural standpoint is the integration of those flavors into what we know today as Greek food. But at the same time we see, taste, and feel the heritage, honor, and traditions of the forebears who were stubbornly rooted in the Greek soil.

The resounding, echoing, single-word definition of the culinary history of Greece is *pride*. My aim has been to showcase that pride of history, culture, and cuisine and to capture it in a way that allows the culinary world to experience the emotion that defines that pride. For me, it is critically important to express pride of culture because it is something that was ingrained in me as a child by my parents. This clear message of pride overrode everything we did and repeated itself over and over in every aspect of our lives. My parents did not want their children to forget the pride they felt for the country they had left. I, my siblings, and my contemporaries from the Greek community were instilled with this pride. As the next generation, we were groomed to carry the torch—and we did so in every way. I can assure you that if you asked any one of us where we came from, we would all shout "Greece!" because that is, unequivocally, who we are.

Food just happens to be my means of expressing that pride in my deep ties to Greek soil, to my heritage and culture. My art has allowed me to express the lessons that I learned and the emotions that I felt. When I was in the kitchen, I began to explore how to express those emotions to allow them to reach the dining public. It was then that I started to focus on the soul of Greece, because the soul is what reflects the values that shaped the culture and how those values are mystically ingrained into the food.

The cooking I do at Anthos represents my cerebral approach to the exploration of the question "What is Greece?" I realized immediately when I started cooking at Anthos that when people identified with that soul in my cooking, I was able to take them back to a moment of time in their lives that had been etched into their memories. By bringing them back to that moment, I was taking them on an emotional journey. At Anthos, not only are we giving the gift of food, we are also giving the gift of reliving a memory. That is the glory of food.

This last chapter is a way of showing my father, in words, where I am. I know he always looked at me, at all of my siblings and me, as his greatest work. And now, when I look at my son, Gabriel, I feel the same. Those values that were instilled in me—humility, pride in my culture, the importance of family and my role in caring for them, thinking of others before I think of myself—are the building blocks of my approach as I'm conceptualizing and creating the dishes at Anthos. I see the excitement of a boy who is hunting for the first time with his father and uncles, and the dreams he has of becoming a man; I see the pride and care my mother took when preparing festive meals for relatives and friends; and I see myself as a young man, grappling with my identity, and now, a man, at peace with myself.

I recognize that the recipes in this chapter are challenging, but I hope you will try at least one and blend the collective memories of my culture with a history of your own.

In this chapter, we will be very specific—no more laissez-faire. The recipes in this chapter are ambitious and unapologetically restaurant-style, as they are a sampling from my restaurant Anthos. This is my life today.

Some of the ingredients may be difficult to find but, having said that, you can find anything on the Internet. If you have the time and the passion, I encourage you to cook a dish in one of the earlier chapters, then try one of the related—but far more evolved—recipes in this chapter. In this way, you can experience my vision for today's Greek cuisine. Not only will it allow you a taste of the past, but also a glimpse of the future.

Cooking these dishes will allow you to understand the evolution I made from the hearty, home-style food in the rest of this book to cooking very haute, sophisticated food. For me, it has been a wonderful, inspiring, and eye-opening journey. Every recipe has been carefully calculated; the depth of each flavor is layered with a complementary or contrasting flavor. The resulting experience is exciting, sometimes unexpected, and always exactly what I have planned it to be. So clear your schedule, invite your very closest friends, and let yourself explore and experience haute Greek cuisine.

EVOLVED TRADITION AND INSPIRATION

All of the dishes in this chapter fall into one of two categories. In the first, we try to capture the essence of a traditional Greek dish, then express the tradition in an evolved way. With my new approach, the conceptualization of these dishes is grounded in the guests' ability to make the connection between the traditional and the evolved, both on the palate and in the mind. In the second category, we follow inspiration and journey beyond the traditional definitions of Greek cuisine. We continue to work with the ingredients common in Greek cuisine in these dishes, but allow ourselves to expand on techniques, unusual flavor combinations, and presentation to allow for the exploration of the soul of Greece.

In every one of the dishes in this chapter and at Anthos, I bring both a cerebral and a theatrical element. I want the cerebral part of the experience to develop quickly, but in two distinct phases: first a reaction to the theater involved in the presentation, and the second when the guest is actually eating the dish.

When you see, taste, and compare these dishes to the more traditional dishes earlier in the book, you will find that they are far more refined and elegant, not just in the preparation and presentation, but also on the palate. The original dishes are firmly rooted in my heart. They have taught, guided, and challenged me as my parents did and still do. The newer dishes are like my children: the next generation. They are reflections of lessons learned and traditions honored. They pay homage to the Greek blood that flows in my veins and the pride I carry in the crusade to show the culinary world the glory of Greece.

Note: For the recipes in this chapter, it will be helpful to have on hand some tools and equipment more commonly found in restaurant kitchens, such as a chinoise and a tamis sieve.

POACHED HALIBUT WITH CYPRIOT SHELLFISH SALAD, CUCUMBER-YOGURT BROTH & CAVIAR

SERVES 4

When I was honored to be asked by Michael Batterberry to prepare the fish course for the thirtieth anniversary of *Food Arts* magazine at the Plaza Hotel, I wanted to do something progressive yet firmly rooted in Greek cuisine.

The light dish that I came up with plays off the cucumber salad you saw earlier in this book (page 24). In that traditional dish, I have always loved the summer brightness of the cucumbers, the briny undertones of the olives, the piquant salinity of the feta, and the way the vinaigrette unifies them as one. So, in creating this dish, we first focused on the ingredients. The goal: to capture each element in a new, unique, and more refined manner while always paying homage to the simple, rustic roots. Once we had captured the soul of the ingredients, we could reflect on them, adding unexpected textures to showcase the underlying lightness that was to define the completed work.

To begin, we juice the cucumbers and emulsify the juices with sheep's milk yogurt to emulate the flavor of the feta, which gives us a richly textured broth. We do see just a hint of the feta, but here it is dehydrated, bringing in a texture that serves to intensify that sharp, salty-briny flavor. Then we added a new element: the fish. The flaky white flesh of the delicately poached whitefish crumbles into the cool, milky broth with just a hint of green. Suddenly, this evolves into a very sophisticated dish.

The bold, aggressive flavors are still here, but they're more subdued. The fresh, the light, and the bold mesh together to create a unified final product that lets me express each of the elements on the palate, one by one.

When you look back on that original cucumber salad—especially if you tasted the two salads side by side—you'd see the thought process involved in evolving this dish. The cucumber salad played a creative role: it was the inspiration.

FOR THE CUCUMBER-YOGURT BROTH

½ English cucumber, about three quarters of the peel removed

1 cup sheep's milk yogurt

4 tablespoons extra-virgin olive oil

Kosher salt and cracked black pepper

continued

Poached Halibut with Cypriot Shellfish Salad continued from page 228

FOR THE COURT BOUILLON
AND HALIBUT

1 tablespoon coriander seeds

1 cinnamon stick

1 tablespoon whole black peppercorns

4 shallots, sliced

2 cloves garlic, sliced

1 stalk celery, sliced

¼ fennel bulb, sliced

1 fresh bay leaf

6 sprigs thyme

6 sprigs oregano

1 cup water

1 quart dry white Greek wine,
preferably from Santorini

1 pint fish fumé

4 (4-ounce) pieces of halibut

Kosher salt and white pepper

FOR THE LEMON GELÉE

6 sheets gelatin

1½ cups fresh lemon juice

½ cup simple syrup (60 percent sugar
to 40 percent water)

2 teaspoons kosher salt

FOR THE PICKLED SARDINES

4 whole, very fresh sardines

1 teaspoon coriander seeds

1 teaspoon whole black peppercorns

1 teaspoon fennel seeds

1 fresh bay leaf

1 sprig thyme

Zest of 1 lemon

1 cup dry white wine

1 pint white wine vinegar

½ cup kosher salt

½ cup sugar

Extra-virgin olive oil

FOR THE DRIED THÁSSOS OLIVES
AND DEHYDRATED FETA

½ cup Thássos olives, pitted

4 ounces feta cheese

FOR THE CYPRIOT SALAD

White wine as needed

12 live razor clams

8 breakfast radishes, with greens

4 black radishes, cut into batons

12 baby cucumbers, with blossoms

4 sprigs coriander blossoms

Extra-virgin olive oil

Fresh lemon juice

Sea salt and cracked black pepper

FOR THE DILL OIL

1 ounce fresh dill sprigs

1 pint extra-virgin olive oil

1 tablespoon kosher salt

TO ASSEMBLE

Cucumber-Yogurt Broth

Court Bouillon

Poached Halibut

4 dominos Lemon Gelée

Pickled Sardines

2 tablespoons Dried Thássos Olives and
Dehydrated Feta

Sea salt and cracked black pepper

Cypriot Salad

Dill Oil

4 tablespoons sturgeon caviar

❖ CUCUMBER-YOGURT BROTH ❖

Push the cucumber through a juice extractor. In a bowl, whisk together the cucumber juice, yogurt, and olive oil. Season with kosher salt and pepper.

❖ COURT BOUILLON AND HALIBUT ❖

In a dry pan, toast the spices. Add the vegetables and herbs and 1 cup of water. Sweat the vegetables for 10 minutes, without browning. Add the white wine and reduce by half. Add the fish fumé, reduce the heat, and simmer for 20 minutes. Strain the bouillon and reserve.

Season the halibut with kosher salt and white pepper. Warm the Court Bouillon to 125°F, cover the fish, and poach at a very gentle simmer until fish is warm in the center, about 10 to 12 minutes.

❖ LEMON GELÉE ❖

Soften the gelatin in ice water.

Meanwhile, combine the lemon juice and simple syrup in a small saucepan. Add the kosher salt and warm gently over low heat until the salt dissolves (the liquid should never get hotter than 175°F).

Squeeze the excess water from the softened gelatin sheets. Add the sheets to the hot lemon solution and stir to dissolve. Strain the liquid through a chinoise.

Pour the liquid into a small mold or tray so it is about 1 inch deep. Refrigerate for 1 hour, until firm. Cut into domino shapes just before serving.

❖ PICKLED SARDINES ❖

Remove the fillets from the sardines and trim them to a nice, neat shape.

Lightly toast the spices in a dry saucepan. Add the bay leaf, thyme, lemon zest, and wine. Reduce the liquid by half. Stir in the vinegar, kosher salt, and sugar.

Place the sardines in a container and cover with the cold pickling liquid. Let stand for 30 minutes. Drain off the pickling solution and store the sardines in olive oil until serving.

continued

❧ THÁSSOS OLIVES AND DEHYDRATED FETA ❧

Most home ovens don't offer a temperature less than 170°F. In order to get the temperature low enough to create a similar effect as a dehydrator, prop the door open slightly with a balled-up dish towel.

Place the olives on a baking sheet and bake at 170°F for about 2 hours, or until fully dried. Pulse the olives in a food processor until coarsely chopped.

Crumble the feta and spread on a baking sheet lined with a Silpat (a silicone baking mat). Bake at 170°F until fully dried but not brown. Crumble between your hands into a powder.

❧ CYPRIOT SALAD ❧

In a steamer set over barely simmering white wine, steam the clams until they open. Cool the clams slightly and cut into julienne.

Just before serving, mix the radishes, clams, cucumbers, and coriander blossoms together very gently. Season the mixture lightly with olive oil, lemon juice, sea salt, and pepper. The baby vegetables are delicate; make sure the blossoms and greens stay intact.

❧ DILL OIL ❧

In a blender, purée all the ingredients on high speed until smooth. Pass through a fine tamis sieve. Note: You will have Dill Oil left over for another use.

❧ TO ASSEMBLE ❧

Warm the Cucumber-Yogurt Broth. Remove the warm Poached Halibut from the Court Bouillon. Place each piece of fish in the bottom of a large individual serving bowl. Place a domino of the Lemon Gelée in the center of each piece of fish, and put a Pickled Sardine on top of the lemon. Garnish the top of the fish with the Dried Thássos Olives and Dehydrated Feta, a few grains of sea salt, and some pepper.

Loosely mound the Cypriot Salad on the fish so it is slightly falling off into the center of the bowl; let the baby vegetables fall at random. Drizzle the Dill Oil over the salad. Place a small quenelle of caviar opposite the fish on the plate.

At the table, pour the warm Cucumber-Yogurt Broth around the edges.

SKORDALIA POTATO-GARLIC SOUP WITH CRISPY
BACALIAROS CONFIT & BEET TARTARE

SERVES 4

All over Greece, you will see Cod *Skordalia* (page 98), the inspiration for this dish, with very few, if any, regional variations. This is a universally beloved dish throughout Greek cuisine.

The traditional dish is one of my mother's favorites. I created this refined version because I wanted to show her how we could evolve something so close to her heart. Here, we capture the soul of the traditional by also bringing in another typical tavern combination of roasted beets with yogurt. These are dishes not usually found on the same plate, but they work together to unify the new, more refined plate that we serve at Anthos.

The same assertive, acidic flavors are here, but the boldness is mellowed with a dairy product: instead of heavy cream, it's sheep's milk yogurt. The grassy sheep-milk flavor of the yogurt acts as the unifying element for everything else on the plate, adding both texture and flavor to the acid of the lemon and heat of the garlic that defines *skordalia*. We emulsify the yogurt and the potato-garlic purée to create a very rich and elegant velvety soup that is still construable as skordalia.

Rather than roasting the beets, we represent them as an assertively spiced tartare, allowing us to incorporate additional depths of flavor. The cod, *bacaliaros*, has been turned into a confit. Then we make a wildly flavorful Mediterranean salad with the confit, adding capers and lots of fresh herbs. For texture, we add another piece of cod—this time, it's fried. As soon as the bowl is placed in front of the guest, a server comes by and pours the *skordalia* soup over the elements already in the bowl. The guest is encouraged to take a spoon and swirl all the elements together. Now, the purple swirls of beet tartare move throughout the silky white soup, the ingredients in the salad disperse, and the crispy, flaky fried cod retains a little bit of its texture.

In each spoonful you get a little of everything, and all the flavors become one. That's the beauty of soup. It's one of the rare dishes where you can actually control the experience of the palate from beginning to end. As with all of my Anthos dishes, the theater is a part of this experience too. It's knowing what is in the bowl when it arrives as separate elements, then having them melded together before your eyes.

When my mother ate this soup at the restaurant, she immediately identified its roots. Tears came to her eyes as she asked, "How do you come up with these things?" My reply: "A lifetime of memories from the meals that you created when I was growing up."

continued

Skordalia Potato-Garlic Soup continued from page 233

FOR THE BEET TARTARE

2 large red beets, peeled and roughly chopped

2 tablespoons capers

2 tablespoons red wine vinegar

1 tablespoon Dijon mustard

1 tablespoon grated fresh horseradish

1 teaspoon finely chopped dill

1 teaspoon finely chopped fresh mint leaves

1 teaspoon finely chopped parsley

Kosher salt and cracked black pepper

FOR THE BACALIAROS CONFIT SALAD

½ pound fresh cod (*bacaliaros*)

1 quart extra-virgin olive oil

6 cardamom seeds

5 cloves garlic, crushed

2 fresh bay leaves

3 tablespoons fresh lemon juice

2 tablespoons capers

1 teaspoon finely chopped dill

1 teaspoon finely chopped fresh mint leaves

1 teaspoon finely chopped parsley

Kosher salt and cracked black pepper

FOR THE POTATO-GARLIC SOUP

5 cloves garlic, peeled

½ cup white wine vinegar

2 large Idaho potatoes, peeled, boiled until tender, and put through a ricer

2 cups whole milk, warmed

1 cup sheep's milk yogurt

Kosher salt and freshly ground white pepper

FOR THE BACALIAROS

Canola oil, for deep-frying

1 cup all-purpose flour

½ cup water chestnut starch

Kosher salt and cracked black pepper

1 can beer, or as needed

6 ounces fresh cod (*bacaliaros*), cut into 4 rectangles

TO ASSEMBLE

Beet Tartare

Bacaliaros Confit Salad

Bacaliaros

4 caperberries, thinly sliced, for garnish

❖ BEET TARTARE ❖

Place the beets and capers in a food processor and pulse until coarsely chopped.

In a bowl, fold together the beet mixture, vinegar, mustard, horseradish, and fresh herbs. Season with kosher salt and pepper. Reserve.

❧ BACALIAROS CONFIT SALAD ❧

Combine the cod, olive oil, cardamom, garlic, and bay leaves in a saucepan. Set over low heat and bring the temperature of the oil to 180°F. Poach for about 20 minutes, maintaining the temperature, until the fish is flaky. Cool to room temperature, still in the oil.

Remove the fish and flake into a bowl. Add the lemon juice, 2 tablespoons of the poaching oil, capers, and fresh herbs. Season with kosher salt and pepper, and reserve. (The oil used for poaching should be discarded after 24 hours. If you would like to use some for sautéing during that time, scoop the oil carefully from the top, leaving behind any albumen or bits of fish.)

❧ POTATO-GARLIC SOUP ❧

Place garlic and vinegar in a blender; pulse until smooth. Add the potatoes, milk, and yogurt; blend until smooth. Season with salt and pepper and pass through chinoise. Reserve.

❧ BACALIAROS ❧

In a heavy pot or deep fryer, heat the oil to 375°F.

In a bowl, combine the flour, water chestnut starch, ½ teaspoon kosher salt, and ¼ teaspoon pepper; add enough beer to make a smooth batter.

Dip the cod pieces in the batter, then fry until crispy and golden. Remove with a spider and drain on absorbent paper.

❧ TO ASSEMBLE ❧

To serve, form the Beet Tartare into quenelles and place a quenelle to one side of each large individual serving bowl. Place some *Bacaliaros* Confit Salad next to the beets. Top the salad with a piece of fried *bacaliaros*, and garnish with sliced caperberries.

At the table, pour the Potato-Garlic Soup over the Beet Tartare.

RAW MEZE PLATTER: TUNA, TAYLOR BAY SCALLOPS, SARDINES, HAMACHI & BOTAN SHRIMP

SERVES 4

In Greece, there is little tradition of raw fish, sashimi. This dish falls into the category of inspiration, and it has become one of my signatures.

In New York City over the last decade or so, sushi has become very popular. I became fascinated by the technique of cutting the fish and the beauty of the pristine flavors, and the unique textures of an elaborate *omakase* meal. By breaking barriers and allowing ourselves the freedom to play within a larger spectrum at Anthos, we have successfully combined the ingredients and flavors found in Greece to create what we refer to as "Greek sashimi." Until I opened Onera five years ago, "modern" Greek cuisine was expertly represented by groundbreaking Greek institutions such as Periyali, Molyvos, and Mylos. These restaurants refined the traditional dishes and remained loyal to the very bold, aggressive flavors of Greece. I wanted to try another approach—not better, but different. This raw plate is a perfect illustration of my new approach. Unlike Japanese sushi chefs, who look at the fish as the pivotal ingredient, I see the fish as a platform to create mini-compositions, all using quintessentially Greek ingredients that are meant to be experienced in one bite. Other than in a soup, it is rare that I can be certain all the elements are present in every bite. With the one-bite experience we have designed here, every part of it—beginning, middle, and end—is controlled by me.

The fish is like an artist's canvas. We begin with the fish: what is the flavor, what is its texture? Tuna is totally different from fluke and Spanish mackerel. Then, we enhance each unique fish with small notes of various fruits, raw and cooked vegetables, nuts, and prepared elements rooted somewhere in the Greek culinary lexicon, even if loosely. There are marmalades, pickled vegetables, gelées—an unlimited range of techniques we can use to capture the romance of the evolution on the palate. Even though this recipe is a new dish, not found in Greek cuisine, an echo or memory of traditional Greek fare remains. These raw *meze* capture those elusive memories better than any other dish.

At Anthos, the raw platter is not a static presentation, it changes with my thoughts and the market, but there are always five fish with five little compositions. Here, each of the five is created separately and then united for serving.

continued

Facing page, clockwise from top left: Hamachi Meze, Botan Shrimp Meze, Sardine Meze, Taylor Bay Scallop Meze, and Tuna Meze

Raw Meze Platter continued from page 236

TUNA MEZE

FOR THE DEHYDRATED WATERMELON

1 cup finely diced fresh watermelon,
   rind reserved for pickling

FOR THE PICKLED WATERMELON RIND

1 teaspoon coriander seeds

1 teaspoon whole black peppercorns

1 teaspoon fennel seeds

1 fresh bay leaf

1 sprig thyme

1 cup dry white wine

1 pint white wine vinegar

½ cup kosher salt

½ cup sugar

FOR THE GRILLED MANOURI

1-ounce slice *manouri* cheese,
   about 1½ inches thick

Extra-virgin olive oil

Kosher salt and cracked black pepper

TO ASSEMBLE

½ cup finely diced fresh watermelon

Dehydrated Watermelon

Pickled Watermelon Rind, cut into a
   small dice

A little of the pickling liquid

Extra-virgin olive oil

½ teaspoon Dried Lemon Zest (page 270)
   or ¼ teaspoon fresh-grated lemon zest

4 ounces yellowfin tuna, sliced into
   4 pieces

Small, picked sprigs dill

Grilled *Manouri*

❧ DEHYDRATED WATERMELON ❧

Spread the diced watermelon on a Silpat (silicone baking mat) and place in a 170°F oven. Prop the door open slightly with a balled-up dishtowel and dry until very hard. It should resemble hard candy.

❧ PICKLED WATERMELON RIND ❧

Lightly toast the spices and herbs in a dry saucepan. Add the wine and reduce by half. Stir in the vinegar, kosher salt, and sugar. Strain the liquid over the diced rind and let it soak overnight, or as long as possible. Lift the rind from the pickling liquid before serving.

❧ GRILLED MANOURI ❧

Paint the *manouri* with olive oil and season with kosher salt and pepper. Grill on both sides until char-marked. Reserve.

❧ TO ASSEMBLE ❧

Mix together the fresh watermelon, the Dehydrated Watermelon, and the Pickled Watermelon Rind. Dress lightly with a little pickling liquid, olive oil, and Dried Lemon Zest. Place about 1 teaspoon of the watermelon salad on top of each piece of raw fish. Garnish with a dill sprig and a small wedge of Grilled *Manouri*.

FOR THE TAYLOR BAY SCALLOPS

2 tablespoons finely diced fennel

2 tablespoons finely diced green apple

2 tablespoons finely diced *pastourma* (or prosciutto, or speck)

2 cured anchovies, minced

1 teaspoon Dried Lemon Zest (page 270) or ½ teaspoon fresh-grated lemon zest

Extra-virgin olive oil

Fresh lemon juice

Sea salt and cracked black pepper

12 Taylor Bay scallops, cleaned; 4 shells reserved

TO ASSEMBLE THE MEZE

Rock salt

4 Taylor Bay scallop shells

Taylor Bay Scallops

Sea salt and cracked black pepper

Coriander flowers

❖ TAYLOR BAY SCALLOPS ❖

Toss together the fennel, apple, *pastourma*, anchovies, and Dried Lemon Zest. Dress lightly with olive oil, lemon juice, sea salt, and pepper. Fold in the scallops and reserve.

❖ TO ASSEMBLE ❖

In a small vessel, make a layer of rock salt to secure each shell upright and level. Mound the scallop *meze* in the shell, and garnish with sea salt, cracked pepper, and a coriander flower.

continued

Anthos garnishes

Raw Meze Platter continued from page 239

SARDINE MEZE

FOR THE THÁSSOS OLIVE OIL

1 cup Dried Thássos Olives (page 232)

¼ cup Thássos olives, pitted

1 to 2 tablespoons extra-virgin olive oil

FOR THE PICKLED SARDINES

4 whole, very fresh sardines

1 teaspoon coriander seeds

1 teaspoon black peppercorns

1 teaspoon fennel seeds

1 fresh bay leaf

1 sprig thyme

Zest of 1 lemon

1 cup dry white wine

1 pint white wine vinegar

½ cup kosher salt

½ cup sugar

Extra-virgin olive oil

FOR THE CUCUMBER PLANKS

½ English cucumber, peeled

TO ASSEMBLE

Thássos Olive Oil

Pickled Sardines

Extra-virgin olive oil

Small pinch dry Greek oregano

Sea salt and cracked black pepper

Cucumber Planks

2 teaspoons Greek or sheep's milk yogurt

2 Thássos olives, pitted and slivered

Small, picked sprigs dill

❖ THÁSSOS OLIVE OIL ❖

Place the Dried Thássos Olives in a blender and purée to a fine powder, scraping down the sides. Add the fresh olives bit by bit, puréeing after each addition, until the olive purée is a thick, loose paste. Slowly incorporate the olive oil, 1 tablespoon at a time, until the purée is only just pourable.

❖ PICKLED SARDINES ❖

Remove the fillets from the sardines and trim them to a nice, neat shape.

Lightly toast the spices in a dry saucepan. Add the bay leaf, thyme, lemon zest, and wine. Reduce the liquid by half. Stir in the vinegar, kosher salt, and sugar. Chill the liquid.

Place the sardines in a container and cover with the cold pickling liquid. Let stand for 30 minutes. Drain off the pickling liquid, and keep the sardines in the olive oil until serving.

❖ CUCUMBER PLANK ❖

Cut four slices of cucumber ⅛ inch thick; trim to the same size as the sardines.

In each vessel, make a small pool of the Thássos Olive Oil. Paint each Pickled Sardine with a little olive oil and season with a few grains of oregano, sea salt, and black pepper.

Place a sardine on each Cucumber Plank and place on top of the pool of olive oil. Make a small dot of yogurt and a dot of Thássos Olive Oil in the center of each sardine. Garnish with a sliver of Thássos olive and a dill sprig.

HAMACHI MEZE

FOR THE SPICE-RUBBED HAMACHI

1 teaspoon Cretan Spice Mix
  (page 270)

1 teaspoon Dried Lemon Zest
  (page 270) or ½ teaspoon fresh-grated
  lemon zest

2 ounces hamachi (yellowtail)

Extra-virgin olive oil

Sea salt

FOR THE PICKLED CELERY HEARTS

1 teaspoon coriander seeds

1 teaspoon whole black peppercorns

1 teaspoon fennel seeds

½ cup dry white wine

1 cup white wine vinegar

2 tablespoons kosher salt

2 tablespoons sugar

1 small, pale yellow celery heart,
  leaves reserved

FOR THE OUZO-MACERATED CHERRIES

1 cup ouzo

4 tart dried cherries

TO ASSEMBLE

Spiced Rubbed Hamachi cubes

Ouzo-Macerated Cherries

Pickled Celery Heart

Reserved celery leaves

Extra-virgin olive oil

❖ SPICE-RUBBED HAMACHI ❖

Combine the Cretan Spice Mix and the Dried Lemon Zest.

Slice the hamachi across the loin into four 1-inch cubes. Paint the hamachi cubes with olive oil and press the spice-lemon mix into the top surface only of each cube. Season with sea salt and reserve

❖ OUZO-MACERATED CHERRIES ❖

In a small saucepan, reduce the ouzo by half. Add the cherries, and simmer until reconstituted and soft. Reserve.

continued

❧ PICKLED CELERY HEARTS ❧

In a dry pan, lightly toast the spices. Add the wine and reduce by half. Add the vinegar, kosher salt, and sugar. Simmer the pickling liquid for 20 minutes.

Meanwhile, slice the celery heart ⅛ inch thick and place in a heatproof container. Pass the hot pickling liquid through a fine sieve over the celery heart. Let it soak overnight, or as long as possible.

❧ TO ASSEMBLE ❧

In each vessel, place a Spice-Rubbed Hamachi cube. Put an Ouzo-Macerated Cherry and a pinch of the Pickled Celery Heart up against one side of the cube. Garnish with tiny celery leaves, and drizzle with a little olive oil.

BOTAN SHRIMP MEZE

FOR THE OVEN-DRIED TOMATOES

2 Roma tomatoes, peeled, quartered, and seeded

3 cloves garlic, smashed

Extra-virgin olive oil

Sea salt and cracked black pepper

1 sprig thyme

FOR THE TOMATO VINEGAR SYRUP

17-ounce bottle of Mutti Tomato Vinegar (from Parma, Italy)

FOR THE BOTAN SHRIMP TARTARE

4 botan shrimp, shelled but with tails left on

Oven-Dried Tomatoes

¼ teaspoon ground coriander

¼ teaspoon Dried Lemon Zest (page 270) or a tiny pinch of fresh-grated lemon zest

½ teaspoon minced chives

Sea salt and cracked black pepper

Extra-virgin olive oil

1 tablespoon Dehydrated Feta (page 232)

TO ASSEMBLE

Oven-Dried Tomatoes

Tomato Vinegar Syrup

4 reserved tail-on botan shrimp pieces

Botan Shrimp Tartare

Tiny leaves basil

❧ OVEN-DRIED TOMATOES ❧

Preheat the oven to 250°F. Toss the tomatoes with the garlic, a little olive oil, sea salt, black pepper, and thyme.

Place the tomatoes rounded-side down on a parchment-lined baking sheet. Bake until the tomato pieces are wrinkled but not black, about 6 hours. Cut the pieces into julienne strips.

❧ TOMATO VINEGAR SYRUP ❧

In a saucepan, reduce the vinegar over medium heat to a thick syrup. Cool.

❧ BOTAN SHRIMP TARTARE ❧

Slice down the center of each shrimp toward, but not through, the tail. Lift off half of the butterflied shrimp, leaving the tail attached to the other half. Reserve the tail-on shrimp.

Mince the tail-free shrimp halves into a tartare. In a bowl, combine with the Oven-dried Tomatoes, coriander, Dried Lemon Zest, chives, a little sea salt and pepper, and a drizzle of olive oil. Toss together and fold in the Dehydrated Feta.

❧ TO ASSEMBLE ❧

Place a dot of the Tomato Vinegar Syrup in the base of each vessel. Place a piece of tail-on shrimp over the syrup. Mound the tartare on top of the tail, and garnish with tiny basil leaves.

HOMAGE TO THE OLD

All the dishes at Anthos pay homage to the old ways. The ultimate praise a student can offer to his or her teacher is to evolve the teacher's lessons, to present and represent what was learned in new and different ways. I take great pride in being Greek and in cooking Greek food. I am honored to use my chosen profession to show people the possibilities of Greek food. This is my way of giving back.

PSAROKORIZO: SEA URCHIN TSATZIKI WITH CRAB & LOBSTER RISOTTO WITH YOGURT & CAVIAR

Every once in a while, a chef creates a dish and the kitchen brigade suddenly steps back and becomes very quiet. Everyone knows that something very special has just happened. This is one of those dishes. It is theatrical and cerebral and one of the most spectacular presentations we serve at Anthos.

My inspiration was the classic Lenten dish Spinach Rice (page 167). I wanted to play around with the *idea* of that dish, which is made with rice stewed together with spinach and tomatoes, but I wanted to refine it and bring in another dimension. We began with lobster and crab, using their bones to make a really rich, classic French-style stock, to enrich the rice. To take it a step further, we brought in the briny influence of sea urchin and added a little fat by incorporating yogurt in the form of *tsatziki*. We discovered that when we added sea urchin to the *tsatziki*, it not only mellowed its inherent bold flavor but also enhanced the underlying notes of pure ocean brine. Now that we had created the dish, we decided to plate it in a way that would showcase all the individual elements. After the plate is delivered to the table, the lobster- and crab-rich rice is spooned onto the plate from a cooking vessel. The guest is then asked to fold all the ingredients together, unifying the complexity of all the individual flavors at the table. The guest ultimately becomes the last cook, adding the final dimension of design and finishing the plate. Visualize the egg's richness and the yogurt's creamy texture engulfing the lobster and crab as the sea urchin starts to break down in the hot rice, and the oils begin to come out and bloom, creating layer upon layer of flavor—all in front of your eyes.

FOR THE SEA URCHIN TSATZIKI
3 tablespoons distilled white vinegar
3 cloves garlic, peeled
¼ cup Greek or sheep's milk yogurt

1 cup sea urchin tongues (available at some fish markets and Japanese markets)
Kosher salt and cracked black pepper

FOR THE RISOTTO

4 ounces (1 stick) unsalted butter

2 tablespoons extra-virgin olive oil

½ Spanish or sweet onion, finely chopped

1 cup Vialone Nano, Carnaroli, or Arborio rice

1 quart white wine

1 quart Lobster Broth (recipe follows), warm

Kosher salt and cracked black pepper

2 teaspoons finely chopped dill

2 teaspoons finely chopped parsley

¼ cup grated *graviera* cheese

¼ cup Tasmanian red crabmeat, picked over

FOR THE LOBSTER BROTH

1 pound (4 sticks) unsalted butter

1 pound lobster shells and heads

6 shallots, roughly chopped

4 cloves garlic, smashed

1 stalk celery, roughly chopped

1 bulb fennel, roughly chopped

1 tablespoon cracked black pepper

1 teaspoon coriander seeds

¼ cup tomato paste

1 quart ouzo

1 cup white wine

3 quarts light chicken stock, homemade

TO ASSEMBLE

Sea Urchin *Tsatziki*

4 tablespoons Greek or sheep's milk yogurt

4 free-range or pasture-raised egg yolks

8 sea urchin tongues

4 tablespoons Osetra caviar

Small sprigs dill and parsley, deep-fried

Risotto, warm

❧ SEA URCHIN TSATZIKI ❧

In a blender, combine the vinegar and garlic, and purée until smooth. With the motor running, add the yogurt 1 tablespoon at a time, emulsifying between each addition. Add the sea urchin tongues slowly, in the same way. Pulse until very smooth. Pass the mixture through a chinoise and season with kosher salt and pepper.

❧ RISOTTO ❧

Warm a heavy saucepan over medium heat and add the butter and olive oil. When the butter foams, add the onions and sweat them until tender.

Add the rice to the onions and sear for 1 to 2 minutes, stirring. Add the white wine and reduce until the pan is dry.

Add the Lobster Broth a little at a time, stirring frequently. Keep adding broth until the rice is almost tender but still has a little bite at the center of each kernel. Season liberally with kosher salt and pepper; stir in the fresh herbs and the *graviera*. Fold in the crabmeat. Reserve, warm.

continued

Psarokorizo continued from page 247

❧ LOBSTER BROTH ❧

Warm a large stockpot over medium-high heat and add the butter. When it foams, add the lobster parts and all the vegetables. Sauté until the vegetables are light brown. Add the spices and tomato paste, and cook, stirring all the time, until the paste is dark brown but not scorched.

Add the ouzo and deglaze the pan. Simmer briskly to reduce until the pot is almost dry. Add the white wine and simmer to reduce by half. Add the chicken stock, reduce the heat, and partially cover the pan. Simmer for 1 hour.

Pulse in a food processor until fairly smooth. Pass the broth through a chinoise to remove the shell bits. Reserve.

❧ TO ASSEMBLE ❧

Make a large swoosh of *Tsatziki* in the bottom half of a bowl. On the opposite side, place a small pool of the yogurt. Gently place an egg yolk in the yogurt, to resemble a sunny-side-up egg.

Place two sea urchin tongues and a quenelle of caviar in the bowl, opposite the "egg." Top with the fried herbs.

At the table, spoon the hot Risotto over the "egg," and stir in the yolk.

THE SOUL OF THE SEA

Sea urchin captures the flavors of the ocean better than any other seafood I know. Whenever I taste sea urchin, I am transported back to an island in Greece. There, we eat the urchins right out of the shell—just rinse with a little sea water and squeeze a little lemon over the top. Immediately you get a rush of the muddy-murky flavor of the ocean floor and that wonderful briny flavor. It reminds me so much of the sea; I close my eyes and I am there.

SMOKED OCTOPUS WITH FENNEL PURÉE,
LEMON CONFIT & PICKLED VEGETABLES

SERVES 4

No protein symbolizes the identity of the Greek culinary lexicon better than octopus. Grilling it, as tradition mandates, enhances the flavor while showcasing the unique textural aspects of this eight-legged marvel of the sea.

This dish reflects on that tradition with a creative spin. First we braise the octopus, to tenderize it. Then we break from tradition and cold-smoke it to capture the smokiness of the open flame without influencing the texture. Next we affect texture by pan-roasting the octopus in oil to crisp it on all sides. This allows us to infuse the oil with herbs and garlic, so as the flesh is crisping, it is being basted with multiple layers of added flavors. As you chew, you get a wonderfully crunchy exterior that exquisitely contrasts with the fork-tender interior achieved in the slow braise. The result is a tender, smoky, crispy, and garlicky flesh before we even begin to compose the dish.

At this point, the octopus would typically be finished with a squeeze of fresh lemon and a drizzle of extra-virgin olive oil. In this new dish, we replace the acidity typically provided by the fresh lemon juice with a pickled vegetable salad that allows us to incorporate both the perfect level of acidity and additional depth of flavor and texture. We bring back the lemon element in a slightly sweet guise, a lemon confit that is caramelized during the final pan-roast. Shaved fresh fennel adds brightness to these complex flavors; a cold julienne of smoked octopus head offers a balance of temperatures to the assembly. The completed dish evokes memories of its peasant roots, but it is presented in a style that is at once earthy and evolved.

FOR THE PICKLED PEARL ONIONS	FOR THE PICKLED CHANTERELLES
1 teaspoon coriander seeds	1 teaspoon coriander seeds
1 teaspoon whole black peppercorns	1 teaspoon whole black peppercorns
1 teaspoon fennel seeds	1 teaspoon fennel seeds
½ cup dry red wine	½ cup dry white wine
1 cup red wine vinegar	1 cup white wine vinegar
2 tablespoons kosher salt	2 tablespoons kosher salt
2 tablespoons sugar	2 tablespoons sugar
1 pint whole pearl onions, peeled	8 chanterelle mushrooms, stems peeled and grit rinsed away

continued

FOR THE LEMON CONFIT

⅔ cup sugar

⅓ cup water

1 lemon

Kosher salt and cracked black pepper

1 shallot, thinly sliced

1 clove garlic, thinly sliced

FOR THE SMOKED OCTOPUS

4- to 6-pound octopus

Kosher salt and cracked black pepper

Extra-virgin olive oil

10 shallots

10 cloves garlic, smashed

1 large bulb fennel, quartered

2 stalks celery, thinly sliced

10 sprigs thyme

½ bunch dill

3 fresh bay leaves

1½ tablespoons whole black peppercorns

1 tablespoon coriander seeds

1 tablespoon fennel seeds

4 lemons, sliced

4 quarts dry white Greek wine, warm

1 quart applewood smoking chips, soaked

FOR THE FENNEL PURÉE

1 pound fennel bulbs, quartered and cored

½ pound Idaho potatoes, peeled

3 shallots

Extra-virgin olive oil

2 cloves garlic, smashed

Kosher salt and freshly ground white pepper

1 tablespoon fennel pollen

2 quarts whole milk

TO ASSEMBLE

4 Smoked Octopus legs, at room temperature

Extra-virgin olive oil

Pickled Chanterelles and Pickled Pearl Onions

1 small, pale yellow celery heart, thinly sliced on a bias

Lemon Confit slices

½ bulb fennel, shaved paper-thin

Pale yellow leaves from the celery heart, torn into small pieces

Fennel Purée

Smoked Octopus head, at room temperature

❧ PICKLED PEARL ONIONS ❧

In a dry pan, lightly toast the spices. Add the wine and reduce by half. Add the vinegar, kosher salt, and sugar. Simmer for 20 minutes.

Meanwhile, place the onions in a heatproof container. Pass the hot pickling liquid through a fine sieve, pour it over the onions, and let them soak overnight, refrigerated, or as long as possible.

❧ PICKLED CHANTERELLES ❧

In a dry pan, lightly toast the spices. Add the wine and reduce by half. Add the vinegar, kosher salt, and sugar. Simmer for 20 minutes.

Meanwhile, place the mushrooms in a heatproof container. Pass the hot pickling liquid through a fine sieve, pour it over the mushrooms, and let them soak overnight in the refrigerator, or as long as possible.

continued

❖ LEMON CONFIT ❖

Make a simple syrup with the sugar and water. Slice the lemon paper-thin, preferably with an electric slicer. Gently remove the seeds, leaving the slices intact.

Layer the lemon slices in a small, heatproof dish. Season each slice with kosher salt and pepper, and top with the shallot and garlic slices. Barely cover the slices with the warm simple syrup; bake at 200°F for 1 hour, or until the lemon is tender. Remove the confit to a sheet of parchment paper and reserve.

❖ SMOKED OCTOPUS ❖

Cut the head from the octopus, leaving about 2 inches of the body attached to each leg. Remove and discard the beak. (You will use only 4 of the legs and the head for this dish. Reserve the other 4 legs to make another octopus dish in this book, like the Octopus and Salami on page 44.)

Season the octopus legs and head liberally with kosher salt and pepper. Place a large skillet over the highest heat and let it get smoking hot. Sear the octopus in batches, to avoid overcrowding the pan. Film the skillet with a little olive oil and when it is hot, add 2 of the legs, tentacle-sides down. Sear to a really nice reddish brown, 2 or 3 minutes, turning. Remove the octopus to a Dutch oven or roasting pan and, after returning the skillet to superhot, sear the remaining legs and the head.

Preheat the oven to 325°F. Add the shallots, garlic, fennel, celery, herbs, and spices to the skillet and pan-roast until golden brown. Add the lemon slices and deglaze the pan with 2 cups of the white wine. Pour the braising liquid over the octopus, add the remaining wine, and press a sheet of parchment over the top. Cover the pan with a lid or aluminum foil and roast in the oven until fork-tender, about 1 to 1½ hours, depending on the size of the octopus. Cool to room temperature in the braising liquid. Transfer the octopus to a rack to dry slightly. (Do this the night before, if you like, and refrigerate.)

In a tabletop or outdoor smoker, ignite the wood chips and let them begin to smolder. Cold-smoke all the braised octopus pieces for 15 minutes.

Cut the octopus head into very thin julienne. Cut each octopus leg in half crosswise. Reserve all the pieces in the refrigerator. Thirty minutes before serving, bring the legs and the head julienne to room temperature.

❖ FENNEL PURÉE ❖

Cut the fennel, potatoes, and shallots into similar-sized, rough chunks, so they will cook evenly. Warm a large, heavy pot over medium heat. Film the pot with a little olive oil, then add the fennel, potatoes, shallots, and garlic, and sweat until softened but not colored, about 10 minutes. Season liberally with kosher salt and pepper and add the fennel pollen.

Add the milk, partially cover the pan, and simmer until the vegetables are almost falling apart. Drain the vegetables, reserving the cooking liquid. Purée the vegetables in a blender, in batches if necessary, adding just enough of the braising liquid to keep it moving, until the mixture is very smooth, about the consistency of yogurt. Pass the purée through a chinoise or a tamis sieve, pushing down hard. Reserve.

❖ TO ASSEMBLE ❖

Preheat a large cast-iron pan until very, very hot. Add about ¼ inch of olive oil to the pan and when it is very hot, pan-roast the octopus legs in batches, to prevent overcrowding, until very crispy and golden brown on all sides.

Turn the legs over and add the Pickled Chanterelles and Pickled Pearl Onions, celery, and Lemon Confit to the pan. Roast everything together for 2 to 3 minutes, tossing, to infuse the flavors throughout the fat and caramelize the Lemon Confit slices. Transfer everything to a large bowl with most of the pan juices. Add the shaved baby fennel and celery leaves, and toss to blend. Pull the lemon slices out of the salad, to use for garnish.

Make a small pool of the Fennel Purée on each plate. Place the upper, larger half of an octopus leg on top and spoon some warm pickled vegetables over and around it. Lean the smaller end of the octopus leg against the assembly and top with a slice of Lemon Confit and a few pieces of the julienned octopus head.

ANTHOS SHELLFISH YOUVETSI

This recipe is a perfect example of the technical differences between home and haute cooking. The Shellfish Youvetsi on page 79 explores the simpler—though still wonderful—home-style version of this dish, which should not take you more than half an hour to put together. To produce the following recipe, along with the balance of a typical menu at Anthos, twenty-five people work feverishly all day.

I have provided this recipe to allow you to reflect on these differences. For you to fully absorb this illustration, I highly recommend preparing the home version first, then studying it. Make mental and written notes of the nuances you find to be particularly interesting. Then prepare this version and explore these two opposing worlds.

FOR THE SAFFRON BROTH

1 pound (4 sticks) butter

1 pound *merguez* sausage, casings removed, crumbled

1 tablespoon whole black peppercorns

1 tablespoon coriander seeds

2 stalks celery, sliced

2 leeks, white part only, sliced

2 white onions, sliced

4 bulbs fennel, sliced

Cloves from 1 head garlic, sliced

1 tablespoon saffron threads

1 tablespoon smoked paprika

2 fresh bay leaves

10 sprigs thyme

1 quart ouzo

2 quarts dry white wine

6 quarts water

1 pound whitefish (halibut or cod) bones, roasted in the oven until golden

FOR THE SAFFRON ORZO

1 tablespoon extra-virgin olive oil

4 cloves garlic, sliced

1 teaspoon saffron threads

1 fresh bay leaf

1 teaspoon smoked paprika

1 quart white wine

1 quart white *verjus*

2 quarts water

Large pinch of kosher salt

1 pound orzo pasta

FOR THE BRAISED GEODUCK, WHELKS & PERIWINKLES

2 pounds (8 sticks) whole butter, divided into 3 equal quantities

9 shallots, sliced

9 sprigs thyme

6 fresh bay leaves

6 teaspoons whole black peppercorns

6 teaspoons coriander seeds

1 geoduck clam, whole

3 quarts dry vermouth

3 quarts dry white wine

3 quarts fish fumé, hot

6 whelks, scrubbed

1 pound periwinkles, scrubbed

continued

TO ASSEMBLE

2 cups *merguez* sausage, sliced

1 pinch saffron threads

1 pinch smoked paprika

½ cup sliced shallots

½ cup sliced garlic (8 to 10 cloves)

½ cup sliced scallion, white part only

3 quarts Saffron Broth

12 Manila clams

24 bouchot mussels

28 cockles

16 Taylor Bay scallops

12 razor clams

Braised Periwinkles, drained

Braised Whelks, drained

Braised Geoduck, peeled, sliced, and drained

12 Hawaiian blue prawns

Saffron Orzo

¼ cup each: small, picked sprigs dill, parsley, cilantro, fino verde basil, bronze fennel, and chive blossoms

1 tablespoon cold, unsalted butter

Juice of 1 lemon

❧ SAFFRON BROTH ❧

In a large stockpot, melt the butter until it foams. Add the sausage and cook, rendering out most of its fat into the butter.

Add the peppercorns and coriander seeds, and toast in the fat. Add the celery, leeks, onions, fennel, garlic, saffron, and paprika. Pan-roast over medium heat until all the vegetables are tender and lightly caramelized. Add the bay leaves and thyme.

Deglaze the pan with the ouzo, and reduce until the pan is dry and the pan juices begin to caramelize again. Now deglaze the pan with the white wine. Reduce the wine by half, then add the water and roasted fish bones.

Simmer, partially covered, for 45 minutes. Purée everything in a strong blender for a long time, until completely broken down. Pass the mixture through a fine china cap, scraping energetically. Now pass it through a chinoise, again scraping well to extract the maximum amount of liquid.

❧ SAFFRON ORZO ❧

In a large, heavy pot, warm the olive oil. Brown the garlic slightly, and add the saffron, bay leaf, and paprika. Toast the spices for a moment, then deglaze the pot with the white wine; reduce the wine by half.

Add the *verjus* and water, and bring to a boil. Add the kosher salt and orzo, and simmer until the orzo is tender. Drain well. Spread the orzo on a sheet tray to cool until serving time.

In this recipe, you will braise the three types of shellfish until tender, separately but in the same way. Beginning with the geoduck, use one third of the braising ingredients for each type of shellfish. The geoduck will take about 2 hours, the whelks about 1 hour, and the periwinkles about 20 to 30 minutes.

In a wide, shallow sauté pan, warm one third of the butter until it foams. Add one third of the shallots, thyme, and spices. Sauté gently until tender but not colored. Add the geoduck and 1 quart of the vermouth. Over medium heat, reduce until the vermouth is completely gone and the butter thickens and separates.

Deglaze the pan with 1 quart of the white wine; simmer until reduced by half, to cook off the alcohol. Add 1 quart of the hot fumé and bring to a simmer. Simmer until the geoduck is tender. Remove from the heat and let it cool in the braising liquid.

Cook the whelks and the periwinkles in the same way. (The periwinkles are done when they begin to emerge from their shells.)

Peel and slice the geoduck. Reserve all the braised shellfish in their liquid. At serving time, lift them from the liquid with a slotted spoon; the braising liquid will be gritty, and so may not be reused.

❧ TO ASSEMBLE ❧

In a very large, heavy sauté pan with a lid, warm the *merguez* sausage over low heat until most of the fat has rendered out and the sausage begins to brown. Add the saffron and paprika, toast slightly, then add the shallots, garlic, and scallion. Sauté gently until softened. Add the Saffron Broth and bring up the liquid to a simmer.

Add the shellfish in the following order, according to the cooking time required: Manila clams, bouchot mussels, cockles, Taylor Bay scallops, razor clams, Braised Whelks, Braised Periwinkles, Braised Geoduck, Hawaiian blue prawns.

Simmer all until the shellfish are open and tender, then use a slotted spoon to transfer them to individual, warmed serving bowls, dividing evenly. Fold the Saffron Orzo into the pan juices and warm through. Fold in the picked fresh herbs. Finish by swirling in the cold butter and lemon juice. Spoon the orzo and all the juices over the shellfish.

BRAISED LAMB PASTITSIO

SERVES 4

The largest hurdle I have encountered in my efforts to showcase the evolution of Greek food has undoubtedly been the relatively limited knowledge of Greek cuisine in general. Imagine the difficulty in trying to encourage the proliferation of a cuisine that is relatively unknown—the roots of the tradition must be fully understood first before its proposed evolution can be taught. As challenging as it may sound, this has always been my goal. Somehow, through the grace of luck and hard work, we have succeeded beyond even my wildest dreams.

It has always struck me as curious that the food of neighboring Italy has not only broken through the "ethnic" barrier, it has also become ingrained in what now defines American cuisine. My hope is that Greek food follows in these footsteps, and that this book will open your eyes to the reasons why it should. Greek cuisine is simple, based on recognizable and easily sourced ingredients that pay particular attention to the seasonality and topography of the country's broad, engaging regions. It is also a cuisine of multiple underlying and medically proven health benefits, such as those attributed to "the Mediterranean diet," not to mention the bold, enticing flavors that define Greek cooking to the core. I ask you to go beyond the obvious language barrier that I believe has slowed its pace in American culture. The proof lies within these pages. I challenge you to cook them and say otherwise.

That being said, the inclusion of this particular dish was very calculated. I venture to say that if you have encountered one Greek dish, *pastitsio* is probably it. My hope is that upon completing this refined version of a cornerstone of Greek cooking, you will close your eyes, take a bite, and allow yourself to be transported to a new realm of Greek cuisine.

FOR THE LAMB PASTITSIO

5 tablespoons extra-virgin olive oil

1 cup minced white onion

½ cup minced carrot

½ cup minced celery

2 tablespoons minced garlic

2 pounds ground lamb (well marbled, from the shoulder)

1 cup whole milk

1 cup rich lamb, beef, or roasted chicken stock, plus more if necessary

4 ounces large sprigs oregano, sage, and rosemary, tied with twine

FOR THE FETA MACARONIA

1 pound feta cheese

2 cups milk

2 cups durum flour

continued

Braised Lamb Pastitio continued from page 258

FOR THE BÉCHAMEL SAUCE

Extra-virgin olive oil

1 Spanish or sweet onion, thinly sliced

1 leek, white part only, minced

4 cloves garlic, thinly sliced

4 scallions, white part only, minced

1 Idaho potato, peeled and cut into
¼-inch dice

2 cups milk

½ cup water

1 teaspoon ground cloves

2 cinnamon sticks

3 large eggs, slightly beaten

Pinch of freshly grated nutmeg

½ cup grated *kefalotiri* cheese or sharp
Pecorino Romano

TO ASSEMBLE

Lamb *Pastitsio*

Flour, beaten egg, and bread crumbs,
as needed to sauté

Feta Macaronia

Extra-virgin olive oil

4 tablespoons goat butter

3 ounces lobster mushrooms, washed,
dried, and sliced

1 cinnamon stick

Kosher salt and cracked black pepper

12 Thássos olives, cracked and pitted

3 cloves Garlic Confit (page 264)

Small handful picked sprigs fresh
oregano

10 grape or pear tomatoes, halved

1 tablespoon very finely chopped fines
herbes (dill, parsley, and/or chives)

Béchamel Sauce, warm

¼ cup pale yellow celery leaves

1½ ounces *kefalotiri* cheese, shaved

❧ LAMB PASTITSIO ❧

Heat a large skillet over medium-high heat. When the pan is hot, add 3 tablespoons
of the olive oil. Reduce the heat and add the onion, carrot, celery, and garlic. Sweat
the vegetables until they are translucent. Add the lamb and cook until no longer pink,
about 6 minutes. Through a sieve, strain off all the fat and liquid. Discard the liquid
and return the mixture to the pan.

Adjust the heat to medium-low and add the milk, stock, and herb sprigs. Simmer very
gently until all the liquid has been absorbed by the meat, about 3 hours. If the liquid
is totally absorbed before the meat is completely tender, adjust by adding more stock,
little by little, just enough so the meat does not stick. (The goal is to reduce the liquid
to a glaze without drying out the meat.)

Remove the remains of the herb sprigs. Spoon the mixture into a half sheet tray or 7 x
10-inch roasting pan to a thickness of 2 inches. Make sure to press all the air out of the
meat and smooth the top, so it will cool perfectly flat. Cover and refrigerate for at least
1 day. (The mixture must set for 24 hours to prevent it from breaking when sliced.)

❖ FETA MACARONIA ❖

Dehydrate the feta as directed on page 232. When the feta is hard and dry, pulse it in a food processor until grated. Measure out 2 cups of the dehydrated feta and reserve any that remains for another use.

In a food processor, combine the feta, milk, and durum flour; pulse until the mixture comes together on the stem. Remove to a floured board and knead for about 4 minutes. Wrap the dough and chill for at least 1 hour, or up to 1 day.

Roll the dough into a long cylinder, then roll out to flatten slightly. Ideally, crank the dough through the pasta extruder of a heavy-duty stand mixer to make a hollow, tube-shaped pasta like bigoli, perciatelli, or bucatini. Or, you can pass it through a pasta machine, setting the rollers down after each pass, to no. 5. Then, place the spaghetti attachment on the machine and pass the strip of dough through to make spaghetti. Reserve on parchment or freeze.

❖ BÉCHAMEL SAUCE ❖

In a large, heavy pot, warm a thin film of olive oil over medium-low heat. Add the onion, leek, garlic, and scallions, and cover the pan. Sweat the vegetables until tender and do not allow them to color.

Add the potato, milk, water, cloves, and cinnamon. Simmer just until the potato is cooked. Remove the cinnamon, and purée the mixture in a blender until smooth. Temper the eggs with a little of the warm sauce, and return the tempered egg mixture to the sauce. Stir in the nutmeg and *kefalotiri*. Reserve.

❖ TO ASSEMBLE ❖

With a 1½-inch ring mold, cut 20 disks of the Lamb *Pastitsio*. (Add the trimmings to the béchamel.) Dredge the disks in flour, then in egg, and finally in bread crumbs. Return to the refrigerator for at least 1 hour.

Bring a pot of well-salted water to the boil for the Feta Macaronia.

In a very large sauté pan over medium heat, warm 1 tablespoon each of the olive oil and the goat butter. When the butter foams, add the disks of breaded *pastitsio* and sauté on one side until golden brown, about 4 minutes. Flip over and add the lobster mushrooms and cinnamon stick. Season liberally with kosher salt and pepper, and cook for about 2 minutes more. Add the olives, Garlic Confit, and oregano. Remove the cinnamon stick.

Boil the pasta until *al dente*. Drain it and add to the *pastitsio* mixture. Add the tomatoes to the mixture. Add the fresh herbs to the warm béchamel.

Twirl the Feta Macaronia lengthwise and arrange 5 disks of the *pastitsio* on each plate. Surround with the vegetable mixture. Spoon a little béchamel over the *pastitsio*, and finish with a drizzle of olive oil, the celery leaves, and the shaved *kefalotiri*.

the aegean pantry

I make a lot of different confits in both my restaurant and home kitchens, and this technique is very simple for even the home cook to execute. The benefits are enormous: from each of the confits below you have a whole repertoire of great dishes newly available. There's no trick, and you don't need a sous chef or a professional kitchen.

The technique of simmering food in fat (lard or oil) at a low temperature was actually developed at a time when there was no refrigeration. People looked for various ways to preserve their food, and they realized that anything submerged in oil would not be exposed to aerobic bacteria, the ones that need oxygen to survive. Meat and, later, vegetables could be kept far longer than when exposed to the air. In today's haute cuisine, we know these flavors and love what they can add to a dish. So, not only are you preserving a vegetable that can be ready to add to a recipe at a moment's notice, you are also making the dish even more tasty.

With a little care and attention to basic hygiene (see "Preserving Hygiene" on page 268) all my vegetable confits will last up to three weeks in the refrigerator. With that in mind, I suggest you double these recipes. Once you taste the results of adding a tablespoon of Garlic Purée to a simple pan sauce, or enjoy a great potato salad made with Artichoke Confit, you'll see the benefit of this advice.

In this chapter I also include a number of sauces and vinaigrettes that are called for earlier in the book.

❖ GARLIC CONFIT ❖

MAKES 3 CUPS

If you get nothing else out of this book, you are going to thank me for this recipe. If you like Italian food—if you like *my* food—you will want to keep this confit on hand. You can keep it in the refrigerator for weeks, and the oil will add another level of flavor to *Lado-lemono* or any of the vinaigrettes in this book. *Always* save the confit oil from any of my vegetable confits for another use, such as in a vinaigrette or for drizzling over a finished dish. If you have access to peeled garlic cloves, this confit makes itself.

3 cups garlic cloves, peeled
1 fresh bay leaf or 2 dried leaves
8 to 10 sprigs fresh thyme
Kosher salt and whole black peppercorns

About 2 cups blended oil (50 percent canola, 50 percent extra-virgin olive), as needed

Put the garlic cloves in a heavy, covered braising pan or Dutch oven. Add the bay leaf and thyme, a scant tablespoon kosher salt, and 15 or 20 black peppercorns. Barely cover with the oil.

Cover the pan and braise in a 300°F oven until the cloves are pale golden and very tender, about 1 hour to 1 hour and 15 minutes. Cool it to room temperature.

Transfer the garlic and all of the oil to a sterilized jar. Press a square of plastic wrap down directly onto the surface of the oil. Place another square of plastic over the rim of the jar and twist on the lid or secure with a rubber band. With every use, replace the square of plastic that touches the oil and use a perfectly clean fork or tongs *each time* to prevent cross-contamination from other surfaces in your kitchen. As long as the cloves and Garlic Purée, below, are covered with oil, they will last for at least 3 weeks in the refrigerator.

GARLIC PURÉE

MAKES ABOUT ¾ CUP

Substitute this purée for butter to finish and emulsify pan sauces, in addition to countless other uses. You can even substitute store-bought caramelized garlic for the Garlic Confit.

About 1 cup cloves garlic from
    Garlic Confit (above)

With a slotted spoon, transfer the garlic cloves to a cutting board, allowing all of the oil to drain back into the container. Chop the garlic fine (or purée it in a mini food processor). Film with confit oil and store in the refrigerator.

❖ CHICKPEA CONFIT ❖

MAKES ABOUT 3 CUPS

Cloves from 1 head of garlic, separated
and peeled

1 teaspoon cumin seeds

1 teaspoon mustard seeds

2½ cups cooked chickpeas or 28-ounce
can best-quality chickpeas (such as
Goya), well rinsed and well drained

Kosher salt and whole black peppercorns

Blended oil (50 percent canola, 50
percent extra-virgin olive), as needed

In a Dutch oven or a heavy pot, combine the garlic, cumin, mustard seeds, and chick-peas. Season liberally with kosher salt and pepper, and barely cover with blended oil. Cover the pot and cook at 325°F until aromatic but not browned, about 45 minutes.

When the mixture is cool, transfer it, with all the oil, to a sterilized glass container and use as you like. If the chickpeas are covered with oil, the confit will last for at least 3 weeks in the refrigerator. Always save the oil for another use, for example, in a cumin vinaigrette or for sautéing.

❖ FENNEL CONFIT ❖

MAKES ABOUT 24 PIECES

6 bulbs baby fennel or 3 medium bulbs

2½ to 3 cups blended oil (50 percent
canola, 50 percent extra-virgin olive)

5 cloves garlic, smashed

1 fresh bay leaf or 2 dried leaves

8 to 10 sprigs thyme

1 teaspoon fennel seeds

Kosher salt and cracked black pepper

When using baby fennel, quarter, leaving the core intact. If using medium bulbs, halve the fennel lengthwise through the core. Place each half cut-side down and slice length-wise into 4 or 5 thin wedges, again through the core. Do not trim away the core, as this will help the wedges hold together.

Place the fennel pieces in a covered braiser or Dutch oven and barely cover with blended oil. Add the garlic, bay leaf, thyme, and fennel seeds. Season with a scant tablespoon of kosher salt and a generous grinding of black pepper. Cover the pan and braise in a 300°F oven until tender but not falling apart, about 1 hour. Cool the fennel slightly and transfer it to a sterilized glass container, with all the oil. Cool the confit to room temperature, cover, and refrigerate for up to 3 weeks.

When ready to serve, pull the fennel pieces from the oil with a clean fork or tongs, so you don't cross-contaminate the confit (see "Preserving Hygiene"). Always reserve the oil for another use.

MAKES ABOUT 16 PIECES

1 lemon, halved
8 baby artichokes or 4 medium arti-
    chokes
2½ to 3 cups blended oil (50 percent
    canola, 50 percent extra-virgin olive)
5 cloves garlic, smashed

1 fresh bay leaf or 2 dried leaves
8 to 10 sprigs thyme
1 teaspoon fennel seeds
20 to 30 whole black peppercorns
Kosher salt

Fill a bowl with cold water and squeeze in the juice of the lemon. Drop in the lemon halves. Pull off most of the artichoke leaves (down to the pale yellow), trim off the pointed top about half an inch above the base, and trim the dark green parts off the stem and base with a sharp vegetable peeler. Cut in half lengthwise. Scoop out the choke with a small spoon, and drop each half into the lemon water as soon as you're finished with it.

Drain the artichoke pieces and place them in a small, covered braiser or Dutch oven, packing them in as densely as possible. Barely cover with the blended oil. Add the garlic, bay leaf, thyme, fennel seeds, and peppercorns. Season with a scant tablespoon of kosher salt. Cover the pan and braise in a 350°F oven for 10 minutes, then turn the temperature down to 325°F and braise for 30 minutes to 1 hour more (depending on their size), until the pieces are tender when pierced with a sharp knife, but not mushy.

Cool the pieces slightly and transfer to a sterilized glass container with all the oil. Cool the confit to room temperature, cover, and refrigerate for up to 3 weeks.

When ready to serve, pull the pieces from the oil with a clean fork or tongs, so you don't cross-contaminate the confit (see "Preserving Hygiene"). Halve again length-wise, or cut into bite-size chunks. Always reserve the oil for another use.

☀ Deep-fry a few pieces of Artichoke Confit and add to a salad or some orzo. Or, use as a garnish for a piece of grilled chicken. It's also great in a sandwich of leftover steak or turkey with a little mayonnaise, or in an omelet.

CREAMY ARTICHOKE VINAIGRETTE

You can make a wonderful, thick, and creamy vinaigrette by putting some of the con-fit artichokes into a blender or food processor with some of the artichoke oil, plus a little red wine vinegar. This vinaigrette gains great sweetness and complexity from the artichokes. It is terrific drizzled over a piece of grilled chicken or a little salad.

❖ LEEK CONFIT ❖

MAKES 4 PIECES

2 leeks, cut an inch above green part, roots removed (be sure to remove tough or dry, papery outer layers)
1 teaspoon mustard seeds
1 teaspoon cumin seeds
1 teaspoon fennel seeds
2 star anise pods or pieces

3 cloves garlic
½ fresh bay leaf or 1 dried leaf
Kosher salt and whole black peppercorns
About 2 cups blended oil (50 percent canola, 50% extra-virgin olive), as needed

Halve the leeks lengthwise and place cut-side down on a sheet of parchment inside a roasting pan just large enough to hold the four halves in a single layer. Add the mustard, cumin, and fennel seeds, star anise, garlic, bay leaf, about 2 teaspoons kosher salt, and 15 or 20 black peppercorns. Barely cover with blended oil. Cover the top with another sheet of parchment, pressing gently down onto the surface of the oil.

Cover the pan with a lid or aluminum foil. Braise in a 375°F oven until very tender, about 1 hour and 20 minutes. Cool to room temperature. If you will not be using all the leek pieces right away, transfer the leeks with all of their oil to a sterilized jar. Press a square of plastic wrap directly onto the surface of the oil. Place another square of plastic over the rim of the jar and top with the lid or a rubber band. Every time you use some of the confit, replace the square of plastic that touches the oil, and use a perfectly clean fork or tongs each time to prevent cross-contamination from other surfaces in your kitchen.

PRESERVING HYGIENE

Use care when making any of the vegetable confits or the candied fruits. Save olive and pickle jars, or any large glass jar. Sterilize the jar with boiling water, then drain upside down on a clean towel until perfectly dry. After sterilizing, handle the outside of the jar only. When the confit vegetable or candied fruit is finished cooking, cool it quickly and place it in the clean jar while the confit is still warm (but not hot, or you risk breaking the jar). Once the confit is in the jar, continue the quick-cooling process by immersing the jar in cold water. The more quickly you cool the food, the better it will keep. Cut a square of plastic wrap and press it down on top of the oil's or syrup's surface. Then, since most jar tops are not truly airtight once the vacuum seal has been broken, place another square of plastic over the mouth of the jar and twist on the cap (or secure with a rubber band). When you are ready to retrieve a piece of vegetable or fruit, or a spoonful of the confit oil for a vinaigrette, always use a perfectly clean spoon. If you set the spoon down on a cutting board or use it to stir something, grab a clean spoon to dip back into the jar.

❖ LADOLEMONO ❖

MAKES ABOUT ¾ CUP (REALLY SHOULD BE DOUBLED OR TRIPLED)

¼ cup fresh lemon juice
1 tablespoon Dijon mustard
1 tablespoon dry Greek oregano

Kosher salt and cracked black pepper
½ cup extra-virgin olive oil

In a bowl, combine the lemon juice, mustard, oregano, ½ teaspoon kosher salt, and a generous grinding of pepper. Whisk to blend the mixture completely and, whisking all the time, drizzle in the olive oil. This sauce will separate; whisk or shake in a jar before using.

❖ DRIED LEMON ZEST ❖

Using a Microplane zester, remove the zest from any quantity scrubbed and dried lemon or other citrus fruit—lime, orange, ruby-red grapefruit—without picking up any of the white pith. Spread the zest out on a baking sheet and place on a windowsill or any dry place. Let it dry overnight; all of the bitter oil in the skin evaporates and you are left only with concentrated lemon flavor. This can become an instant gremolata, but of course you can use fresh-grated lemon zest if you don't have it on hand. The Microplane, by the way, makes it significantly easier to remove the fragrant and flavorful zest without picking up the bitter white pith beneath.

❖ CRETAN SPICE MIX ❖

Mix together 1 teaspoon each of cumin, fennel, and mustard seeds along with 3 cardamom pods and 10 peppercorns. Toast the spices in a 350°F oven or a toaster oven for 5 to 10 minutes. Cool, transfer to a spice grinder, and grind to a powder.

❖ GRILLED ONIONS ❖

Slice peeled Spanish or sweet onions crosswise about ¼ inch thick, keeping the slices together. Brush with olive oil and season liberally with kosher salt and pepper. Grill on a medium-hot charcoal or gas grill, or a ridged cast-iron griddle pan, until slightly char-marked and soft. Toss in a bowl with a drizzle of extra-virgin olive oil and fresh lemon juice, at which point the onion slices will fall apart into a jumble of rings.

❖ ROASTED BELL PEPPERS ❖

Using tongs or a long fork, hold a whole pepper directly in the flame of a gas stove, turning, until blackened and flaking all over. Transfer to a bowl and cover with plastic wrap. Let stand for 5 to 10 minutes. Slip off the skin, and remove seeds, white ribs, and stems.

❖ RED WINE & FETA VINAIGRETTE ❖

MAKES 1¼ CUPS

½ cup red wine vinegar
1 small onion, sliced and grilled
  (facing page)
6 basil leaves
1 teaspoon picked thyme
¼ cup crumbled feta cheese
2 tablespoons Dijon mustard

6 cloves garlic, smashed
2 shallots, thickly sliced
2 tablespoons dry Greek oregano
1 tablespoon kosher salt
1 tablespoon coarsely cracked black pepper
¾ cup extra-virgin olive oil

In a food processor, combine the vinegar, onion, basil, thyme, feta, mustard, garlic, shallots, oregano, salt, and pepper. With the motor running, drizzle in the olive oil until smooth. Season with salt and pepper.

❖ LEMON-DILL VINAIGRETTE ❖

MAKES ¾ CUP

½ cup fresh lemon juice
2 tablespoons chopped fresh dill
1 teaspoon Dijon mustard
3 cloves garlic, smashed
1 small shallot, sliced

1 tablespoon kosher salt
Generous grinding of black pepper
¾ cup extra-virgin olive oil

In a food processor, combine lemon juice, dill, mustard, garlic, shallot, salt, and pepper. With the motor running, drizzle in the olive oil until smooth.

VINAIGRETTES:
HOT OR COLD, BROKEN OR EMULSIFIED

Most vinaigrettes can be used hot or cold, and the temperature affects not just their flavor but also the way they interact with the food. A broken vinaigrette, one that has not been machine-emulsified in a blender or food processor, makes a lovely plate sauce, whether you warm it up in a pan or just drizzle it onto hot food. An emulsified vinaigrette makes a smoother, more refined dressing.

❖ WHITE ANCHOVY VINAIGRETTE ❖

MAKES 1¾ CUPS

Use this wonderful, rustic, and chunky vinaigrette either warm or cold. Makes a great "plate sauce" for cooked protein and vegetables.

Cured white anchovies, sometimes labeled as *boquerónes*, are available at well-stocked deli counters, Italian groceries, and on the Internet. If you can't find them, you can substitute high-quality salt-cured anchovies (be sure to soak them in cool water or milk for 10 minutes, then rinse carefully but well to remove excess salt).

4 white anchovies
4 shallots, thickly sliced
1 tablespoon small, picked sprigs dill
1 tablespoon small, picked sprigs parsley
8 leaves fresh mint

1 tablespoon Dijon mustard
1 teaspoon dry Greek oregano
1 cup distilled white vinegar
½ cup extra-virgin olive oil
Kosher salt and cracked black pepper

In a small food processor, combine the anchovies, shallots, dill, parsley, and mint. Pulse until finely chopped but not puréed. Transfer to a bowl.

Add the mustard, oregano, and vinegar. Whisk together and, whisking all the time, drizzle in the olive oil. Season with salt and pepper. Since this is a broken vinaigrette, it will separate quickly. Whisk again to bring it together just before serving.

❖ RED WINE–BLACK PEPPER VINAIGRETTE ❖

MAKES 1¼ CUPS

½ cup red wine vinegar
1 small Grilled Onion (page 270)
6 leaves basil
1 teaspoon picked thyme
2 tablespoons Dijon mustard
6 small cloves garlic, smashed

2 shallots, thickly sliced
2 tablespoons dry Greek oregano
1 tablespoon kosher salt
1 tablespoon coarsely cracked
    black pepper
¾ cup extra-virgin olive oil

In a food processor, combine the vinegar, grilled onion, basil, thyme, mustard, garlic, shallots, oregano, salt, and pepper. With the motor running, drizzle in the olive oil until smooth. Add salt and pepper if desired.

☀ To make White Wine Vinaigrette, substitute white wine vinegar for the red wine vinegar in the recipe above.

❖ GREEK BÉCHAMEL SAUCE ❖

MAKES ABOUT 1¾ QUARTS

Greek béchamel differs from French béchamel or Italian besciamella due to the inclusion of whole eggs. When a dish is baked, the eggs in the sauce create a custard. This basic ingredient is what makes many Greek dishes so special. Because of the large quantity of flour and the resulting thickness of the roux, you really can't step away from the stove while you are preparing this sauce. Plus, you'll need muscle to stir it thoroughly. The larger recipe, with eggs, makes the correct amount for *Pastitsio* (page 212). The smaller recipe, without eggs, yields 1 quart. The smaller recipe should be used for Greek Creamed Spinach (page 66), Open Goat Moussaka (page 158), *Spanakopita* (page 214), and the mac and cheese variation of *Spanakopita* (page 214). If you make the smaller quantity of béchamel for Stuffed Baby Eggplants (*Papoutsakia*, page 174), stir 1 beaten egg into 1 cup of the warm béchamel.

Note: Béchamel sauce made without eggs may be kept for up to 1 week in the refrigerator. Press a piece of plastic wrap down on the surface, to keep a skin from forming. Warm over very low heat or in a double boiler and add the eggs just before using, if the recipe calls for them.

5 ounces unsalted butter	Large pinch nutmeg, preferably
10 ounces all-purpose flour	freshly ground
1½ quarts whole milk, warm	1½ to 2 teaspoons kosher salt
2½ teaspoons ground cinnamon	Cracked black pepper
	5 large eggs, lightly beaten

In a large, heavy pot, melt the butter over low heat, whisking with a large balloon whisk. Add the flour and whisk to a very crumbly roux, not a smooth paste. Whisk constantly and energetically for about 5 minutes to cook off the raw flour taste, but do *not* allow to brown (slide the pot off and on the heat every now and then if you sense it is getting too hot).

Still whisking constantly, drizzle in the warm milk until smooth. Continue cooking, adjusting the heat as necessary to keep the mixture at a very low simmer, until very thick. Whisk in the cinnamon, nutmeg, kosher salt to taste, and a generous amount of pepper.

Scoop out about ¼ cup of the warm sauce. In a bowl, whisk the sauce into the eggs to temper them. Remove the pan from the heat and whisk all the egg mixture back into the béchamel.

❧ BÉCHAMEL SAUCE WITHOUT EGGS ❧

MAKES SCANT 1 QUART

2½ ounces unsalted butter
5 ounces all-purpose flour
3¼ cups whole milk, warm
1 teaspoon ground cinnamon

Pinch nutmeg, preferably freshly ground
½ to 1 teaspoon kosher salt
Cracked black pepper

In a large, heavy pot, melt the butter over low heat, whisking with a large balloon whisk. Add the flour and whisk to a very crumbly roux, not a smooth paste. Whisk constantly and energetically for about 5 minutes to cook off the raw flour taste, but do *not* allow to brown (slide the pot off and on the heat every now and then if you sense it is getting too hot).

Still whisking constantly, drizzle in the warm milk until smooth. Continue cooking, adjusting the heat as necessary to keep the mixture at a very low simmer, until very thick. Whisk in the cinnamon, nutmeg, kosher salt to taste, and a generous amount of pepper.

❧ CANDIED CHERRIES ❧

MAKES ABOUT 1 PINT

1 cup water
1 cup granulated sugar
1 cinnamon stick

Whole peel from 1 scrubbed orange
1 pint Bing cherries, washed, dried,
    stemmed, and pitted

In a saucepan, combine the water and sugar to make a simple syrup. Stir to dissolve and add the cinnamon stick and orange peel. Add the cherries and bring to a boil. Reduce the heat to low, partially cover the pan, and simmer the fruit gently in the syrup until the liquid is reduced by about half.

Remove the pan from the heat and cool for 10 to 15 minutes. Transfer all the fruit to a sterilized jar and cool the jar down quickly in an ice water bath (this will improve the keeping time). Press a square of plastic wrap down directly onto the surface of the syrup. Place another square of plastic over the rim of the jar and twist on the lid or secure with a rubber band. Replace the square of plastic that touches the preserves each time you use some and use a perfectly clean spoon *each time* to prevent cross-contamination from other surfaces in your kitchen.

SPOON FRUIT PRESERVES

In Greece, when you receive a visitor into your home, one of the most traditional offerings is called "spoon fruit." It is toothachingly sweet, so you'd scoop up a spoonful of the fruit and place it—spoon and all—into a glass of ice-cold water, as an antidote to the sweetness. Whenever a particular fruit was in season, my mom would make these sweet fruit preserves and put them up in jars so we could have them all year round. Because of the high sugar content, these preserves will keep for a long time if you observe good kitchen hygiene during preparation and whenever you dip into the jar to retrieve pieces.

❖ CANDIED QUINCE ❖

MAKES 2 CANDIED QUINCES

My mom always used cherries, but quince is a quintessentially Greek fruit.

2 quinces, each about the size of a large
  apple, peeled, quartered, and cored
2 cups granulated sugar
4 cups water
7 cloves

2 cinnamon sticks
Zest of 1 whole orange, removed in
  one thin strip with a vegetable peeler,
  without any of the bitter white pith

Cut the quince quarters into long strips about ¼ inch thick and wide.

In a saucepan, combine the sugar and water to make a simple syrup. Stir to dissolve and add the cloves, cinnamon sticks, and orange zest. Add the quince and bring to a boil. Reduce the heat to low, partially cover the pan, and simmer the fruit gently in the syrup until it looks slightly pink from the cinnamon and cloves, and is very tender and almost completely translucent but not falling apart. This may take up to 1½ hours.

Remove the pan from the heat and cool for 10 to 15 minutes. Transfer the mixture to a sterilized jar and cool the jar down quickly in an ice water bath (this will improve the keeping time). Press a square of plastic wrap down directly onto the surface of the syrup. Place another square of plastic over the rim of the jar and twist on the lid or secure with a rubber band. Replace the square of plastic that touches the preserves each time you use some and use a perfectly clean spoon *each time* to prevent cross-contamination from other surfaces in your kitchen.

※ If you can find fresh lovage, add 2 sprigs to the simple syrup while you poach the quince.

❖ CANDIED ORANGE PEEL ❖

MAKES 1½ TO 1¾ CUPS

If you blanch the peel three times instead of just two, you will tame more of the bitterness from the pith, but you'll also lose some of the bright orange flavor. If you like sweet-and-sour flavors, add half a cup of distilled white vinegar.

And why not make more? As long as you sterilize the jar and are sure to use a perfectly clean spoon *each time* you dip into the jar to retrieve pieces of candied peel, this will last months in the refrigerator.

3 oranges, scrubbed under hot water to remove any wax
2 cups water, plus water for boiling
1 cup sugar

2 cinnamon sticks
5 cardamom pods
1 large star anise pod or pieces

Trim off the top and bottom half inch of each orange to expose the flesh. Cut into quarters lengthwise. Scrape out and reserve the flesh, leaving all of the white pith behind. Press the flesh through a strainer to get the pulp-free juice. Add water to the juice to make up to ½ cup, if necessary, and reserve.

Put the pieces of peel into a saucepan, cover with water, and bring to a boil. Drain and repeat with fresh water. Drain. Cut the peel into 1-inch strips (or, cut into ¼-inch strips, roll into a spiral, and secure each one with a toothpick).

In the empty saucepan, combine the sugar and 2 cups water and stir to dissolve over low heat. Add the orange peel, reserved orange juice, cinnamon, cardamom, and star anise. Bring to a simmer. Simmer uncovered until the liquid is very thick and syrupy, about 1½ hours. Don't leave it alone for too long; you will need to adjust the heat downward gradually as the liquid reduces, to keep it at a gentle simmer and not a rolling boil.

Cool the mixture for 10 to 15 minutes. Transfer it to a sterilized jar and cool the jar down quickly in an ice water bath (this will improve the keeping time). Press a square of plastic wrap down directly onto the surface of the syrup. Place another square of plastic over the rim of the jar and twist on the lid or secure with a rubber band. Replace the square of plastic that touches the preserves each time you use some and use a perfectly clean spoon *each time* to prevent cross-contamination from other surfaces in your kitchen.

RECIPES BY TYPE OF DISH

MEZE

Chickpea Spread 194 Eggplant Spread 188 Fava Spread 190 Figs Stuffed with Feta Wrapped with Pastourma 197 Four Cheese–Stuffed Zucchini Blossoms 32 Fried Calamari & Whitebait with Crispy Chickpeas & Lemon 200 Fried Pork & Beef Meatballs 184 Little Sausages 186 Mussels with Gigante Beans & Feta 221 Raw Meze Platter: Tuna, Taylor Bay Scallops, Sardines, Hamachi & Botan Shrimp 236 Roasted Pepper & Feta Spread 195 Sweet-&-Sour Eggplant & Onion Stew 22 Taramosalata 191 Tsatziki 189 Venison Sausage 130 Warm Feta with Tomato, Olive & Pepper Salad 196

SOUPS

Beef & Rice Meatballs in Egg-Lemon Soup 172 Lentil Soup 90 Skordalia Potato-Garlic Soup with Crispy Bakaliaros Confit & Beet Tartare 233 White Bean Soup 92 Whole Chicken Soup with Avgolemono & Orzo 88

SIDES & SALADS

Artichoke Fricassee 209 Artichokes & Potato 36 Bulgur Salad with Roasted Peppers, Capers, Raisins, Celery & Onion 34 Cucumber Salad, Celery, Leek & Tsakistes Olives with Lemon-Dill Vinaigrette 24 Dried Fruit Salad with Thyme-Honey Vinaigrette 107 French Fries 154 Greek Salad 213 Grilled Summer Squash, Feta & Mint Salad 29 Potatoes, Olives & Capers with Anchovy Vinaigrette 217 Sausage, Peppers, Onion & Tomato 102 Shaved Fennel, Cabbage, Olive, Onion & Graviera Salad with Red Wine–Black Pepper Vinaigrette 25 Spanakopita 214 Spinach Rice 167 Stewed English Peas & Mushrooms 27 Stewed String Beans, Zucchini & Potato 28 Stuffed Baby Eggplants 174 Sweet-&-Sour Eggplant & Onion Stew 22 Tomato & String Bean Salad 104 Twice-Cooked Gigante Beans 215 Wild Bitter Greens, Roasted Peppers, Grilled Onion, Oil-Marinated Dried Tomato & Kefalotiri 20

FISH & SHELLFISH

Anthos Shellfish Youvetsi 254 Cod Skordalia with Pickled Beets 98 Cretan Spiced Tuna with Bulgur Salad 54 Fried Calamari & Whitebait with Crispy Chickpeas & Lemon 200 Fried Red Mullet with Lentils, Lemon & Oil 50 Grilled Cuttlefish Stuffed with Spinach 49 Grilled Porgies 175 Grilled Sardines with Chopped Salad & Skordalia Soup 47 Grilled Swordfish with Tomato-Braised Cauliflower 52 Halibut, Fennel, Clams & Sausage with Fennel Broth 58 Mussels with Gigante Beans & Feta 221 Octopus with Chickpea Salad 218 Octopus, Salami & Apples with Anchovy Vinaigrette 44 Ouzo & Orange–Braised Snails 51 Poached Halibut with Cypriot Shellfish Salad, Cucumber-Yogurt Broth & Caviar 228 Psarokorizo: Sea Urchin Tsatziki with Crab & Lobster Risotto with Yogurt & Caviar 246 Roasted John Dory with Crab-Yogurt-Orzo Salad & Butternut Soup 56 Roasted Scallops with Cauliflower, Tart Dried Cherries & Capers in Brown Butter Sauce 55 Roasted Skate with Walnut Baklava, Yogurt & Candied Quince 46 Shellfish Youvetsi 79 Shrimp with Orzo

& Tomato 176 Smoked Octopus with Fennel Purée, Lemon Confit & Pickled Vegetables 249 Striped Bass Plaki 219 Whole Grilled Loup de Mer 96

BEEF, PORK & POULTRY

Beef Stew with Leeks 70 Hanger Steak with Braised Dandelion, Lemon & Oil 100 Pan-Roasted Chicken with Lemon Potatoes 170 Pork Soffrito with Spicy Peppers & Cabbage 72 Sausage, Peppers, Onion & Tomato 102 Souvlaki: Chicken & Pork Shish Kebab 74 Steak with Bone Marrow Htipiti 66 Stuffed Peppers with Beef & Rice 173 Sweetbreads with Caperberries, Artichokes & White Wine 201

LAMB & GOAT

Braised Goat 157 Braised Lamb Pastitsio 258 Braised Lamb Tongue with White Beans & Mushrooms 147 Dumplings with Sausage, Dandelion Greens, Sun-Dried Tomato & Pine Nuts 80 Grilled Lamb Chops 148 Grilled Lamb Heart with Crispy & Shaved Fennel Salad 146 Kefi Lamb Gyro 150 Lamb Burger 152 Lamb Shanks with Orzo 166 Open Goat Moussaka 158 Poached Goat Avgolemono 155 Roasted Leg of Lamb 142 Sun-Dried-Tomato-Crusted Loin of Lamb with Wilted Arugula & Tsatziki 145 Whole Spit-Roasted Lamb 208

DAIRY & PASTA

Grilled Watermelon & Grilled Manouri 30 Manti: Ravioli of Four Cheeses with Crispy Shallots, Brown Butter & Sage 76 Pasta with Kima 93 Pastitsio 212 Potato, Egg, Tomato & Peppers 103 Yogurt with Candied Quince & Crushed Jordan Almonds 108

GAME

Braised Quail with Fennel & Apricots 128 Grilled Quails with Sweet-&-Sour Charred Onion & Red Wine Glaze 124 Grilled Rabbit Confit 116 Pheasant with Spaghetti 122 Rack of Venison with Leek Confit & Candied Cherries 133 Roasted Pheasant with Candied Orange Peel & Leek Confit 123 Rustic Braised Rabbit with Hilopites Pasta 118 Venison Stew 129

INDEX

METRIC EQUIVALENTS

The recipes in this book use standard U.S. measurements. The information below is intended to help cooks outside the United States successfully work with these recipes.

WEIGHT

FORMULAS
Ounces to grams: multiply ounces by 28.35
Pounds to grams: multiply pounds by 453.5
Pounds to kilos: multiply pounds by .45

EXACT EQUIVALENTS
1 ounce   28.35 grams
1 pound   453.59 grams, .45 kilograms

APPROXIMATE EQUIVALENTS
¼ ounce	7 grams
½ ounce	14 grams
1 ounce	28 grams
1¼ ounces	35 grams
1½ ounces	40 grams
1⅔ ounces	45 grams
2 ounces	55 grams
2½ ounces	70 grams
4 ounces	112 grams
5 ounces	140 grams
8 ounces	228 grams
10 ounces	280 grams
15 ounces	425 grams
16 ounces (1 pound)	454 grams

VOLUME

FORMULAS
Cups to milliliters: multiply by 2.4
Cups to liters: multiply cups by .24

EXACT EQUIVALENTS
1 teaspoon	4.9 milliliters
1 tablespoon	14.8 milliliters
1 ounce	29.57 milliliters
1 cup	236.6 milliliters
1 pint	473.2 milliliters

APPROXIMATE EQUIVALENTS
¼ cup	60 milliliters
⅓ cup	80 milliliters
½ cup	120 milliliters
⅔ cup	160 milliliters
1 cup	230 milliliters
1¼ cups	300 milliliters
1½ cups	360 milliliters
1⅔ cups	400 milliliters
2 cups	460 milliliters
2½ cups	600 milliliters
3 cups	700 milliliters
4 cups (1 quart)	.95 liter
4 quarts (1 gallon)	3.8 liters

LENGTH

FORMULA
Inches to centimeters: multiply inches by 2.54

TEMPERATURE

FORMULA
Fahrenheit to centigrade: subtract 32 from Fahrenheit, multiply by 5, then divide by 9 (F–32) x 5/9

APPROXIMATE EQUIVALENTS
250°F	120°C
275°F	135°C
300°F	150°C
325°F	160°C
350°F	180°C
375°F	190°C
400°F	200°C
450°F	230°C

ACKNOWLEDGMENTS

THERE ARE MANY PEOPLE TO THANK for help with this book. Some of you I have thanked already, but some I must acknowledge here in writing.

Jason Hall, corporate chef, D&M, LLC, for the hours spent writing recipes and the tireless days spent together in the kitchen bringing them to life. For always holding the bar high. For his love of food and the culinary art.

Steve Koustoumbaris, executive chef, Kefi restaurant, for the weeks we spent cooking, tasting, and adjusting. For his love of family and food. For his love of being Greek. For his unselfish heart.

Costas Kalandranis, executive chef, Anthos restaurant, for his unparalleled dedication. For his sincerity in all that he does. For his unquenchable thirst to explore.

Ellen Shapiro, writer extraordinaire. For her ability to capture my voice. For the person she is. For her willingness to share emotions.

Brigit Binns, recipe cowriter, for her relentless measuring and weighing. For putting up with me in the kitchen.

Barbara Kafka, for your kind words. For being in my corner. For always telling it the way it is.

Michael Sand, editor and believer, for his commitment to the book and his fortitude in not "making any changes unless it made it better."

Christopher Hirsheimer and Melissa Hamilton, inspired photographers and visionaries, for the soulful photography. For their vision. For sharing their unsurpassed talent. For caring.

Michael Psaltis, agent, for all his help. For listening to me talk. For making it happen.

Donatella Arpaia, business partner, for believing in my cooking.

All my staff at all the restaurants both in the front and back: I am able to accomplish because of you.

Little, Brown and Company, publishers, for taking a chance.